Research and Development in Expert Systems

THE BRITISH COMPUTER SOCIETY WORKSHOP SERIES

Editor: P. Hammersley

The BCS Workshop Series aims to report developments of an advanced technical standard undertaken by members of The British Computer Society through the Society's study groups and conference organisation. The Series should be compulsive reading for all whose work or interest involves computing technology and for both undergraduate and post-graduate students. Volumes in this Series will mirror the quality of papers published in the BCS's technical periodical *The Computer Journal* and range widely across topics in computer hardware, software, applications and management.

Some current titles:

Data Bases: Proceedings of the International Conference 1980
Ed. S. M. Deen and P. Hammersley

Minis, Micros and Terminals for Libraries and Information Services
Ed. Alan Gilchrist

Information Technology for the Eighties BCS '81
Ed. R. D. Parslow

Second International Conference on Databases 1983
Ed. S. M. Deen and P. Hammersley

Research and Development in Information Retrieval
Ed. C. J. van Rijsbergen

Proceedings of the Third British National Conference on Databases
(BNCOD 3)
Ed. J. Longstaff

Research and Development in Expert Systems
Ed. M. A. Bramer

Research and development in expert systems

Proceedings of the Fourth Technical Conference of the
British Computer Society Specialist Group on Expert Systems
University of Warwick
18–20 December 1984

Edited by
M. A. Bramer

Head of Computing Science, Thames Polytechnic

QA
76.9
E96
B75
1984

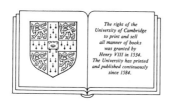

The right of the
University of Cambridge
to print and sell
all manner of books
was granted by
Henry VIII in 1534.
The University has printed
and published continuously
since 1584.

CAMBRIDGE UNIVERSITY PRESS
on behalf of the British Computer Society

Cambridge

London   New York   New Rochelle

Melbourne   Sydney

Published by the Press Syndicate of the University of Cambridge
The Pitt Building, Trumpington Street, Cambridge CB2 1RP
32 East 57th Street, New York, NY 10022, USA
10 Stamford Road, Oakleigh, Melbourne 3166, Australia

First published 1985
Reprinted 1985, 1986

Printed in Great Britain at the Cambridge University Press

Library of Congress catalogue card number:

ISBN 0 521 30652 3

CONTENTS

PREFACE

The papers in this volume are those presented at the fourth annual conference of The British Computer Society Specialist Group on Expert Systems, held at the University of Warwick in December 1984, augmented by a specially written overview paper contributed by the Programme Chairman, Max Bramer.

The conference was organized by the committee of the Specialist Group in conjunction with the Alvey Directorate, and was administered for the Group by British Informatics Society Ltd. (BISL).

The conference included presentations on a range of aspects of Expert Systems research and development. In particular, there were papers on Expert Systems Shells, Reasoning and Inference in Diagnostic Systems, the Man-Machine Interface, the Representation of Knowledge, and Knowledge Elicitation and Acquisition, plus a variety of applications.

Apart from the initial overview paper, which aims to place the remaining work in context, the papers in this volume are those presented at the conference arranged in the order of their presentation. Eighteen of these are refereed papers. In addition, the papers by Dr. Karen Sparck Jones and Professor Aaron Sloman are the texts of their invited lectures.

The Programme Committee would particularly like to thank Kate Norman and her colleagues at BISL for all their help in assembling this volume.

The British Computer Society Specialist Group on Expert Systems
Programme Committee

Max Bramer (Chairman)
Bernard Kelly (Deputy Chairman)
Tom Addis
Alan Bundy
Ian Croall
John Lumley
Abe Mamdani
Alan Rector
John Tait
Brian Ward

EXPERT SYSTEMS: THE VISION AND THE REALITY

M.A.Bramer
School of Mathematics, Statistics and Computing
Thames Polytechnic
Wellington Street
London SE18 6PF

1. Introduction

The field of Expert Systems development and its parent field of Artificial Intelligence (A.I.) are ones on which considerable interest has been focussed in recent years, not least as a result of the Japanese Fifth Generation initiative and the various national and international responses, such as the British Government's Alvey Programme for Advanced Information Technology.

As recently as 3 or 4 years ago the Artificial Intelligence community was a small and endangered species. In Britain its ranks had been decimated by the publication of the ill-considered but highly damaging Lighthill Report to the (then) Science Research Council (Science Research Council, 1973).

It was not until the publication of the Report of the Alvey Committee (Department of Industry, 1982) that Artificial Intelligence was rehabilitated in official circles in this country, under the new name of IKBS (Intelligent Knowledge-Based Systems).

It is amusing (in an ironic way) to note the comment in the Alvey Report that "The need to train additional personnel .... is particularly pressing in the IKBS area, where there are at present few active participants."

In a short period the problems of the British A.I. community, and particularly those involved in Expert Systems development, have changed from being those of a small group regarded with suspicion to being those of a rapidly growing community in high fashion.

Naturally, many would argue that if they must have problems they would prefer those of the second kind and certainly there have been benefits. A substantial rise in the number of individuals working in a field can ultimately only be for the good, even if some do no more than load their existing work on to a topical bandwagon.

The availability of A.I. tools and languages outside the academic world of DEC-10s, Vax's etc. has always been low, but here also the position has markedly improved in the last few years. Artificial Intelligence languages (most notably Prolog) are now far more widely discussed, implemented and even used than before.

A traditional (and largely valid) criticism of such languages, outside a few privileged institutions, is that they are implemented in a rudimentary fashion without much attention to input/output, graphics, error handling, documentation, or the needs of those who do not find either successions of CARs, CDRs and opening and closing parentheses, or clauses in first-order predicate logic entirely natural formalisms to use. This criticism is becoming less valid as time goes by - an inevitable result of the rapid growth of the user community.

Probably the greatest benefit of the explosive growth of interest and work in Expert Systems development is the much greater openness of commerce and industry to the ideas, techniques and tools of Artificial Intelligence and the far greater willingness to experiment with building systems of their own.

The most negative aspect of the developments of the last few
years is probably that of expectations raised unrealistically high.
It is all too easy for newcomers to a field (perhaps ones
who are important or influential in their own fields) to misjudge it and
make claims that are overblown or even patently absurd - some recent
suggestions about emulating the neural connections of the brain being in
the latter category.
The danger of overhigh expectations - particularly those of
immediate success - lies in the reaction that many follow when, ultimately,
claims are unfulfilled.
The term "The A.I. Winter" has been coined in the United
States to describe the collapse of confidence that may occur if
expectations are not met. Many in Britain would find the phrase "The
Second Lighthill" equally chilling.

2. The vision

Although Expert Systems have only recently become well-known,
the first Expert System - Dendral - was developed in the mid-1960s and
the parent field of Artificial Intelligence can be traced back (well
beyond the invention of the name) to the work of Alan Turing and the
earliest days of computers.
Moreover, the idea of constructing an intelligent artifact is
one which seems to have had a strong and persistent appeal long before
the age of computers, as McCorduck (1979) has demonstrated with examples
going back as far as Homer's Iliad.
In recent times, the talking, seeing and thinking computer
has been a regular feature in popular culture. Indeed, the layman might
well be excused for assuming that computers were already far more
intelligent than mere humans.
Although many (including some in the A.I. community) would
reject the idea of a machine being 'intelligent' in any literal sense,
the idea that certain relatively limited intellectual tasks such as
medical diagnosis, debugging computer programs or translating into
foreign languages might be programmable has gained increasing credence
with the passage of time, and the existence of at least 50 Expert Systems
in a variety of fields to show the way. Perhaps the most notable such
system is the MYCIN medical consultation system for diagnosing the cause
of bacterial infections.
The failures and false trails taken by Artificial Intelligence
workers in the early years can increasingly be seen in their correct
context. What stage did Mathematics, Physics, Chemistry, Astronomy and
Medicine reach in their first quarter centuries? It is only by making
mistakes and following false trails that such fields can ever advance.
An important aspect of Expert Systems which distinguishes
them from much early work in Artificial Intelligence is the focussing on
relatively small (but important) areas of expertise about which the
system might have several hundred painstakingly derived rules, rather
than on general methods of solving large classes of 'idealized' problems
into which it is often disappointingly difficult to fit any real-life
problems at all.
The Japanese launching of their Fifth Generation project, at
an international conference in Tokyo in the Autumn of 1981, helped to
crystallize an interest which had already been growing in the West, but
placed the development targets well beyond those that most Western

researchers would have set for themselves. The report of the Japan
Information Processing Development Center - the Jipdec Report (JIPDEC,
1981) stated the target in these words: "The Fifth Generation Computer
Systems will be knowledge information processing systems having problem-
solving functions of a very high level. In these systems, intelligence
will be greatly improved to approach that of a human being".

Feigenbaum and McCorduck (1983) remark that "the Japanese
expect these machines to change their lives - and everyone else's....
Their Fifth Generation plans say unequivocally that the Japanese are
the first nation to ... have acted on a truth that has been emerging
and reiterated for nearly two decades. The world is entering a new
period. The wealth of nations, which depended upon land, labor, and
capital during its agricultural and industrial phases ... will come in
the future to depend upon information, knowledge, and intelligence."

There is little doubt of the potential value of Expert Systems
in a world in which leading experts are rare, costly and inaccessible -
as well as inevitably mortal.

At a much lower level, many organisations have individuals,
perhaps at junior levels, whose expertise (for example in stock control,
in fault-finding or in scheduling) is not written down anywhere and would
be hard to replace. Capturing these skills in a computer program is an
attractive prospect if only as a safety measure.

Sadly, the development of Expert Systems is not as straightforward a matter as articles in the popular press (or sometimes even the
technical press) would often seem to imply. The theoretical problems
involved in developing Artificial Intelligence systems have not suddenly
ceased to exist, simply because it may sometimes be inconvenient to
recognize them. The growing body of work on building Expert Systems has
provided valuable experience and insight for those actively involved, but
the field is still in a state which can be described as 'pre-paradigmatic',
in the terminology of Kuhn (1962), with many problems left to solve before
Expert Systems building can emerge as a science rather than the craft
it is now.

Some of the most important problem areas, both theoretical
and practical, are discussed in the remaining sections of this paper.

3. Expert System shells

An idea which has appealed to many as an aid to developing
working systems rapidly is to make use of a standard framework or shell,
and a number of commercially available shells have appeared in the last
few years.

Probably the best known shell is EMYCIN (the domain -
independent 'Empty MYCIN' - essentially MYCIN with the system's knowledge
of bacterial infections removed to provide a framework in which other
systems can be built).

At the present time, almost all commercially-available shells
are based on either EMYCIN or its fairly close relative PROSPECTOR.

The potential value of using a shell is well illustrated by
Feigenbaum (1979). In describing the development of PUFF, an Expert
System for diagnosing pulmonary function disorders constructed within
the EMYCIN framework, Feigenbaum points out that the development time
taken to reach a working system based on the analysis of some 250 test
cases was less than 10 man-weeks of effort by knowledge engineers, with
less than 50 hours of interaction with subject experts - a trifling

amount of effort compared with the development of most commercial data
processing systems.
          Using a shell can greatly reduce the development time of an
Expert System by providing, for example, explanatory facilities as
standard. Its weakness - and it may prove a severe one - lies in the
restrictions it imposes, the implications of which may often not be
apparent to the user.
          The most significant of these restrictions is the overall
representation chosen. In the case of EMYCIN, this comprises in broad
terms a number of inherently different objects (called contexts), joined
in a tree structure, each context having its own set of properties,
which are either supplied by the user or deduced by goal-directed
reasoning.
          Commenting on this representation, Van Melle (1980) remarks:
"EMYCIN was not designed to be a general-purpose representation language.
It is thus wholly unsuited for some problems .... The framework seems
well suited for some deductive problems, notably some classes of fault
diagnosis .... It is less well suited for 'formation' problems, ...
simulation tasks, and tasks involving planning with stepwise refinement."
          Similar comments can be (and should be) made about every shell
but seldom are.
          Van Melle goes on to discuss the system's 'backward chaining'
form of reasoning and comments: "Backward chaining works well for simple
deductive tasks, but as soon as a problem poses additional constraints on
the means by which reasoning can or should be performed, more sophisticated
control mechanisms may be required."
          The choice of a suitable control mechanism is one of the key
problems of Artificial Intelligence programming. Being restricted to one
specific standard mechanism, whichever one it is, is certain to prove too
restrictive over a wide range of problems. The 'universal inference
engine' that is usable for any conceivable problem is surely the holy
grail of Expert Systems programming.
          One approach to overcoming the problem of a fixed control
mechanism may be the idea of an 'adaptable shell', where the system
builder is able to select a control mechanism judged suitable for the
problem in hand, within certain limits, whilst retaining the advantages
of using a standard package (such as the ability to use standard input/
output routines and explanatory capabilities). However, this approach
has not been much developed as yet.

4. Logic programming and Prolog

          On the assumption that the large majority of serious Expert
Systems will be written 'from scratch' in some programming language
rather than constructed using a shell for the foreseeable future, it is
worthwhile to consider the question of which language is most suitable
for Expert Systems development.
          There are essentially two principal positions that are
adopted on this matter: The American view "Lisp is the best possible
language for building Expert Systems" and the British view "Prolog is
the best possible language for building Expert Systems".
          This is to parody a little, but not excessively so.
Language advocates are traditionally impervious to argument and unmoved
by counter-example. Any defects found in the chosen language simply act
as a spur to further embellishments to the language not to any reappraisal

of the choice itself. The theological aspects of programming language preference may prove excellent material for Social Science Ph.D. theses in years to come.

Advocates of Lisp do at least have around 50 working Expert Systems to which to point, as well as a long history of use in building Artificial Intelligence systems of all kinds. Substantial and fully-implemented Expert Systems in Prolog are still rare.

A typical Expert System in Prolog is far too often either half-a-dozen rules implementing a toy example, or a partially implemented system to perform some extremely complex task. Such work is often advanced as demonstrating the self-evident value of using Prolog for building Expert Systems, but in fact it shows very little. It is often only in building the last 10 or 20 percent of a complex computer system that serious difficulties show up.

Bramer (1982) remarked in connection with the building of Expert Systems as Production Systems implemented in Lisp· "The potential value of the idea of logic programming is considerable .... Advocates of logic programming have so far paid little attention to a critical evaluation of its strengths and weaknesses or to comparisons with the use of production systems. This is however, an important area to pursue in the future." Little has changed since then.

Logic programming is often used as a synonym for Prolog programming, but in fact this is a case where the vision and the reality are markedly different. Logic programming is the vision: a truly declarative rule-based programming language firmly based in mathematical logic is an attractive idea and one which has come to prominence as a core component of the Japanese Fifth Generation project. The compromises needed to implement this vision with today's technology produce Prolog, a practical programming language but one with serious flaws.

For illustration, a typical Prolog program consists of a number of rules, such as
        grandfather-of(X,Y):-father-of(X,Z),parent-of(Z,Y).
and a number of facts, such as:
        father-of(john,mary).

In a genuinely declarative language, these lines could be written in any order and the individual components of a premise (since they are joined by logical 'and' connectives) could also be written in any order, without changing the meaning of the program. In Prolog this is in general not so.

"Basic" Prolog uses a fixed control mechanism, selecting rules from the top downwards and then evaluating them from left to right. This is closely related to a depth-first search of an AND-OR tree. Since search control is one of the central problem areas in Artificial Intelligence programming (see, for example, Nilsson (1980)), any fixed control mechanism can easily be predicted to be unsatisfactory over a wide range of problems.

Experience rapidly indicates that this is indeed so, and practical Prolog programming makes extensive use of so-called "extra-logical" features (such as 'cut' and 'fail') which alter the standard order of tree search and in some situations suppress automatic backtracking to find alternative solutions to goals or subgoals (the 'non-determinism' of Prolog programming which in other situations is a highly desirable feature of the language).

These compromises combine to severely downgrade the clarity
and ease of use of the language. To take an example from Bundy and
Welham (1977), the procedure 'thnot', defined by

```
thnot(L):-L,!,fail.
thnot(L).
```
approximates to negation, whereas the procedure 'repeat', defined by

```
repeat(L):-L,fail.
repeat(L).
```
provides a looping construct.

The considerable difference made by the presence of the 'cut'
symbol ,!, seems a most undesirable feature, but it is typical of Prolog
programming. To use the language well, the programmer needs a clear
mental image of the detailed workings of the Prolog interpreter and the
precise search control mechanism of his or her own programs - a long way
from the logic programming vision.

Leaving aside the above, there is another important
consideration which deserves attention. Expert systems written in Lisp
are frequently not written "directly" in that language but in some
higher-order representation, such as Production Rules. Much of the value
of Lisp lies in its suitability for constructing interpreters for such
higher-order "languages".

Prolog also appears to be a good systems implementation
language (with which, say, a frame or a blackboard representation could
easily be constructed). However, it would seem that many users of Prolog
do not see it in this light but appear to regard first-order logic as a
universal representation language in its own right.

Sloman (1984) argues at length for a multiplicity of
knowledge representation formalisms.   Even if a representation is
found which in principle is 'universal', such as the Roman Numeral
notation for natural numbers, it may still be virtually worthless for
some purposes, such as when performing division. The 'heuristic power'
of the familiar decimal representation for natural numbers is much
greater for division (and most other purposes) than the Roman Numeral
one. However, there are some purposes for which other notations (such
as binary, octal or hexadecimal) are preferable to the decimal one.

Thus, to prove that a first order logic representation is
adequate in theory in all conceivable situations is in reality to show
very little. Only experience can show whether a given representation is
satisfactory in practice for any particular application.

In considering programming languages is should not be
forgotten that there are other possible options apart from Lisp and
Prolog. The most important of these is POP-2, a language which in
appearance and syntax is not dissimilar to Fortran or Algol-60 but which
incorporates powerful facilities for list processing, manipulating
complex data structures etc. In its revised form as POP-11, this
language is gaining increasing popularity as a central component of the
Poplog environment available on the Vax and other systems.

Perhaps the best conclusion that can be drawn from the
language controversy is that any Artificial Intelligence language will be
much better than none. Going much beyond that in favour of one
particular language is more a matter of religious belief than provable
argument.

There are, of course, those who would argue that Expert
Systems can perfectly well be written in conventional languages, such
as Basic, and that the use of special "Artificial Intelligence"
languages is mere elitism.
    This is a little too reminiscent of the slogan "Real
Programmers don't use Pascal" to be taken seriously. It is probably
easiest to conceed that the sufficiently determined can do virtually any
job with virtually any tools, however unsuitable they may be.

5. Knowledge acquisition

    If the choice of programming language and the choice between
a language and a shell are the most contentious topics in developing
Expert Systems, the acquisition of knowledge is probably the hardest.
    The lack of emphasis placed on the techniques (or problems)
of extracting expert knowledge and converting it into a suitable form
(generally rules) in the 'popular' literature on Expert Systems might
lead the unwary to conclude that it presents no difficulties.
    Nothing could be further from the truth. Knowledge
acquisition is, in fact, the most difficult aspect when developing even
today's systems with a few hundred rules, and presents a formidable
obstacle to the construction of the systems with tens of thousands of
rules that may envisage existing in the future.
    The most effective methods of acquiring knowledge from
experts, such as observation 'in the field' or in-depth interviewing,
are inherently slow, a major problem given that experts' time is often
in short supply. Further problems can arise when trying to represent
the knowledge so acquired in rule form. Rules obtained in this way may
well be inconsistent as well as incomplete and repeated reference back
to human experts for clarification of inconsistencies substantially
increases the amount of time involved.
    Combining knowledge extracted from several different experts
is a possible way of overcoming the problem of incompleteness, but may
lead to considerable problems if the experts should prove to make use of
fundamentally different 'models' of the task domain.
    A recent report by Welbank (1983) examines a variety of
knowledge acquisition techniques for Expert Systems. The report concludes
that as a field of expertise knowledge acquisition "is at a very early
stage of development, where different experiences are still being
gathered, and general principles have not emerged".
    Some have argued that the best way to overcome the problems
associated with traditional techniques of knowledge acquisition is to
move towards automatic methods of rule generation based on analysis of
example cases.
    Given a database of examples, machine induction can quickly
generate a rule base which completely accounts for all the examples, and
in general this can be performed in many different ways. Some of these
ways will produce rule bases that are worthless (such as a separate
rule for each example), others may produce rule bases that are valuable
for practical use.
    A rule induction technique which has been well received in
the Expert Systems community is Quinlan's ID3 algorithm, which in
essence is the same as that described in Quinlan (1979).

The danger with any algorithm of this kind is that it may result in a set of rules that is formally correct (in the sense of accounting for all the examples given) but which has low predictive power for cases outside the example set. An extreme example of a rule set with no predictive power at all is the 'one rule per example' case referred to previously.

The problems of machine induction are aggravated by the possibility of 'noise' in data values and the possibility that some necessary attributes (perhaps those which are only significant for a fairly small number of cases) are missing. Under such circumstances, a situation similar to the "overfitting" of a curve to data points can occur. A formal 'solution' for the known cases is always guaranteed, but if it does not capture the underlying causality of the domain, its predictive power will be small.

Such reservations do not, of course, imply that automatic induction of rules should never be used. Even with today's imperfections, it may still be the best way to proceed in many cases, and in the long term developing powerful automatic (or semi-automatic) methods of rule induction seems an essential step if Expert Systems are to be constructed on a large scale.

6. Reasoning with uncertainty

An essential aspect of many Expert Systems is the need to be able to reason with uncertain information. This 'uncertainty' can arise either because of the inherent imprecision of rules in the chosen domain or because data values are themselves imprecise. 'Birds Can Fly' is an example of an imprecise rule. 'The patient may be allergic to Penicillin' is an example of imprecise data.

It is sometimes suggested that Expert Systems developers should avoid the problem of 'reasoning with uncertainty' altogether, but in fact it is an essential aspect in many domains.

It is hard to imagine a field where precision is sought in a more painstaking fashion than the framing of legislation. Despite this, even the best legal advisors can only comment on some proposed legal action in terms such as that it is 'very likely to succeed' or 'quite likely to fail'. Natural languages (such as those in which legislation is written) are inherently imprecise and the world itself has a disconcerting tendency not to operate with the 100 percent predictability that many (outside the industry) believe is possessed by computers.

To avoid imprecise rules also means deliberately ignoring valuable information. For example, 'Birds Can Fly' is a rule well-known to children, who can also readily appreciate the principal exceptions. However, writing down the rule in its full precision is an extremely awkward task, which would have to take into account whether the bird was alive or dead, asleep or awake, whether or not it was an ostrich, whether it had a major or a minor wing fracture, and so on. The rule builder would rapidly despair of completing the task.

Refusing to make use of the original short version of the rule because it is imprecise would be no more than perverse , just as it would be for a General Practitioner to refuse to treat a patient on the basis that his or her diagnosis was only based on incomplete knowledge of the patient and a partial understanding of the workings of the human body. In reality, expert judgement frequently depends crucially on manipulating these imprecise 'rules of thumb' and data that is often subjective or unreliable.

Given the importance of uncertain knowledge and rules in Expert Systems, there is an urgent need for further research into effective techniques by which it can be manipulated. At present there are a variety of ad hoc techniques in use, all of questionable validity.

Probably the most influential model of inexact reasoning is the MYCIN model in which probability like 'certainty factors' associated with both rules and data are propagated through an inference network. This model was analysed by Adams (1976), who proved that although it is presented as an alternative to standard probability theory, a substantial part of the model can be derived from and is equivalent to probability theory, with assumptions of statistical independence, although there are also important differences.

Adams was able to identify a number of shortcomings in the MYCIN model, in particular that there are interdependence restrictions which need to be applied to the estimation of certain parameters (the 'measure of belief' and the 'measure of disbelief' in a hypothesis) to maintain internal consistency, but which are not included in the model. It also turns out that the use of certainty factors as a means of ranking hypotheses is suspect since examples can be given of cases where, of two hypotheses, the one with the lower probability would have the higher certainty factor.

The use of EMYCIN (and variants of EMYCIN) as a domain-independent expert system building tool makes Adams' analysis potentially of great importance, but it still does not seem to be widely known. Nor is this an indictment of one system alone, since methods of reasoning with uncertainty in other systems do not seem appreciably better founded in theory.

It is interesting that such an apparently flawed method as the MYCIN model gives results which seem perfectly acceptable in practice. Adams comments that the "empirical success of MYCIN ... stands in spite of theoretical objections of the types discussed ... It is probable that the model does not founder on the difficulties pointed out because in actual use the chains of reasoning are short and the hypotheses simple. However, there are many fields in which, becuase of its shortcomings, this model could not enjoy comparable success."

In a recent paper, Spiegelhalter and Knill-Jones (1984) have reviewed much of the relevant work to date, comparing statistical and knowledge-based models used in clinical decision support systems, arguing for the use of "weights of evidence" as a means of overcoming many of the previous criticisms of statistical systems and recommending a synthesis between the knowledge based and the statistical approaches in many cases.

7. Reasoning in rule-based systems.

Although rule-based programming has been widely acclaimed as a central element in constructing expert systems (indeed, some seem to regard rule-based program and Expert System as synonymous terms!), there are substantial theoretical problems associated with such systems.

Probably the most important problem is that of inconsistency. What is there to prevent an inconsistent set of rules such as

        if A then B
        if B then C
        if C then not-A

occurring in a rule base, perhaps as three rules interspersed amongst thousands?

At the present time, the answer has to be 'little or nothing'. In a sufficiently large rule set, it is unlikely that the (human) programmer will even notice the inconsistency and detecting inconsistencies automatically presents considerable problems. Unfortunately, there is a well-known proof that in an inconsistent rule set, it is possible to prove any proposition whatsoever.

Another problem, although a less serious one than consistency is that of <u>circular reasoning.</u> Suppose that a rule set contains the rules

    <u>if</u> C <u>then</u> A   (1)
    <u>if</u> A <u>then</u> B   (2)
    <u>if</u> B <u>then</u> C   (3)

and the system wishes to establish the truth or falsity of C, by backward chaining.

Rule (3) indicates the need to establish B, which, by Rule (2), requires the establishment of A. Finally, invoking Rule (1) requires the establishment of C again.

Detecting such a circularity is extremely easy when it happens (the program goes into an infinite loop), but it is hard to rectify. In the above example, which rule is in error?

In reality, a circularity may occur when using rules of the same kind as those shown above but in a more complex form, for example

    <u>if</u> C and P and Q <u>then</u> A
    <u>if</u> A   and   X <u>then</u> B
    <u>if</u> B and Y and Z <u>then</u> C

which does not seem at all unreasonable even in isolation, and would be most difficult to pinpoint in a large rule set.

A further problem which is often dealt with badly is that of <u>missing knowledge</u>. The following example (again from MYCIN) illustrates the problem. Suppose the system is making use of the rule (given here in a simplified notation):

    <u>if</u> site is blood
    <u>and</u> stain is gramneg
    <u>and</u> morphology is rod

    <u>then</u> conclude identity is pseudomonas   (certainly 0.4)

and is unable to establish the value of 'stain' (the gramstain of some organism). Does this imply that 'stain is gramneg' is false?

Clearly the answer must be negative. The 'closed world assumption' that any truth value which cannot be established must be false clearly is not appropriate for most Expert System domains. There is no reason to imagine that MYCIN has all the rules that could possibly exist to conclude a value for gramstain, so no implication can be drawn about the truth of 'stain is gramneg', one way or the other.

The system actually treats all such cases as indicating falsity, which is clearly not correct. A better approach might be to make use of <u>a priori</u> probabilities based on observed frequencies of occurrence.

It is notable that the problems described do not seem to have led to any difficulties in practice as far as it is possible to determine this. Such problems must also be seen in perspective: programs written in Fortran (or other conventional languages) have a far less sound theoretical base than those written in (say) Prolog, however flawed the latter may be at present.

8. Conclusions

In this paper, a number of the current research problems of Expert Systems development have been highlighted. Although the 'vision' and the 'reality' are today very far apart, this is no reason to abandon new work on Expert Systems, just the reverse.

It is rather as if aviation had now reached the era of the bi-plane. The methodology is sufficiently far advanced and has scored enough successes to demonstrate feasibility. The vision of the future (like the idea of regular transatlantic flights) is enticing, but the field is not yet far enough advanced to make it a reality.

To realise the potential of Expert Systems, theoretical and methodological advances are needed, but whether these are more likely to arise from research laboratories and academe or to occur naturally as new and more challenging application areas are explored remains an open question.

References

Adams, J.B. (1976). A probability model of medical reasoning and the MYCIN model. Mathematical Biosciences, 32, 177-186.

Bramer, M.A. (1982). A survey and critical review of expert systems research. In Introductory readings in expert systems, ed.D.Michie, pp. 3-29. London : Gordon and Breach.

Bundy, A. & Welham R. (1977). Utility procedures in Prolog. University of Edinburgh, Department of Artificial Intelligence, Occasional Paper No.9.

Department of Industry (1982). A programme for advanced information technology: the report of the Alvey Committee. London : Her Majesty's Stationery Office.

Feigenbaum, E.A. (1979). Themes and case studies of knowledge engineering. In Expert Systems in the micro-electronic age, ed.D.Michie, pp. 3-25. Edinburgh University Press.

Feigenbaum, E.A. & McCorduck, P. (1983). The fifth generation. Addison-Wesley.

JIPDEC (1981). Preliminary report on study and research on fifth-generation computers 1979-1980. Japan Information Processing Development Center.

Kuhn, T.S. (1962). The structure of scientific revolutions. University of Chicago Press.

McCorduck, P. (1979). Machines who think. San Francisco: W.H.Freeman,

Nilsson, N.J. (1980). Principles of Artificial Intelligence. Palo Alto, California: Tioga.

Quinlan, J.R. (1979). Discovering rules by induction from large collections of examples. In Expert Systems in the micro-electronic age, ed.D.Michie, pp. 168-201. London: Gordon and Breach.

Science Research Council (1973). Artificial Intelligence· a paper symposium.

Sloman, A. (1984). Why we need many knowledge representation formalisms. In Research and development in expert systems, ed.M.A.Bramer. Cambridge: Cambridge University Press. (This volume).

Spiegelhalter, D.J. and Knill-Jones, R.P. (1984). Statistical and knowledge-based approaches to clinical decision-support systems. with an application in Gastroenterology. J.R.Statist.Soc.(A), 147, 1, pp. 35-77.

Van Melle, W. (1980). A domain-independent system that aids in constructing knowledge-based consultation programs. Stanford Heuristic Programming Project Memo HPP.80-22.

Welbank, M. (1983). A review of knowledge acquisition techniques for expert systems. British Telecom Research Laboratories technical report, Martlesham Heath, Ipswich.

EXPERT SYSTEM SHELLS COME OF AGE

Michael J R Keen
Knowledge Engineering Business Centre
ICL, Kings House
READING, Berkshire, RG1 3PX

Gareth Williams
Knowledge Engineering Group
SPL Research Centre
ABINGDON, Oxon, OX14 3LZ

Abstract

Early expert system "shells" failed to deliver all that was originally expected of them. Drawing on the combined experiences of over 100 projects using shells, a set of requirements was defined for a shell capable of fulfilling those original expectations. The way in which these requirements have been satisfied by the new product is described, together with initial user reactions to the product.

1. Introduction

Following several, much publicised, developments of early expert systems, it was recognised that there are a great many areas in the commercial world where the development of consultative expert sytems would be of considerable benefit. Ready access to knowledge, with the ability to manipulate it, is of ever increasing importance in daily commercial life. Yet most knowledge is not readily amenable to handling by conventional data processing techniques. Knowledge Engineering promises to fill this technological gap.

The early expert systems were developed by highly skilled researchers, at considerable cost using ad hoc methods. Generalisation of this research work led to the development and introduction into the market place of several so called expert system "shells". These aimed to allow newcomers to develop their own expert systems without the need for specialist knowledge engineering skills.

2. Early "Shells"

In order to simplify the task facing the newcomer, all expert system "shells" provide a basic framework for building an expert system:-

- a means of encoding the domain knowledge

- inferencing mechanisms (typically backward chaining) for making use of the encoded knowledge.

Traditionally this involves the separation of the knowledge base from the actual inferencing routines that make use of the knowledge - with the inferencing routines being provided as a standard facility within the shell.
With the complex programming tasks being done by the shell, the task of building an expert system is greatly simplified and the builder is free to concentrate on the knowledge acquisition process - using the more traditional investigatory skills of conventional Systems Analysis.
The better shells go much further in providing help to the builders of expert systems. The use of a Very High Level Language to encode the domain knowledge means that the encoded knowledge is readily understandable by the domain expert, without the need for explanation by the knowledge engineer. The expert is thus able to participate much more closely in the building process, speeding up the whole development activity.
The high productivity that results from the use of a good shell makes it possible to develop systems very much more quickly and cheaply than if the systems had to be built completely from scratch. It becomes cost-effective to explore possible applications by building prototype systems before committing resources to a full scale development programme.
Fine as the early shells were for prototyping, the fact that several of them were LISP based, and thus required specialised computer resources, posed a problem when it came to developing production expert systems. Later ones, particularly those developed in the UK, have generally been based on the use of conventional

computer languages. This has produced systems which
are significantly less "resource hungry" and capable
of being run on conventional computer equipment.
          Although these early shells were
generally successful in meeting their principal
goals, they had their drawbacks. The ability of the
system builder to express knowledge was always
constrained. None was able to cope adequately with
progressive iteration towards an optimum solution -
which is a most common design technique - while many
shells made no provision for linking the expert
system to other software. Several shells forced the
system builder to cope explicitly with the user who
answers "UNKNOWN" to a question - which is
unfortunately a rather common occurence. The
simplest of them were even more restrictive and some
did not provide ordinary arithmetic.
          The quality of the MMI produced was
equally variable. In the worst cases, the user
might be presented with questions in a totally
inappropriate form, for instance he might be asked:

"How certain are you that it is hot?"

when all the system builder wanted to ask was:

"What is the temperature?"

          Even in the better systems, the MMI
was frequently unattractive to the user due to a
limited capability for textual manipulation. Only
with a few of the LISP-based shells running on
specialised hardware did the MMI reach an acceptable
standard - though here the effect was in danger of
being spoilt by excesses.
          Consultation style also left much to
be desired. Shells using cost-directed inferencing
frequently produced a "jerky" conversation while
purely goal directed backward chaining systems
produced a rather more coherent, but frequently very
pedestrian style.
          Thus, despite the many and obvious
advantages offered by shells for the cost-effective
development of expert systems, it can be seen that
there were drawbacks which prevented their full
potential from being exploited in a production
environment. Even so, the best of them did attract
a considerable number of users.

3. Practical Experience

          Considerable experience has been built
up in the use of expert system shells by the
knowledge engineering teams in SPL and ICL. Over
one hundred projects of various sizes have been
tackled - ranging from simple demonstrations up to
major prototypes and full systems with tens of
thousands of lines of source. These projects have
involved applications of many different types. As
well as the simple "single- shot" consultative
system, SAGE has been used to build:-

●   multi-stage design systems (Keen 1983)

●   plant fault diagnosis systems

●   slow speed signal monitoring systems
    (Williams 1984)

●   signal classification systems.

          Several of these systems have involved
interfacing SAGE to other software - to perform
complex mathematical calculations, to accept monitor
signals, to access a relational database, to
interface with the host operating system, etc.
          We had also received a great deal of
feedback from our customers.
          Thus , together, ICL and SPL felt they
had an excellent chance of knowing what was needed
to advance the state-of-the-art in expert system
shells and enable them to fulfill their original
promise.

4. Identified Needs

          In analysing the experiences gained
using expert system shells, it became clear that
there were four fundamental needs for improvements
underlying the many detailed requirements that we
identified. These were for:

a) An expressive capability that is both more
   flexible and more powerful than any currently
   available - this need applying both at the
   descriptive and control levels of a system.

b) More responsiveness in control than is found in a
   conventional backward- chaining system.

c) A much more user friendly MMI that is suitable for use with many different types of end user.

d) Assistance to system builder, particularly when the building of large knowledge bases involves the partitioning of the building process so that more than one person can work on the task at the same time.

At the same time, it was recognised that there was much that was good in the existing product and it was essential to carry forward the best of this:-

● The use of a coherent and readily understandable VHLL for encoding the knowledge has already demonstrated its worth in SAGE and would need to be carried forward. Similarly, diagnostic facilities such as explanation and tracing had obvious importance.

● It was clear that the declarative style backward chaining system was a good basis from which to start as it was applicable to so many problems and, in general, produced systems that were intelligible to the end user.

● The use of a conventional programming language as the basis for the implementation was also considered important. We wanted to be able to deliver expert systems using conventional computer equipment and not be constrained to running on specialised, expensive hardware.

● The existing SAGE division into separate knowledge base building and interpretation phases (as against incremental building) was also to be retained. This produces a much more compact run time system and provides for a fairly "tamper-proof" knowledge base.

There was one further and very fundamental requirement - namely that any shell intended for developing and running live commercial systems (as distinct from toy demonstrators) must be built using proper software engineering techniques. We needed a reliable product that could be maintained on a great many sites worldwide for years to come. Anything less than a properly engineered product would not be good enough.

5. The Solution

The existing SAGE product was selected as our starting point - extending its capabilities with new features to meet the needs identified above. This decision brought with it the advantage that we would be building upon a stable, tried and tested product - so hopefully avoiding the teething troubles normally associated with an implementation from scratch.

Its expressive capability was considerably enhanced by the addition of further scalar fact types - numbers now being split into integers and reals, and string facts being included for the manipulation of names and other texts. Power was added to this expressiveness with the introduction of structured facts : arrays (of facts of the same type) and records (of facts of mixed type) - both of which will be familiar to Pascal programmers. These new fact types were backed up with corresponding rule writing and question asking capabilities.

The existing external software interface was extended to include all these new fact types, thereby enabling them to be passed to and received from external user written procedures.

All user level commands can now also be issued from within the system - ensuring that they are used in an expert manner. As well as the more obvious uses - to initiate logging and to save and restore consultations - this facility enables strict control to be applied to accessing the contents of the knowledge base via the use of a masking command.

To improve the responsiveness of the generated systems, a limited amount of "forward chaining" has been added. This takes the form of interrupt actions - or "demons" - which are actioned immediately that some condition is seen to hold. These can be used, for instance, to provide a cross check on the consistency of answers to questions, with any inconsistency being immediately notified to the user. It seems to us that the use of demons in an otherwise backward chaining environment strikes the right balance between the unpredictability of pure forward chaining and the pedestrian style of the pure backward-chainer.

Controlled iteration is provided by powerful wiping facilities that enable the values of individual facts, or even whole areas of the system, to be cleared along with all consequences of these original values. This makes it very simple for the system builder to create all manner of standard iteration capabilities for the end user without the need to work through all the consequences at a detailed level.

MMI is greatly improved by the use of variable text. At the trivial level, the ability to include the user's name within the text of the conversation is an important aid to user friendliness; at a higher level, text manipulation gives greater fluidity and polish to a conversation while needing little effort from the system builder.

Conversation style is further improved by a greater variety of question styles and the freedom to use one's own text instead of the standard prefixes and suffixes supplied by the shell. When combined with variable texts, the impact can be significant - for instance how much better it is to ask:

"How old is John?"

where the name John is actually variable text evaluated from the answer to an earlier question (or possibly even a database access), than to ask:

"What is the age of your no 1 son?"

Even the best and most careful user will occasionally answer a question wrongly; mere mortal users will make such mistakes more frequently. Whether a wrong answer is due to a misunderstanding of the phrasing of a question or simply to a lack of attention on the part of the user, historically the user was always committed once the question had been answered. Correction was often a matter of restarting the consultation from the beginning. To combat this, we have included a correction facility which enables the user to "unwind" the consultation to a previously answered question, to change that answer and then resume a normal consultation. We feel that such a facility is vital if the system is really to live up to the ideal of being user-friendly.

System building has been aided by
better partitioning within the knowledge base.
Facts are exported and imported explicitly, thereby
providing a degree of protection for the knowledge
in one area of the system from that in another area.
This makes it very much easier to divide up the
knowledge acquisition task with individual team
members each working on different areas of the
knowledge.

6. Conclusions

Or

"What do you think of it so far?"

In creating the new product, we set
out to advance the state-of-the-art in expert system
shells and enable them to fulfill their original
promise. We have kept the advantages of the best of
the early consultative shells:-

- the use of a readily understandable VHLL for
  encoding knowledge

- a primarily backward chaining environment.

- systems capable of running on readily available
  conventional computer systems

- separation of knowledge base building from live
  use of the system

while at the same time adding:-

- a greatly enhanced expressive capability

- more responsiveness

- the capacity to build a much more friendly user
  MMI

- facilities to help the system builder.

How far have we succeeded in meeting
our original design objective? Well, versions of
the new product have been on trial both within
ICL/SPL and on selected customer sites since May of
this year and feedback from all these users
indicates that we have succeeded rather well.

Newcomers rapidly take to the new product and, irrespective of background, find the language very quick and easy to learn. On training courses, students rapidly take to the language style and without exception manage to produce, within their first week's exposure to the new product, what would have been considered a sophisticated expert system just 2 or 3 years ago. Overall, the new product has that most elusive of qualities - that is is "liked" by those who use it. One user coined a most apt phrase, saying that the system is "builder friendly".

At the more technical level we have greatly improved the scope and quality of the expert systems that can be built. As well as being ideal for the construction of many types of free-standing consultative systems, we are now fully able to link with other software (to access databases etc) to produce integrated solutions to commercial and industrial problems. Moreover, the facilities that have been included make it the ideal tool for building some of the non-consultative types of expert system described earlier.

Despite all these improvements, the system remains sociable. It doesn't swamp the host machine any more than other conventional users, and is perfectly suited to co-existing in a traditional multi-user DP environment.

Overall, with the new product, we believe that we have significantly advanced the state-of-the-art in expert system shells and that we are now able to deliver the original promise of shells. There are lessons here for all producers and users of shells: given the improvements we have described, there is no excuse not to use a shell to build those prototypes which were too difficult to consider or those full systems that required a higher degree of responsiveness or user-friendliness than was previously available.

The jobs that were obviously crying out for the use of knowledge engineering techniques are now feasible and with greater benefits.

References

Keen, M J R (1983) An expert system for computer performance prediction: Expert Systems 83, Cambridge.

Williams, G (1984). SAGE, an expert system shell: Computer Aided Decision Making, London.

EX-TRAN 7 (EXPERT TRANSLATOR); A FORTRAN-BASED SOFTWARE
PACKAGE FOR BUILDING EXPERT SYSTEMS

M. A-Razzak, T. Hassan and R. Pettipher*
Intelligent Terminals Ltd, George House, Glasgow
*ITT-ESC, Harlow, Essex

Abstract

An expert system inference engine and inductive genenrator
has been coded in Fortran-77. The expert can supply rules either
explicitly or via induction files of example cases. Rules are
generated as Fortran-77 code and can link to Fortran external
routines. Flexible rule structuring allows hierarchical dependency to
be established between rules in the resulting expert system.
Successful applications have been developed using EX-TRAN 7 by client
companies.

1.   Introduction

Design and construction of expert systems is now
proceeding nation-wide and world-wide not only in academic
laboratories but also under the aegis of large industrial firms.
Medicine, plant pathology, chemistry, molecular genetics, structural
analysis, financial auditing, income tax advice, administration,
computer networking, circuit-board fault finding, and adaptive control
are among successful applications. The need now is for a software
tool with which to build and test expert systems quickly and easily.
Recently developed techniques of rule induction (Quinlan
1979 & 1982) are combined in EX-TRAN 7 (A-Razzak & Hassan 1984) with
other useful features to make the above-stated goal attainable even
when large and complex systems are to be built.

2.   Features of EX-TRAN 7

Among EX-TRAN's features are the following:

-    Simple and clear rule-based solutions are generated for the
target problem.

-    Flexible rule structuring allows hierarchical dependency to be
established between rules. Rule structure is controlled by the user
from a text file. The structure of the expert system, using the same
set of rules, can be completely changed by changing text in this
file.

-       External Fortran subroutines can be linked with the expert
system for purposes of capturing data, supporting the
attribute-testing (or "if") component of generated if-then rules, or
for triggering action sequences from the "then" component. Such
external routines can also support intermediate calculations necessary
in the course of executing rules.

-       Rules for the problem can either be directly supplied to
EX-TRAN 7 or they can be inductively inferred by EX-TRAN 7 from
user-supplied sample decisions using the system's inductive learning
module. This latter capability is essential in problems where there
is no complete "how to do it" rule explicitly available from the
expert.

-       EX-TRAN 7 automatically generates Fortran-77 code representing
the rules to be used in the final run-time expert system.

-       User commands are available for interactive guidance of the
system at all stages of its operation.

-       The operation of the resulting expert system incorporates an
"explain on demand" facility. This makes the system a conceptually
transparent aid to the domain expert and a useful auto-tutoring
facility for the less expert.

3.   Usage of EX-TRAN 7

        The principal flowchart for building an expert system
using EX-TRAN 7 is shown in figure 1. The first step for the user,
who is at this stage the domain specialist (or expert) and who may be
aided by a knowledge engineer, is to define the problem to be
considered. A problem is defined to EX-TRAN 7 in terms of the factors
affecting it (attributes) and in terms of its possible outcomes
(classes). In practice, the attributes and/or classes of a problem
may themselves be problems. Hence a problem may be considered as a
main problem and several subproblems.
        Figure 2a shows the simplest form of a problem in which
there are simple attributes and simple classes. Figure 2b shows a
problem with attributes as subproblems and with simple classes.
Figure 2c shows a problem with simple attributes but with classes as
subproblems. Finally, figure 2d shows a combination of attribute
subproblems, class subproblems, simple attributes and simple classes
in a problem.
        The construction of the links between problems, which
determine the execution level of the problem and the type of its
dependency, whether attribute subproblem or class subproblem, is
easily achieved through text in a non-compiled file called the
"problem text file".

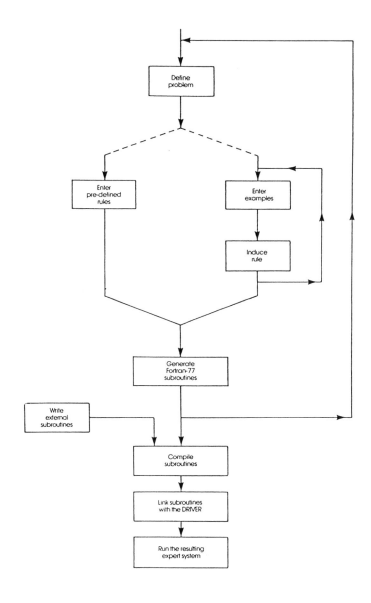

Figure 1   Flowchart for building expert systems using EX-TRAN 7

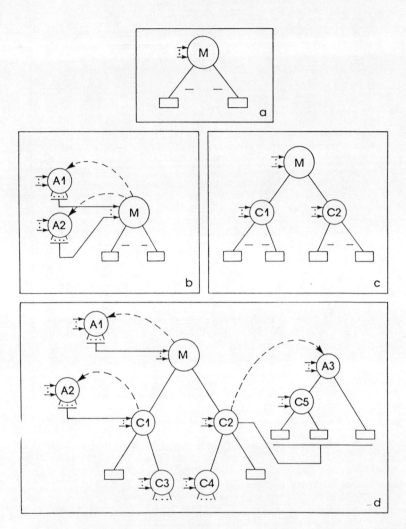

Figure 2   Problems with: a) simple attributes and classes; b)
             attributes as subproblems and simple classes; c) simple
             attributes and classes as subproblems; d) attributes and
             classes as subproblems

General notes on Figure 2

A circle indicates a problem (main problem or subproblem)
A box indicates a terminal class value: dashes between boxes stand
  for additional values
A dashed line indicates execution of an attribute subproblem
" M " stands for main problem
" C " stands for class subproblem
" A " stands for attribute subproblem
" ⇉ " stands for some number of primitive attributes

The structuring facilities of EX-TRAN 7 together with the simple technique of constructing links between problems allows the user efficiently to analyse his problem and create a suitable structure to define it.

Each problem in the final structure is then considered separately to generate a rule representing its means of solution. The user may enter examples which represent individual cases with solutions. He then induces a classification rule from them. Alternatively, he might enter a pre-defined rule to solve the problem. No programming knowledge is required in any of these operations.

The process of entering examples and inducing rules can be repeated until a satisfactory rule is obtained. Fortran-77 subroutines representing the rules are then generated to be used when running them under the DRIVER (see below). Several problems can be handled in a single session and the process of generating a rule is repeated for each of them. These subroutines, in addition to external subroutines written by the user to perform certain tasks, must be compiled and linked with the DRIVER object files (explained below).

4.   Structure of EX-TRAN 7

EX-TRAN 7 is composed of two parts: ACL-TRAN (Analog Concept Learning Translator) and DRIVER (Rule Driver). ACL-TRAN is responsible for checking and managing examples entered by the user, inducing rules from such examples, checking pre-defined rules entered by the user and generating from the rules the required Fortran-77 subroutines. The DRIVER is responsible for running the rules generated by ACL-TRAN. These will form the consultation facility of the resulting expert system.

Figure 3 shows the general block diagram of the structure of EX-TRAN 7. The expert interacts with ACL-TRAN to develop a rule for his problem. The problem is defined either in a file called the "problem text file" which is also used later by the DRIVER, or in the "attribute file". Several problems can be defined together in the "problem text file", while only a single problem can be defined in the "attribute file". An example file may be used to enter a batch of examples. A rule file may be used to enter a pre-defined rule.

When the developed rules are satisfactory, ACL-TRAN may be asked to translate them to Fortran-77 subroutines. ACL-TRAN also generates such "intermediate subroutines" as are necessary for the DRIVER operation. The expert may also write and link external subroutines to perform needed calculations, or actions including user interrogation data-capture, control, etc.

After compiling and linking these subroutines with the DRIVER object files, the expert system is ready. A non-expert user may then interact with the DRIVER to reach decisions, making use of the experience which the expert has put into the system.

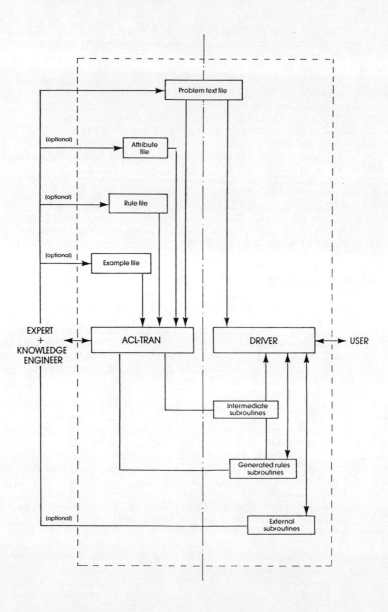

Figure 3   Block diagram showing the structure of EX-TRAN 7

5.   Performance of EX-TRAN 7

Expert systems built by use of EX-TRAN 7 have a number of useful commands that can be used during consultation. The rule under execution can be displayed in "natural language" form with a marker indicating the current position of execution reached. At any time the user can ask the system "Why" this question was asked or "How" that decision was reached, or whether there are any comments available to explain the question or the decision etc. In addition, the user may edit his previous answers or climb backwards in the executed rule to change his answers. A decision log file is automatically opened at the start of the consultations session to log all the decisions reached during the session. The user can also write his own notes or request the printing of the rule under execution to the decision log file. These commands, among others, make the consultationn session informative and user friendly. The combination of:

(1)   commands available to the domain expert during system construction and

(2)   run-time commands for the non-expert or semi-expert user

facilitates the development of expert systems which, either through problem size and complexity or through lack of full articulateness in available experts, would otherwise be impossible to produce.
EX-TRAN 7 was finalised for commercial release on June 30th 1984. Pre-release versions were meanwhile in use by corporate clients for building and testing trial expert systems. These included an expert circuit-board fault finder and an intelligent front end for a large library of Fortran-77 numerical routines for analysis of seismic data. Both expert systems have been found fully satisfactory for their operational requirements.

6.   Technical details

EX-TRAN 7 is available "off the shelf" for VAX 750 and 780 computers running UNIX or VMS operating systems. Since it is written in standard Fortran-77, EX-TRAN 7 can be run under other operating systems supporting Fortran-77. However, although the language is standard, the compilers under different operating systems may differ. Hence minor modifications will usually be needed to suit the specific compiler.
Concerning the memory requirements for EX-TRAN 7, we should speak about the requirements for ACL-TRAN and DRIVER separately since they are separate modules. The memory size of both modules depends on the size of the problem considered. However a base value of 200 Kbytes of memory is needed for ACL-TRAN and 300 Kbytes for DRIVER. These values include the memory required by the code of the module plus the code and data requirements of the Fortran library subroutines. These values are calculated under the UNIX operating system.

To give an idea of the effect of the size of the problem on the size of memory, consider the following example: an ACL-TRAN module allowing for 500 examples, 200 nodes for the induced rule and handling a problem with 25 attributes, 25 values per logical attribute and 25 class values, requires 360 Kbytes.

A DRIVER module running the rules of 20 problems of the size mentioned above requires 380 Kbytes. The number of problems and the problem settings given in the above example is considered large. Again, these values are calculated under the UNIX operating system.

References

A-Razzak, M. and Hassan, T. (1984). EX-TRAN 7 User Manual. Glasgow: Intelligent Terminals Ltd.

Quinlan, J.R. (1979). Discovering rules from large collections of examples: a case study. In Expert Systems in Micro-electronic Age, ed. D. Michie, pp. 168-201. Edinburgh: Edinburgh University Press.

Quinlan, J.R. (1982). Semi-autonomous acquisition of pattern-based knowledge. In Introductory Readings in Expert Systems, ed. D. Michie, pp. 192-207. London, Paris and New York: Gordon & Breach.

Acknowledgements

Thanks are due for corporate support and facilities to:

- Shell Exploratie en Produktie Laboratorium, Rijswijk, Netherlands
- ITT-ESC, Harlow, Essex, UK
- Standard Electrik Lorenz, Stuttgart, W. Germany.

The design and development of EX-TRAN 7 was in part supported by a five-year technology-transfer contract on "Research and Development in the Field of Artificial Intelligence" granted to ITL by ITT (Europe). The work was supervised by Professor Donald Michie, Director of Research at the Turing Institute and Technical Director of Intelligent Terminals Ltd.

THE MXA SHELL

R A Stammers
SPL International

This paper describes some distinguishing features of MXA, a
blackboard multiple-expert shell developed for prototyping sensor-based
continuous interpretation systems. This description includes the
implementation of pattern-matching via set declarations, the facilities
provided to support meta-knowledge and interaction with the user(s) at
run-time via hypothesis creation and update. These aspects of MXA are
illustrated by a discussion of their use in the Signal Understanding
System, an application in real-time sensor fusion. Although
experimental, this system employs a number of techniques needed for
operational systems.

1.   Introduction

        The MXA shell was created as a tool for research into the
application of expert system techniques to the sensor fusion problem of
producing an integrated continuous interpretation of data from a
diversity of military sensors. This research work is outside the scope
of this paper but aspects of a demonstration Signal Understanding System
(SUS) produced by SPL are described to illustrate the use of MXA
facilities.

2.   Overview of MXA

        The overall design of MXA was influenced by the American HASP
system (Nii et al 1982) but both in original implementation and
subsequent development the functionality has differed considerably.

        MXA incorporates the basic blackboard model of a group of
Knowledge Sources interacting via a database in main memory accessible to
all of them. In the case of MXA each knowledge source consists of a
group of condition-action rules, with procedural knowledge supported by
the ability to use functions and procedures in rules.

        The knowledge representation language is an extension of
Pascal. The MXA compiler generates Pascal which is in its turn compiled.

        The principal objects on the blackboard are hypotheses. Each of
these is an instance of an application-specific type and has the form of
a Pascal record. Typing is strong and static. MXA maintains a creation
time and time of last update for each hypothesis.

        Hypotheses are connected by binary evidential links which
explicitly record how hypotheses support other hypotheses. Each
hypothesis has a likelihood and each evidential link has a degree of
support, showing the relevance of the supporting hypothesis to the
supported hypothesis. MXA incorporates a lazy-evaluation Bayesian method
of maintaining up-to-date likelihoods as hypothesis structures are
modified by rules.

It is the action-parts of rules that create, modify and delete hypotheses and evidential links. The basic operation of an MXA system is via the pattern matching of rule condition-parts against the current state of the blackboard, leading to the firing of action-parts of successful rules, causing modification to blackboard structures, in turn causing further rules to fire. This forward-chaining mechanism is dominant because of the infinite solution space of a typical MXA application.

Data from sensors is input to the blackboard as hypotheses at the lowest level of interpretation. The advantages of this representation are the uniformity with that of higher-level interpretations and the ability to represent the uncertainty inherent in all sensor data. The interface provided by MXA allows a number of mechanisms: a real-time simulator operating in the same timeframe as the application system, input from a file of time-stamped data or direct input from sensors.

MXA also supports the creation of expectations by rules. These expectations have the same structure as hypotheses so that all facilities for operating on hypotheses are equally available for expectations. A time period can be specified to indicate when they are to appear on the blackboard. This expectation mechanism has a variety of uses, as illustrated by the SUS system described later.   One important use is to constrain forward-chaining via a 'generate and test' strategy.

Users can interact with an application system via an interface which provides for the creation, modification and deletion of hypotheses. The primary reasons for this mechanism are to allow users to volunteer information or to request explanation and for the system to ask questions by creating hypotheses whose attributes will be specified by a user. An important aspect is that the mechanism only suspends the system's operation for the minimum time.

In most systems the blackboard will contain several alternative interpretations of the world perceived via the sensors, with varying associated degrees of belief. Thus applications need to contain MMI knowledge sources that extract selected aspects of the interpretation for presentation to the user(s) of the system.

Symbolic debugging facilities are an integral part of MXA. For example, entry to and exit from knowledge sources and rules can be trapped or monitored, the contents of sets formed in rule condition-parts can be examined, the source lines currently being executed can be inspected and the MXA clock can be speeded up or slowed down.

Two central aspects of MXA not yet described deserve more detailed exposition. These are the use of set definitions in rule condition-parts and the role of meta-knowledge.

3.   Set Definition

        In the type of application for which MXA was designed there are
typically several instances of things in the interpreted scene, such as
several unprocessed radar contacts or several planes. For this reason a
principal feature of the knowledge representation language is the
implementation of pattern-matching in rule condition-parts by set
definitions. Whenever the rule is invoked each definition is applied to
the current state of the blackboard and a set is formed consisting of all
hypothesis structures meeting the constraints. To make this more
concrete, here is an example of a rule:

        RULE   Plane-Ship-Combinations

                    "which displays each of our ships and the hostile
                    plane nearest to it"

        IS

        Pairs =   SET_OF (Ship: Surface-vessel; Plane: Aircraft)
                    SUCH_THAT
                          Ship.On_our_side
                    AND NOT plane_on_our_side
                    AND
                    THERE_IS_NO Other: Aircraft WHERE
                    Separation (Other, Ship)<Separation (Plane,Ship)

        IF NOT EMPTY Pairs
        ACTION
                FOR_ALL Elements IN Pairs DO

                ! conjecture that this closest enemy plane
                ! will attack our ship

                Correlation:= CREATE Potential_Attack (Elements, Ship)

                SUPPORT (Elements.Plane, Correlation, 100, -100,
                            Separation (Elements.Plane, Elements.Ship),
                            "proximity could indicate attack")

                END_FOR_ALL OF Elements
        END_RULE

        This rather naive rule illustrates the intent of the knowledge
representation language design that a simple action will follow a
highly-selective condition. In this case, for each combination of ship
and closest enemy plane a hypothesis that the ship could be attacked is
created, with support from the plane hypothesis depending on the distance
between plane and ship.

        The declarative nature of rule condition-parts allows parallel
evaluation of all rules in a knowledge source although in the current
implementation the rules are considered sequentially and thus there is no
form of conflict resolution at the rule level.

Several sets can be defined in one condition-part. Union, intersection and difference operations on the other sets in a rule can be used in the definition of any set. In the degenerate case a rule can omit all set definitions and merely have a Boolean firing condition.

4.   Meta Knowledge

MXA was designed for continuous operation in systems where the flow of sensor data is determined by outside events. There is thus the usual problem of real-time systems: the need to prioritise and schedule the various activities of the system to keep up with the outside world. This is the province of meta-knowledge.

The set of meta-knowledge sources is responsible for deciding what objectives are important at the moment, what strategy should be used to achieve these objectives and which ordinary knowledge sources will be employed in the strategies.

In form, meta-knowledge sources are just like ordinary ones. As a consequence meta-knowledge sources can control the eligibility of other meta-knowledge sources for pattern-matching. Thus there can and normally will be several levels of meta-knowledge in an MXA system.

A simple two-level hierarchy would use a meta-knowledge source to determine objectives, with a set of second-level meta-knowledge sources, each of which specialises in the organisation of ordinary knowledge sources to achieve a given type of objective.

The current implementation of MXA allows arbitrary hierarchies of meta-knowledge; it would be a simple extension to allow general networks.

To provide information to help meta-knowledge sources MXA maintains a "significant-event list". This records changes to the blackboard, together with the knowledge sources "interested" in each change. The MXA compiler analyses rule condition-parts to determine the types of hypothesis where changes could cause the knowledge source to react. The rule-writer can modify this automatic mechanism by explicitly declaring or excluding interests of a rule.

In MXA there is a continual cycle of invocation of the highest-level meta-knowledge source and then the meta-knowledge sources it chooses to nominate, followed by the invocation of the ordinary knowledge source ultimately identified as the best to apply at this stage.

Almost all objectives will require a non-trivial plan of invocation of a set of knowledge sources. A control blackboard is used to construct such plans and to monitor their progress through successive cycles of operation. The more complex plans will use one or more meta-knowledge sources as an integral part to keep the plan up-to-date with current events rather than continue to operate on the basis of the state of the blackboard at the time the plan was created.

As in any real-time system it is inevitable that progress towards one objective will need to be interrupted to tackle some new higher-priority objective. Possibly several objectives will need to be pursued in parallel (conceptually). Resumption of an interrupted plan will in general require review of whether the steps already performed remain valid.

5.   The Signal Understanding System

        This demonstration system illustrates a few of the possible uses
of the MXA facilities discussed above.

        SUS   interprets   radar   data   and   contacts   from   electronic
surveillance measures (ESM), coupled with plans of own-force actions and
intelligence of enemy actions, to build a continually-updated picture of
the immediate environment of a warship.

        Being intended for general demonstration, the rules are invented
(but plausible) and the radar and ESM data is generated by a real-time
simulator. The latter adds noise to the attributes of each contact to
give a realistic scenario.

        The multi-process system runs on a VAX with a BBC micro as the
user interface to give colour graphics. The main window on the BBC
screen displays the area around the ship with the tracks and identities
of vehicles inferred from the sensor data (see Figure 1).

        Track hypotheses are built up from radar contacts, with
evidential links between contacts and tracks explicitly recording the
rationale for each track. A contact can support several tracks, with the
degree of support for each depending on the separation between the
position of the contact and the extrapolated end-point of the track.
Thus in general there are various alternative tracks under consideration
at any time. From time to time a set of knowledge sources are scheduled
to review track hypotheses to perform track repair and to delete
evidential links and tracks according to various criteria. For example,
the lack of support from new radar contacts downgrades belief in a
track. Throughout this construction and manipulation of track hypotheses
their likelihoods are automatically kept up-to-date by MXA.

        For each track a set of possible vehicle classifications is
postulated (eg. surface ship, fixed-wing aircraft, rotary-wing aircraft,
missile). This set is continually refined by eliminating hypotheses
inconsistent with the observed track behaviour (i.e. factors such as
minimum and maximum speed, maximum acceleration, minimum radius of turn
seen to date). Similarly once the vehicle has been classified a set of
precise identifications is postulated and whittled down.

        Vehicle identities are used in the extrapolation of tracks and
to disambiguate crossing tracks, so tracking and identification are part
of an integrated process.

        ESM contacts are correlated with conjectured vehicle
identifications already produced by radar analysis, or in the absence of
suitable radar evidence cause new vehicles to be postulated. As with
radar contacts, the conjectured correlation is explicitly recorded by an
evidential link between the contact and vehicle identification hypotheses.

        Intelligence reports and plans of own-force actions are
represented as expectation structures, with detailed expectations derived
from the overall report or plan, possibly involving alternatives at the
lower levels of interpretation. Expectations at various levels in this
structure, but primarily at the lowest level, are correlated with
hypotheses built up from radar and ESM sensor analysis.

The various activities in SUS need to be scheduled. Meta-knowledge sources build agenda structures on a control blackboard to address each task currently relevant. Examples of tasks are: processing of new sensor data, refinement of vehicle identifications, correlation of sensor-based hypotheses with expectations from intelligence reports and plans, deletion of unlikely tracks and old uncorrelated sensor data, updating of user displays and processing of requests for explanation. Each agenda records the pattern of knowledge sources needed to accomplish the task, plus progress to date. Priorities of agendas are reviewed from time to time and new agendas are constructed so in general several tasks are in hand simultaneously.

Production of the display of the selected interpretation and an overall threat assessment is the responsibility of a set of MMI knowledge sources.

User requests for explanation are input as new hypotheses of a "request" class. Depending on the type of request one of a set of explanation knowledge sources responds to the appearance of the request and examines the relevant blackboard structures to produce the required output. Texts associated with support links can be used in this process.

6.   Concluding Remarks

Although MXA is a first-generation UK blackboard system it incorporates sufficient functionality to support a continuing research programme. A working demonstration system has also been built and MXA is currently being used for experimentation in intelligent alarm analysis.

Figure 1: Signal Understanding System Display

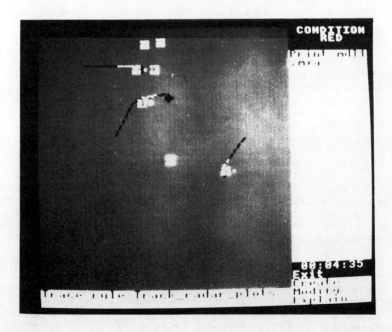

There are six windows currently visible on the screen. The largest is the main graphics display and the others are concerned with displaying system information and with sending commands to the MXA system, the real-time simulator and VMS.

The graphics are drawn asynchronously by both the MXA system (white) and the real-time simulator (black). 'We' are on the ship in the middle of the screen. There are three planes in the area, marked by black icons. The size of any white dot to the right of an icon indicates the systems assessent of the threat it poses.

The two topmost white icons represent uncorrelated ESM signals. The system displays these icons to warn that something is likely to appear on that bearing. The '?' icon represents a plane which the system has not been able to classify very accurately. The icon resting on the curved, black track is an hostile missile. The two icons above the missile represent the same object. The one on the left is an unidentified plane which the system has been tracking for some time. The icon to its right is a flight plan for a plane. The course and other expected parameters will enable the system to correlate the unidentified plane with it.

Acknowledgement

MXA was produced by SPL under contract to the Admiralty Surface Weapon Establishment (now part of the Admiralty Research Establishment).

References

Nii, Feigenbaum, Anton, Rockmore.
Signal to Symbol Transformation : HASP/SIAP Case Study.
AI   Magazine   Spring   1982.

INFERENCE DEFICIENCIES IN RULE-BASED EXPERT SYSTEMS

A.P. White
Centre for Computing and Computer Science,
University of Birmingham, UK.

Abstract

Rule-based expert systems which have scope for inexact reasoning typically exhibit serious deficiencies of statistical inference. This paper attempts to explain and demonstrate these problems. The principal deficiencies are (1) violation of the assumption of conditional independence; (2) use of "fuzzy logic"; and (3) difficulties arising from the use of subjective estimates of probabilities.

1. Introduction

A number of expert systems exist which operate on the principle of rule-based inference. Systems such as MYCIN (Shortliffe & Buchanan, 1975), Prospector (Duda et al, 1979) and AL/X (Reiter, 1980) come into this category. This paper is concerned with certain potentially serious deficiencies which are typically present in the inference processing parts of such systems. It focuses on Prospector in particular because the author has made a detailed study of the inference techniques used in that system.

It would be impossible in a paper of this length to give a full account of the inference system used in Prospector. Interested readers are therefore referred to other sources. Perhaps the most detailed account is given in Section II of Duda et al (1977). A shorter paper by Duda, Hart & Nilsson (1976) gives a general account of subjective Bayesian methods for rule-based inference systems. Appendix D of the Final Report of the Prospector project (Duda et al, 1979) also contains some interesting material, indicating that the Prospector team were aware of at least some of the practical consequences of their faulty theoretical formulation and suggests further ad hoc ways of trying to patch things up. Finally, a paper by Duda, Gaschnig & Hart (1979) gives an actual example of the propagation of probabilities through the inference network. Unfortunately, this contains further errors of a mathematical nature which make the example hard to follow.

The following sections of this paper will attempt to pick out the theoretical shortcomings of the Prospector inference system and explain or demonstrate their practical consequences.

2. Conditional Independence

2.1 The Problem

Rule-based systems such as Prospector are concerned with drawing inferences about the likelihood of various hypotheses, H_j, from the values of various pieces of evidence, E_i. (For example, in a system devoted to medical diagnosis, the hypotheses would represent possible diseases and the pieces of evidence might be symptoms, or the results of laboratory tests).

Typically, Bayes' rule is used to make these inferences:

$$P(H|E) = P(E|H).P(H)/P(E) \qquad (1)$$

For computational purposes, this takes the odds-likelihood form:

$$O(H|E_i) = L_i O(H) \qquad (2)$$

where L_i is the likelihood ratio, defined as:

$$L_i = P(E_i|H)/(P(E_i|\bar{H}) \qquad (3)$$

For each such rule, the expert supplies $O(H)$, the prior odds of H, and a likelihood ratio for each value of E_i, enabling the user of the system to obtain the posterior odds of H given E.

The problem arises when more than one piece of evidence is considered. Suppose we wish to obtain the posterior odds of H, given two pieces of evidence, E_1 and E_2. Here, the likelihood ratio that is required is given by:

$$L = P(E_1 \wedge E_2|H)/P(E_1 \wedge E_2|\bar{H}) \qquad (4)$$

Now, complicated likelihood ratios like (4) are typically not incorporated into the system. Indeed, the provision of a full set of likelihood ratios for all possible combinations of pieces of evidence would be prohibitive in terms of time and impossibly difficult for the expert. The solution that is typically adopted is to assume that E_1 and E_2 are conditionally independent (i.e. independent at each level of H and its complement) so that:

$$P(E_1 \wedge E_2|H) = P(E_1|H).P(E_2|H) \qquad (5)$$

and $\qquad P(E_1 \wedge E_2|\bar{H}) = P(E_1|H).P(E_2|\bar{H}) \qquad (6)$

With these assumptions, L in (4) simply becomes $L_1.L_2$ and odds updating becomes a very simple matter, with the process being extended to any number of pieces of evidence. Thus using O^* to represent the approximate posterior odds, we have, for n pieces of evidence:

$$O^*(H|E_1 \wedge E_2 \wedge \ldots \wedge E_n) = \prod_{i=1}^{n} L_i O(H) \qquad (7)$$

Of course, where conditional independence does not hold, the posterior odds will be in error. Furthermore, the greater the number of steps in the inference procedure, the greater this error is likely to be. This problem has been mentioned by others, e.g. Adams (1976), in his criticism of MYCIN, but seems to have been largely ignored by those responsible for designing expert systems.

2.2 A Demonstration

In order to examine the performance of such a system with more steps in the updating procedure, an example was constructed in which there were six pieces of binary evidence and two mutually exclusive and jointly exhaustive hypotheses, giving a 128 x 8 case table. For the sake of simplicity, all but two of the frequencies were fixed so that all binary vectors corresponding to an H value of zero had frequency counts of ten and all binary vectors corresponding to an H value of unity had frequency counts of one, except that there were ten cases in which both H and all pieces of evidence were present. The remaining frequency count, x, (corresponding to the absence of H and all the pieces of evidence) was varied systematically in approximately equal logarithmic steps, taking nineteen values from one to one million, according to the series: 1, 2, 5, 10, 20, 50, 100, 200, ... ,1000000. The case table is represented in Table 1. For each of the nineteen values of x, both O (the true posterior odds) and O^* (the posterior odds under the assumption of conditional independence) were calculated for different numbers of evidence variables and the log odds ratio, $R = \log(O^*/O)$, was computed. The results are displayed graphically in Fig. 1. Also, the Pearson product moment correlations between H versus E_1 and E_1 versus E_2 are plotted as a function of $\log(x)$ in Fig. 2. (It should be noted that the correlations between all pairs of evidence variables are identical. Hence it suffices to display just one of these). It can be seen in Fig. 1 that both x (the first vector frequency) and S (the number of steps in the updating process) have a profound effect on the value of R, the log odds ratio. (Indeed, R was chosen to be a logarithmic quantity specifically in order to render the graphical display more tractable). For the particular vector frequencies chosen, R increases rapidly, even when only two steps are required in the updating procedure. The more steps that are used, the steeper is the resulting curve. With six pieces of evidence in use, the stepwise posterior odds are too large by a factor in excess of 10^{15} for an x value of 10^6 – a very poor approximation! Indeed, whatever the number of steps (provided it is greater than one) the stepwise posterior odds are at least twice as large as the proper posterior odds when x is greater than a thousand. Also, for smaller values of x, it can be seen that the true posterior odds are underestimated – particularly for large numbers of steps. Altogether, for the vector frequencies chosen, the value of the stepwise posterior odds is unsatisfactory as an approximation to the true posterior odds,

N	H	E_1	E_2	E_3	E_4	E_5	E_6
x	0	0	0	0	0	0	0
10	0	0	0	0	0	0	1
.	.	.	.	.	.	.	.
.	.	.	.	.	.	.	.
.	.	.	.	.	.	.	.
10	0	1	1	1	1	1	1
1	1	0	0	0	0	0	0
.	.	.	.	.	.	.	.
.	.	.	.	.	.	.	.
.	.	.	.	.	.	.	.
1	1	1	1	1	1	1	0
10	1	1	1	1	1	1	1

Table 1. The case table used in the performance demonstration

except for a small range of x values somewhere between a hundred and a thousand. Even this acceptable range shrinks as the number of steps is increased.

It could be claimed that the vector frequencies chosen were contrived to produce a large odds ratio. In a sense, this is true. However, the frequencies are by no means unrealistic. They represent a situation in which the following facts are true:

(a) The hypothesis, H, is more likely to be false than true.

(b) The various pieces of evidence, E_i, are positively correlated.

(c) H is positively correlated with each E_i.

(d) Increasing the value of x increases the rarity of H, the rarity of each E_i and the positive correlations mentioned above.

(e) The more E_i that are present, the more H is likely to be true.

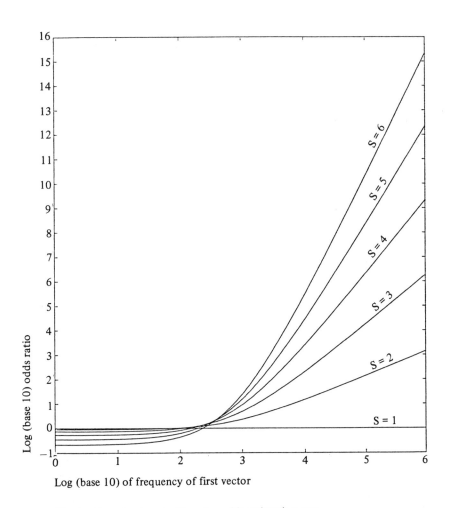

Fig. 1   Error in stepwise Bayesian odds estimation as a
function of first vector frequency and number of steps

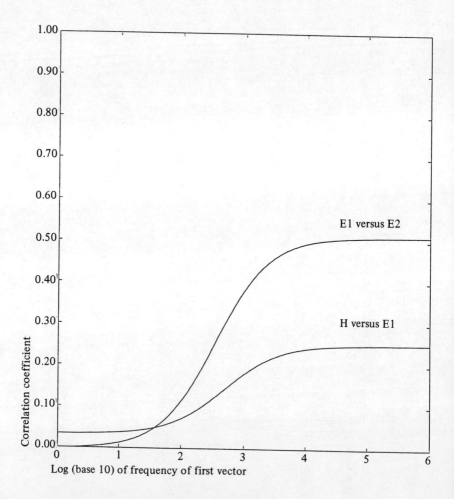

Fig. 2   Pearson product moment correlations
as a function of first vector frequency

Such a state of affairs might represent, say, a situation involving a rare disease, H, and six symptoms, E_i. The symptoms are positively correlated, but only to a moderate extent. The disease is correlated with each symptom considered separately, but only at a rather low level, (see Fig. 2). However, the disease is more likely to be present the more symptoms are known to be present. Increasing x represents a reduction in the prevalence of the disease and the symptoms, whether considered separately or jointly (in pairs). This joint reduction produces an increase in both the correlation coefficients shown in Fig. 2, with both correlations tending to asymptotic values as x gets large. (The asymptotic values are 0.253 for H versus E_1 and 0.512 for E_1 versus E_2 for the data used). The upper limit of one million chosen for x is by no means unreasonable in the context of the present example – it could easily represent the population of some large city, e.g. Birmingham. If it had been decided to model the prevalence of some rare disease in the whole country, an upper limit of fifty million would have been more appropriate. Such a situation could occur if the disease and the symptoms were each so dramatic and striking that the incidence of any case of the disease (or any combination of the symptoms) would not go unnoticed and would be duly recorded by the health authorities. Note also that, although the correlations tend to asymptotic values as x gets large, R (the log odds ratio) does not – it merely gets larger.

   In conclusion, it is quite clear that stepwise Bayesian odds updating as used in expert systems of the Prospector type is quite unsuitable for estimating posterior odds, except in circumstances in which the assumption of conditional independence is met, or nearly so. The greater the number of steps required, the more critical does this condition become. Unfortunately, there are many situations in which conditional independence is likely to be severely violated – one such instance having been described here.

   In fairness, it should be pointed out that, in circumstances where the use of a single production rule would lead to an unwarranted assumption of conditional independence (as described above), it is always possible to replace the offending rule with two or more production rules for dealing with different combinations of evidence values. However, in typical applications, the use of this technique is often ignored and, even where utilised, it tends to be used in an inadequate or inconsistent fashion. This seems to be due partly to lack of statistical expertise in the knowledge engineer and the domain expert and partly to the fact that no objective data are used to test for violations of conditional independence assumptions. This preference for subjective prior probabilities and likelihood ratios is the cause of further difficulties which are described in Section 4.

3. Use of Fuzzy Set Theory

In addition to the Bayesian odds updating process
described in the previous section, systems such as Prospector
attempt to incorporate logical conjunction and disjunction into the
inference network, by using fuzzy set theory (Zadeh, 1965), as
explained in Duda et al (1977).

For conjunction, the probability of the result is defined
as being the minimum of the conjuncts:

$$P(E_1 \wedge E_2 \wedge \ldots \wedge E_n) = \min(P(E_1), P(E_2), \ldots, P(E_n)) \qquad (8)$$

Duda et al (1977) note that this formulation has the disadvantage
that the outcome is insensitive to changes in any probabilities
except the smallest. For disjunction, a similar expression defines
the probability of the result as being the maximum of the
disjuncts:

$$P(E_1 \vee E_2 \vee \ldots \vee E_n) = \max(P(E_1), P(E_2), \ldots, P(E_n)) \qquad (9)$$

Again Duda et al (1977) remark that this definition yields a
disjunction which is insensitive to changes in any probabilities
except the largest.

N	E_1	E_2
a	0	0
b	0	1
c	1	0
d	1	1

Table 2. The case table used to explain fuzzy 'and' and 'or'

Let us examine these formulations more closely, using an
example where two probabilities are combined. Suppose we have the
case table shown in Table 2. Using P to represent the correct
probabilities (as usual) and P^* to represent pseudo-probabilities,
calculated according to fuzzy logic, we have the following
formulae. Correct conjunction and disjunction are given by:

$$P(E_1 \wedge E_2) = d/(a+b+c+d) \qquad (10)$$

$$P(E_1 \vee E_2) = (b+c+d)/(a+b+c+d) \qquad (11)$$

However, fuzzy logic gives:

$$P^*(E_1 \wedge E_2) = (\min(b,c)+d)/(a+b+c+d) \qquad (12)$$

and $\quad P^*(E_1 \vee E_2) = (\max(b,c)+d)/(a+b+c+d) \qquad (13)$

Furthermore, it is true that:

$$0 \leqslant P(E_1 \wedge E_2) \leqslant P^*(E_1 \wedge E_2) \qquad (14)$$

and $\quad P^*(E_1 \vee E_2) \leqslant P(E_1 \vee E_2) \leqslant 1 \qquad (15)$

Thus the 'fuzzy and' is an upper bound on the set of values that can be taken by the true conjunction. Similarly, the 'fuzzy or' is a lower bound on the set of values that can be taken by the true disjunction. In both cases, the fuzzy version is correct if and only if the frequencies for either b or c are zero. It seems that, in general, use of these rules is reserved for situations in which the various E_i are positively correlated, thus rendering computation based on assumptions of independence inaccurate. (Results would be too high for disjunctions and too low for conjunctions). However, to adopt the lower bound for disjunction and the upper bound for conjunction is certainly a gross over-compensation and can lead to serious error during the propagation of probabilities through the inference network.

4. Subjective Probability Estimates and Associated Difficulties

4.1 Inconsistent Priors

Prospector deals with the uncertainty of evidence by allowing the user to give a subjective probability for the existence of each piece of evidence. (This is not actually done directly, but is done via certainty factors, which are described in the next section). Using P' to represent random probability variables, the correct expression for deriving the probability of H becomes:

$$P'(H) = P(H|E)P'(E) + P(H|\bar{E})P'(\bar{E}) \qquad (16)$$

This is a function giving P'(H) in terms of P'(E). The end points of the function yield P(H|E) when P'(E)=1 and P(H|$\bar{E}$) when P'(E)=0. As the function is linear, these endpoints completely determine it. Now, when P'(E)=P(E) (i.e. the prior probability of E), the function should give P'(H)=P(H) (i.e. the prior probability of H). This is where difficulties arise. In general, the prior probabilities tend to be inconsistent, i.e. the point specified by the prior probabilities of E and H does not lie on the function.

This could be due to either of the priors being incorrect, or to either of the endpoints of the function being incorrect. Of course, all four parameters are, in essence, subjective probability estimates and are thereby prone to error, so the problem is not surprising.

This problem is discussed at some length by Duda, Hart & Nilsson (1976). The solution adopted in Prospector was to use a piecewise linear function, given by Duda et al (1977), which passes through all three points - whether they are colinear or not. The function is shown in below, using the same notation as Equation (16):

$$P'(H) = \begin{cases} P(H|\bar{E}) + (P(H)-P(H|\bar{E}))(P'(E)/P(E)), & 0 \leqslant P'(E) \leqslant P(E) \\ \\ P(H) + (P(H|E)-P(H))(P'(E)-P(E))/P(\bar{E}), & P(E) \leqslant P'(E) \leqslant 1 \end{cases} \tag{17}$$

Of course, such a function is not correct and its use must add to the overall inaccuracy of probability propagation.

Perhaps it is worth mentioning at this point that the technique used by AL/X is superficially similar, using a piecewise linear function to derive the likelihood ratio (rather than P'(H)) from P'(E). This is even worse because such a function becomes linear when the corresponding probability function does so, which is certainly not correct. Reiter (1980) gives no recognition of this fact.

Finally, the scheme for dealing with uncertain evidence that is used by MYCIN also uses a piecewise linear function and departs from probability theory in yet another way. This system does not allow the posterior odds to be revised at all if the user judges the evidence to be less likely than its prior value!

It might be thought that the problem of inconsistent priors could be resolved by confronting the expert with his inconsistencies and requesting him to resolve them. However, in practice, it would probably be virtually impossible to revise a large inference network and render it consistent.

4.2 Certainty Factors

Prospector elicits probabilities from the user with the aid of certainty factors. Thus the certainty of E, is defined by Duda et al (1977) as follows (using the same notation as above):

$$C(E) = \begin{cases} 5(P'(E)-P(E))/P(E), & 0 \leqslant P'(E) < P(E) \\ \\ 5(P'(E)-P(E))/P(\bar{E}), & P(E) \leqslant P'(E) \leqslant 1 \end{cases} \tag{18}$$

This again is a piecewise linear function, with an arbitrary scaling from -5 to +5, arranged so that -5 corresponds to absolute certainty of the absence of E and +5 to absolute certainty of its presence. A certainty value of zero represents a state of complete uncertainty and corresponds to the prior probability of E. Thus certainty factors are used to represent the extent to which the probability of E is different from its prior value, rather than the magnitude of the probability value itself.

Of course, an obvious feature of this approach is that the same certainty value can represent widely different values for the subjective probability of different pieces of evidence if the respective priors are widely different. Whether or not this is a desirable feature hinges upon whether users are clear that they are making subjective estimates of deviations of probabilities from their prior values (rather than estimates of probabilities per se) and also upon whether they are better at doing the former than the latter.

5. Concluding Remarks

As a method of inference, Bayesian odds updating appears superficially attractive because it seems to offer the capability of dealing with pieces of evidence one at a time, in a manageable way, in a manner which appeals to the knowledge engineer because a "window" can easily be provided which casts light on the working of the system.

Unfortunately, such a system depends on the assumption of conditional independence and this assumption is made in a cavalier fashion, regardless of the extent of the lack of fit between the model and the subject area that it represents. Undoubtedly, this flaw is exacerbated by the use of subjective probabilities (rather than objective ones, estimated from actual data). To make matters worse, logical conjunctions and disjunctions are dealt with by a most peculiar approach which seems guaranteed to provide particularly poor estimates of the required probabilities in most instances.

The solution seems to be to give up altogether the goal of attempting to encode the knowledge of the expert directly into an expert system and instead to derive an appropriate model of the domain from a data base of past cases, where the values for H are known. This can either be done using automatic induction techniques (e.g. Michalski and Chilausky, 1980) if a logical representation is preferred, or can be achieved by using statistical techniques such as discriminant analysis or logistic regression if a statistical model is required. The objection might be raised that such techniques are all very well, but they do not give us a proper expert system because they lack the capacity to provide a human window into their workings - a characteristic which many see as essential to a bona fide expert system. The obvious rejoinder to such an objection is that we are better of without windows if they are obtained at the cost of distorting that which is seen through them!

References

Adams, J.B. (1976). A probability model of medical reasoning and the MYCIN model. Mathematical Biosciences, 32, 177-186.

Duda, R., Gaschnig, J. & Hart, P. (1979). Model design in the Prospector consultant system for mineral exploration. In Expert systems in the micro-electronic age, ed. D. Michie, pp. 153-167. Edinburgh: Edinburgh University Press.

Duda, R.O., Hart, P.E., Konolige, K. & Reboh, R. (1979). A computer based consultant for mineral exploration. Final Report, SRI Projects 5821 and 6415, SRI International, Menlo Park, California.

Duda, R.O., Hart, P.E. and Nilsson, N.J. (1976). Subjective Bayesian methods for rule-based inference systems. Technical Note 124, Artificial Intelligence Center, SRI International, Menlo Park, California.

Duda, R.O., Hart, P.E., Nilsson, N.J., Reboh, R., Slocum, J. & Sutherland, G.L. (1977). Development of a computer-based consultant for mineral exploration. Annual Report, SRI Projects 5821 and 6415, SRI International, Menlo Park, California.

Michalski, R.S. & Chilausky, R.L. (1980). Knowledge acquisition by encoding expert rules versus computer induction from examples: a case study involving soybean pathology. Int. J. Man-Machine Studies, 12, 63-87.

Reiter, J. (1980). AL/X: An expert system using plausible inference. Oxford: Intelligent Terminals Ltd.

Shortliffe, E.H. & Buchanan, B. (1975). A model of inexact reasoning in medicine. Mathematical Biosciences, 23, 351-379.

Zadeh, L.A. (1965). Fuzzy sets. Information and Control, 8, 338-353.

IMPORTANCE-DRIVEN DISTRIBUTED CONTROL
OF DIAGNOSTIC INFERENCE

David C. Dodson   Alan L. Rector
Dept. of Computer Science Medical Computation Unit
The City University   University of Manchester
Northampton Square   Manchester Royal Infirmary
London EC1V OHB   Manchester M13 9WL

Abstract

        We present a scheme for importance-driven control of
probabilistic diagnostic inference, as implemented in a prototype
system.
        This control scheme is designed to allow, with minimum
delay, thoroughly considered response to the input of observed
attributes. This involves updating all significantly affected
diagnostic assessments and selecting a prominent set of further
requests for input of observations. These requests are selected
on a cost-benefit basis reflecting the system's current global
belief state. Requests are presented simultaneously, each
together with its measure of merit.
        This scheme supports user interactions in which both
computer and user have initiative. The system provides advice and
criticism but neither demands response nor imposes decisions.
        Quantitative inferences of importance constitute the
central feature of this scheme. These inferences proceed through
an inference network in the opposite direction to ordinary inferences of certainty about facts. Control explanations will just
need to express inferences of importance, and are enabled in the
same way as are explanations of certainty. This provides a powerful alternative to meta-level strategic inference, though both
approaches can be combined.
        Issues of time complexity, strategic choice, cognitive
emulation and robustness are touched on.

1. Introduction

        This paper presents a scheme for importance-driven
control of diagnostic inference. This scheme grew out of research
towards medical decision support systems for general practitioners. The authors are developing a framework for such systems
around interacting subsystems for two problem sub-domains: fact-
seeking inference (i.e. diagnosis) and action-planning. A prototype of the latter subsystem is described by Dodson, Harrison &
Rector (1983). These subsystems must interact extensively with
each other and with sub systems mediating user interaction and
patient medical record access.
        Interactions that the diagnostic subsystem must sup-
port have a major impact on its inference control regime. This
paper presents the key features of this impact as demonstrated by

our 'Mark1' prototype. The required style of mixed initiative
user dialogue described in the next section is sufficient to
motivate the chosen control regime. Envisaged interactions with
subsystems other than the user interface do not radically affect
the picture presented here. This regime is well-suited to, and
perhaps necessary for a broad spectrum of time-critical applications of fact-seeking expert systems.

2. Interaction Requirements

Most fact-seeking expert systems elicit findings by
interviewing the user in a relatively inflexible way. The user
has no control over the course of this interaction, which tends to
be lengthy, exhaustive and tiring. This pattern may be invaluable
for interviewing clients. For the busy doctor, however, such
techniques are unacceptable.

General Practice requires a system usable simply as an
interactive patient medical record system, but which can provide
intelligent advice and criticism (Fox & Rector 1982). This added
functionality should neither demand response nor impose decisions.

Convenient use during patient consultation will be
crucial to success. In the few minutes available for each consultation the doctor's attention must go primarily to the patient. A
real-time approach to inference and interaction is clearly essential.

The user must be able to input findings at will,
whether or not the system prompts for them. Users must be able to
perform input in their own time, ignoring prompts and advice from
the system for an arbitrary period of time. When users are ready
to attend to requests for specific inputs, they must be able to
immediately apprehend the importance of each prompt. This should
allow users to regulate their attention to prompts in tune with
their subjective uncertainty. Prompts should therefore be
presented in a menu format in such a way that the importance of
every item can be immediately perceived.

In order to determine the importance of potential
findings, The system's diagnostic assessment needs to be frequently updated. This implies maintaining a goal set of the possible diagnoses for which further evidence is most sought. This
set of 'investigative goals' should include any relatively
unlikely but dangerous conditions warranting consideration. Each
investigative goal needs a measure of investigative importance
with which to bid for consideration in the system's determination
of its behaviour.

A display of likely diagnoses and investigative goals
could largely explain the reasons for input prompts without resort
to interaction. It would also provide the doctor with an interactive medium for both adjusting the system's line of enquiry and
entering their own assessments.

3. The Inference Model

3.1. The Inference Network

Figure 1 shows a small part of an inference network.

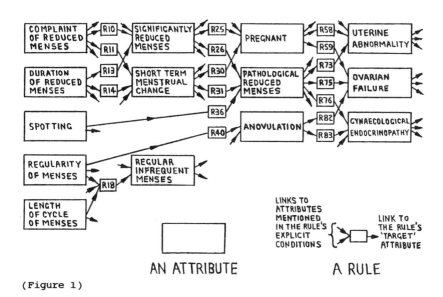

(Figure 1)

As in other diagnostic expert systems there is a set of nodes. Some of these represent rules, the rest represent attributes of a case. The general format for a rule is as follows. (Square brackets indicate optional phrases, angle brackets indicate phrase type names.)

```
<rule> ::= [provided <explicit precondition> then]
              <antecedent> <rule operator> <conclusion> : <strength>
                                     [otherwise <strength>]
<conclusion> ::= <target attribute> [is <value>]
```

Some examples of rules represented in figure 1 are shown below.

r82:   anovulation is_caused_by ovarian failure : possibly
          otherwise definitely_not.

r18:   regular menses and length of cycle of menses > 35 days
          and not change of menses is_associated_with regular
          infrequent menses : very_probably otherwise
          probably_not.

Explicit preconditions (not shown in these examples) have the same
syntax as antecedents. Both are (explicit) 'conditions'. A rule
may also have an implied precondition (or presupposition).
Implied preconditions are taken to be the conjunction of any
attributes presupposed by attributes in the rule's explicit conditions but not presupposed by its target. For instance, 'duration
of change of menses' presupposes 'change of menses' which presupposes 'menses'. In the idiom "X otherwise Y", X specifies the
effect of the rule when all its conditions are true. Y gives the
effect when any preconditions are true but the antecedent is
false.

Every node has not only a measure of belief but also
measures of importance. Both sorts of measure are inferred by
localized plausible reasoning. System control derives from the
interaction of these measures. Though informed by analysis, the
nature of such measures and of the calculus by which they are
inferred is in practice an empirical matter.

3.2. Material Belief

We call the measure of belief in a node its (measure
of) 'material belief'. This more precisely distinguishes it from
a measure of importance, which is a teleological kind of belief.

In our scheme, the material belief in a node does not
consist only of a current certainty. It also includes the maximum
and minimum limits to the certainty the node could achieve, given
further new findings but without altering existing ones. As findings relevant to a node are entered, its certainty limits con-
verge. If all relevant findings are entered, both certainty limits should become equal to the current certainty. A calculus of
current certainty determines a calculus of certainty limits.

The notion of a node having a certainty is a simplifi-
cation for the purpose of exposition. This is only transparent in
the case of propositional or truth-type attributes. In general,
certainties in the prototype do not qualify an attribute itself,
but rather the attribution of a value to an attribute. Thus, in
the case of propositional attributes, the single value 'true' is
assumed. Other types of attributes (nominal and numeric) are
already in limited use, although their full treatment requires
further research.

The certainty measure and certainty calculus used in
the prototype have been found to be technically inadequate. They
are about to be replaced by an extended Bayesian calculus such
that 'certainties' will be probability estimates. Further
description of them is thus inappropriate here, beyond saying that
a certainty/probability mapping was employed.

3.3. Teleological Belief

In our prototype there are two kinds of importance.
Each node has variable potential importance and variable investigative importance.

As a matter of principle, diagnoses are only important

in as much as their implications for treatment are important.
Potential importance thus arises at attributes like "pregnant" and
"ovarian failure" whose probabilities trigger treatment constraints. These attributes are termed 'diagnostic goals'. The
potential importance of a diagnostic goal is simply the importance
of the constraints triggered if it is certainly true. This potential importance is inherited by the immediate indicants of
diagnostic goals and on through to attributes representing
findings as shown on the left in figure 1. This is mediated by a
local calculus of potential importance mirroring the certainty
calculus. The weaker a rule is at transmitting certainty from
attributes in its conditions to its target, the weaker it is at
transmitting importance in the opposite direction.

The second type of importance is investigative importance. This is the importance of looking for more evidence bearing on the material belief status of an attribute. Investigative
importance is obtained by means of what we term an 'importance
actualization' function. This function, diagrammed in figure 2,
is applied to an attribute whenever its belief status is updated.
It yields the attribute's current investigative importance given
its potential importance, its current certainty and its certainty
limits.

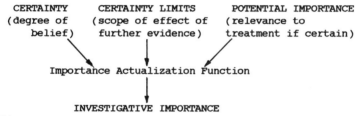

```
   CERTAINTY        CERTAINTY LIMITS         POTENTIAL IMPORTANCE
  (degree of       ( scope of effect of     ( relevance to
     belief)         further evidence)        treatment if certain)


        Importance Actualization Function


              INVESTIGATIVE IMPORTANCE
```
(Figure 2)

Like potential importance, investigative importance is inherited
from goals towards findings. This type of importance originates
at 'investigative goals': attributes of leading investigative
importance upon which attention has been focussed. The inheritance of investigative importance is programmed to depend on local
material beliefs as well as on rule strengths.

The following illustrates this teleology in terms of
figure 1. Suppose the diagnostic attribute "pathological reduced
menses" has considerable POTENTIAL importance. Suppose also that
the certainty of this attribute is "very possible" and that its
certainty limits are quite wide, indicating that some rule or
rules which affect this diagnosis are awaiting further findings.
This enables us to infer, using the importance actualization function, that "pathological reduced menses" has substantial INVESTI-
GATIVE importance. Now, we have several rules for diagnosing
"pathological reduced menses", not all of which are shown. Via
these rules, the attributes mentioned in their conditions each
inherit some of the investigative importance of "pathological

reduced menses" according to their potential to supply new evidence. At each step, this potential is known from the material
beliefs in the nodes involved. Suppose also that most of the
range of certainty limits on "pathological reduced menses" is due
to our not yet having any evidence for "spotting". "Spotting"
will then inherit more of the investigative importance of "pathological reduced menses" than other attributes, and can bid for an
input prompt.

4.   The Inference Control Scheme

4.1.   Coherent Waves of Inference

          An integral part of the scheme is the use of strati-
fied propagation. Nodes in the network have a partial ordering
implicit in the directionality of their interconnexions. The
system's rule base maintenance procedures automatically produce a
stratification of nodes consistent with this partial ordering.
This is illustrated by the arrangement of nodes in columns in figure 1. In global belief update, all strata are visited alter-
nately in "forward" sequence for material belief maintenance and
in "backward" sequence for importance (or teleological belief)
maintenance. This minimizes algorithmic time complexity. (Suppose depth-first traversal were used to realize the consequences
of changing material belief in 'duration of change of menses'.
This could generate a combinatorial explosion of repeatedly visit-
ing nodes such as 'pregnant' and 'ovarian failure' via different
paths.)
          This time-complexity advantage is compounded by pro-
cessing a batch of inputs at a time. Input batching is quite
natural given the batching of prompts implicit in a menu. In a
parallel processing implementation, all nodes in a stratum would
be processed simultaneously, producing a broad front or wave of
update sweeping through the network.

4.2.   The Control Algorithm

          The inference network is initialised to hold the
default material beliefs and importances of attributes. The global belief update procedure thus only has to update significantly
changed beliefs in response to new input. This procedure consists
of these steps.

1)   Material Belief Update: Propagate a wave of signifi-
            cant change of local material beliefs from new find-
            ings towards goals. When the certainty of an attri-
            bute significantly exceeds its default level, it
            becomes evoked as an hypothesis.

2)   A wave of update of potential importance could now be
             propagated back from affected attributes if required.
             The new investigative importance of each affected
             attribute is evaluated. An index of candidate inves-
             tigative goals is maintained in descending order of
             investigative importance.

3)   Attention focusing: A prominent set of investigative
             goals is selected and could be modified by strategy
             heuristics if required.

4)   Investigative importance is propagated from investiga-
             tive goals to queryable attributes. At these attri-
             butes it is divided by ascertainment cost and an index
             of questions is constructed in descending order on the
             resulting measure.

5)   Output of the set of prominent questions, if non-
             empty.

          Prolog has been invaluable as a prototyping language.
Even so, the global update procedure is written algorithmically
using the Logal predicates (Dodson & Rector 1983). This procedure
is well-suited to implementation using microcoding, array processing, or various parallel processing techniques.

4.3. Observations

          Material beliefs affect inferences of importance by
figuring in their calculus. Importances affect material beliefs
by governing the fact-seeking behaviour of the system. Both types
of belief also regulate each other's thresholds of significant
change which are used in update pruning. These interactions
direct investigation in all directions computed to be of salient
importance.
          Our main goal, of course, is appropriate response (in
the form of prompting) to sequences of user inputs. Applied to
gynecological problems, the prototype's sequencing of its
responses is informally acceptable to the doctors involved in
knowledge harvesting. Subject to weaknesses attributable to
incompleteness in the present implementation of our design, it
approximates well to intuitions about evaluation of importance and
pertinence of behaviour.

5. Discussion

5.1. Explanations

          This scheme provides a powerful framework for explana-
tion of inference strategy. Explanations of current inference
control, though not yet implemented, can simply read off current

inferences of importance. For example, "It seems fairly important to ask about 'complaint of reduced menses' because it seems quite important to evaluate whether there is 'pathological reduced menses'" etc..

5.2. Comparison with NEOMYCIN

Our control regime contrasts with that demonstrated in NEOMYCIN (Clancey & Letsinger 1981, Clancey 1983a, 1983b, Warner Hasling 1983). NEOMYCIN apparently succeeds in capturing a rational and exhaustive methodology used by experts. It is controlled by a production system of about 75 meta-rules. As an example, one of these could be paraphrased "if the hypothesis in focus has a sub-type not yet pursued, pursue it". Meta-rules provide a means of declarative control of inferences of certainty. This facilitates explanation of strategy. As such, they state 'first order' strategic knowledge but require a 'second order' strategy for the selection of first-order strategic tasks. Apparently NEOMYCIN has no concurrency of first-order strategic tasks in the conventional sense, only the effect of branching, looping and calling. Clancey (1983b) admits it is unclear how or why meta-rules and thus tasks should be selected in quite the order used and that this impairs explanations of strategy. By imposing a minimum of strategic choices, we suspect our control scheme will be significantly more transparent.

In our approach, strategic knowledge is embedded in the calculi of importance. Such knowledge is thus in effect instantiated at all nodes, identical for all nodes of a given type, and localized in application. The 'meta-level' control problem has been replaced by a base-level problem.

Designed for use in teaching diagnostic methodology, NEOMYCIN's objectives were different from those of our system. In our application, users will want to apply their own methodology in their own time. This makes a highly sequentialized methodology impractical. There is, however, scope for combining both approaches. In our algorithm, the attention focusing step (step 3) provides a point of escape from distributed control. Our prototype uses only a numeric threshold here, but heuristics could abound. For example, the type of heuristics used in INTERNIST (Pople 1982) for pursuing, differentiating or eliminating hypotheses could be incorporated. It may also be useful to allow the user to manually select major strategies like "group and differentiate" and "explore and refine" as used in NEOMYCIN. Such attention focusing will need associated explanatory facilities. Beyond this our control scheme seems transparent enough not to raise questions of self-explanation.

5.3. Local Inference

It is clearly important that our design should tolerate a considerable degree of approximation in rules, user input, and various aspects of belief update. As leading example

of the latter, certainty limits may be optimistic because anta-
gonistic effects of a finding via different paths through the network are ignored.

Our view is that calculi of belief should be domain-
independent, apply locally, and perform interpolations which
satisfy both intuition and mathematical plausibility. This view
partly follows from Berliner's (1982) opposition to "premature
quantization". Berliner observed that relatively smooth transitions of internal evaluation are often essential to successful
behaviour. In particular, attributes may need a degree of quasi-
continuity much greater than that manifested when their values are
linguistically expressed. Applying this view leads to a variety
of hypotheses in cognitive psychology.

Importance calculi require considerable further
research. We are using largely intuitive functions for importance
inheritance and actualization. The case of the importance actualization function is an interesting example. We seem to have
domain-independent intuitions about the 'shape' of this function
which remain only to be fine-tuned. Fine tuning in turn can
accommodate a range of idiosyncrasy without any one setting being
identifiable as best. Within limits, then, user-controllable fine
tuning of cognitive style is possible.

The present prototype seems remarkably tolerant of
weaknesses and omissions in the implementation of our design. Its
known behavioural weaknesses are directly attributable to these
shortcomings. This provides early confirmation that the scheme is
robust.

6. Conclusions

An importance-directed regime for diagnostic inference
control has been implemented in a prototype system. This regime
meets several operational goals associated with time-critical use.
It provides a frequently updated diagnostic assessment and maintains a set of prompts of quantified importance for the input of
findings. User input is not constrained to follow these prompts.
The belief update procedure is well suited to the exploitation of
parallel processing.

The present prototype has shown it is possible to use
concepts of importance derived from treatment needs in the distributed control of a diagnostic system. This is an alternative
to controlling inference by meta-rules. Strategic inferences in
effect run concurrently and merge, avoiding the need to switch
between strategies. This provides a powerful framework for strategy explanation. This distributed component of the control
scheme seems transparent enough not to require self-explanation.
Investigative attention focusing is de-coupled from the distributed component and provides scope for combining our basic scheme
with a meta-rule approach.

Acknowledgements

We wish to thank Alan Bundy for suggesting several useful revisions of this paper. The research reported here was done in the Department of Community Health in The University of Nottingham under a grant from the Medical Research Council.

References

Berliner, H.J. (1982). Multiprocessing and Duality in Intelligence. Proc. European Conference on Artificial Intelligence, Orsay, France (ECAI-82) pp. 28-36.

Clancey, W.J. & Letsinger, R. (1981). NEOMYCIN: Reconfiguring a Rule-Based Expert System for Application to Teaching. Proc. Seventh International Conference on Artificial Intelligence, Vancouver, Canada (IJCAI-81) vol. 2 pp. 829-835.

Clancey, W.J. (1983a). The Epistemology of a Rule-Based Expert System: A Framework for Explanation. Artificial Intelligence vol. 20 no. 3.

Clancey, W.J. (1983b). The Advantages of Abstract Control Knowledge in Expert System Design. Proc. National Conference on Artificial Intelligence, Washington D.C. (AAAI-83) pp. 74-78.

Dodson, D.C., Harrison, M.J. & Rector, A.L. (1983). A Prototype Knowledge-Based Medical Treatment Planner. Proc. B.C.S. Expert Systems 83, Cambridge, UK, pp. 153-161.

Dodson, D.C. & Rector, A.L. (1983). Logal: Algorithmic Control Structures For Prolog. Proc. Eighth International Conference on Artificial Intelligence, Karlsruhe, W. Germany (IJCAI-83) vol. 1 pp. 536-538.

Fox, J. & Rector, A.L. (1982). Expert Systems for Primary Medical Care? Automedica vol. 4 pp. 123-130.

Kulikowski, C.A. & Weiss, S.H. (1982). Representation of Expert Knowledge for Consultation: The CASNET and EXPERT Projects. In Szolovits (1982).

Pople, H.E. (1982). Heuristic Methods for Imposing Structure on Ill-Structured Problems: The Structuring of Medical Diagnostics. In Szolovits (1982).

Szolovits, P. (1982) [Ed.]. Artificial Intelligence in Medicine. Boulder, Colorado: Westview.

Warner Hasling, D. (1983). Abstract Explanations of Strategy in a Diagnostic Consultation System. Proc. National Conference on Artificial Intelligence, Washington D.C. (AAAI-83) pp. 157-161.

AN ANALYSIS OF THE PROBLEMS OF AUGMENTING
A SMALL EXPERT SYSTEM

P L Alvey, C D Myers[1], M F Greaves[2]
Imperial Cancer Research Fund, Lincoln's Inn Fields,
London WC2A 3PX
[1] Current address: Dept of Microbiology, University
of Texas, 5323 Harry Himes Boulevard, Dallas, Texas
[2] Currently: Director, The Leukaemia Research Fund
Centre at The Institute of Cancer Research,
Fulham Road, London SW3 6JB

Abstract

An expert system is being developed to interpret the
results of laboratory tests used in the diagnosis of leukaemia. A
small EMYCIN system gave a satisfactory answer in only 70 cases of
a test set of 100, so it was analysed in detail before a larger
system was built. There were two basic problems: a small number
of simple errors in the rule set, and a poor representation of the
structure of the domain. Correction of the errors could raise the
performance of the system to 94%, but the occurrence of atypical
cases would prevent further improvements. These cases are
completely beyond the scope of the present rules and we fear that
the system could not be modified to handle them without
fundamental changes to its representation of the domain.

1. Introduction

Shells provide the inexperienced with a quick and
convenient method for developing expert systems with mediocre
performance. The ability to produce a system that gets a
proportion of the answers correct usually pleases the system
builder, but this may not be the most appropriate response.
Perhaps the performance gap can simply be filled with more
knowledge, but alternatively it may be the warning sign of future
disaster when the complexity of the system is increased.
At the ICRF an expert system is being developed for
interpreting the results of monoclonal antibody tests on cases of
leukaemia. A small scale system has been produced using EMYCIN,
but when tested on a set of 100 new cases it gave an acceptable
answer in only 70. Before developing a larger system we needed to
know the reasons for the diagnostic shortfall. Was the knowledge
elicited from the expert adequate? Had it been transcribed into
rules that were correct, complete and consistent? Would the
addition of more knowledge make the system better or worse? If
the foundations of the small system were unsound it was important
to find out at an early stage rather than blunder on with an
inappropriate structure. Accordingly we undertook an analysis of
the system to assess the logical integrity of its rules and find
the reasons for its errors.

1.1 Background Information

Considerable improvements have been achieved in the treatment of leukaemia in recent years and this is partly due to the use of the most appropriate method of treatment for each of the different varieties of the disease.

Most doctors are familiar with the four major types of leukaemia. Acute lymphoblastic leukaemia (ALL) and acute myeloblastic leukaemia (AML) are aggressive diseases usually affecting younger people; chronic lymphatic leukaemia (CLL) and chronic myeloid leukaemia (CML) are less severe and tend to affect older people. In addition, chronic myeloid leukaemia can occasionally turn into one of the acute varieties by a process called blast crisis (CML-BC-LYMPHOID, CML-BC-MYELOID).

With the latest laboratory techniques it is now possible to recognize subdivisions within the major types (eg common-ALL, null-ALL), and some of these sub-types are being found to have different prognoses from the others and to respond differently to different treatments. As more knowledge becomes available from current and future research it will be important for clinicians to have information on the sub-types of their cases. At present the tests are only performed in a few laboratories, although the reagents will soon be more widely available. However, the interpretation of the results is not simple. It is somewhat subjective and only a handful of experts have sufficient knowledge to give reliable opinions to clinicians. This is the expertise we wish to emulate in our expert system.

1.2 The ICRF Leukaemia Diagnosis System

The early development of the system was described at the Expert Systems 83 Conference (Myers et al). Briefly, the expert (MFG) gave a running commentary whilst making a diagnosis on 67 samples from various hospitals. "Knowledge" was extracted from transcripts of the sessions and used (by CDM) to create a 67 rule expert system in EMYCIN. The system was not ambitious; it attempted to emulate the subjective opinions of our domain expert (MFG), but only in respect of the diagnosis of the case - no attempt was made to mimic the qualifying comments such as: "compatible with", "probably", "minor population of". Even with this benevolent method of assessment the system only concurred with the expert's view in 70 of the 100 cases in the test set.

2. The Analysis

Analysis of the system was undertaken by one of us (PLA) who had played no more than an advisory role in its initial development. The reviewer had very little knowledge of the domain but was experienced in the use of both EMYCIN and PROLOG.

2.1 Translation into PROLOG

EMYCIN rules have an inconvenient format for logical analysis: the verbose listings, self-referencing rules, multiple conclusions, multi-valued parameters and negative certainty factors all make it difficult to follow or predict the line of reasoning. Therefore the EMYCIN system was translated into Edinburgh University DEC-10 PROLOG to allow the rules making each conclusion to be grouped together and analysed for completeness.

The structure of the system was simple: the top level rules assign specific diagnoses to combinations of the intermediate parameters, cell_lineage and cell_type; and the values of these parameters are derived from raw data. Translation was not difficult; Figure 1 illustrates the translation of a pair of rules with negative and multiple conclusions. These were handled by transferring the negative conclusion of Rule 4 to the subgoals of the translated Rule 3. It was then noticed that the

---

EMYCIN   If: 1) Cell-type = b-cell, and
RULE003   2) Cell-lineage = cll
             Then: Diagnosis = b-cell-cll (1.0)

EMYCIN   If: 1) Cell-type = monoclonal-b-cell, and
RULE004   2) Cell-lineage = cll
             Then: 1) Diagnosis = monoclonal-b-cell-cll (1.0), and
                    2) Diagnosis ~= b-cell-cll (1.0)

Initial PROLOG Translation -

```
   diagnosis(Pt, b_cll ):- cell_lineage(Pt,Sa, cll ),
                           cell_type(   Pt,Sa, b_cell ),
                           \+ cell_type(Pt,Sa, monoclonal_b_cell ).

   diagnosis(Pt, monoclonal_b_cll ):-
                           cell_lineage(Pt,Sa, cll ),
                           cell_type(   Pt,Sa, monoclonal_b_cell ).
```

Final PROLOG Translation -

```
   diagnosis(Pt, b_cll ):-
                           cell_lineage(Pt,Sa, cll ),
                           cell_type(   Pt,Sa, non_monoclonal_b_cell ).

   diagnosis(Pt, monoclonal_b_cll ):-
                           cell_lineage(Pt,Sa, cll ),
                           cell_type(   Pt,Sa, monoclonal_b_cell ).
```

Figure 1 Example of the translation of a pair of EMYCIN rules
Pt and Sa are variables holding the identities of patients and
samples, respectively;   ~ and \+ both represent "not".

subgoals, "cell_type: b_cell / not cell_type: monoclonal_b_cell",
occurred in two other translated rules, and that no other rule
refered to the cell type "b_cell" without the qualification "not
monoclonal_b_cell". Thus it was clear that the system only wanted
to know if the predominant cell type was monoclonal B-cells or
non-monoclonal B-cells. This sub-division was made more explicit
in the final PROLOG version and appropriate changes were made to
the rules concluding values for cell_type.
EMYCIN certainty factors posed a few problems. Most
of the values used were close to 1.0, or -1.0, so the system
builder's intentions were not difficult to deduce. However, other
values made it quite impossible to follow the logic of the domain.
A simplified mechanism was used in the PROLOG system (Figure 2),

```
cell_lineage(Pt,Sa, X ):-
                likely_lineage(Pt,Sa, X, CFx ),
                \+ other_lineage_more_likely_than(Pt,Sa, X CFx ).

likely_lineage(Pt,Sa, X, CFx ):-
                                suggested_lineage(Pt,Sa, X, CFx ),
                                \+ lineage_ruled_out(Pt,Sa, X ).

other_lineage_more_likely_than(Pt,Sa, X CFx ):-
                                likely_lineage(Pt,Sa, Y, CFy ),
                                CFy > CFx.


lineage_ruled_out(Pt,Sa, cll ):- test_result(Pt,Sa, tdt,>,20 ).
lineage_ruled_out(Pt,Sa, aml ):- test_result(Pt,Sa, tdt,>,20 ).

suggested_lineage(Pt,Sa, cml_bc, 1000 ):-
                clinical_diagnosis(Pt, cml ),
                test_result(Pt,Sa, blast_count,>,30 ).

suggested_lineage(Pt,Sa, aml, 800  ):-
                clinical_diagnosis(Pt, aml ).
suggested_lineage(Pt,Sa, aml, 1000 ):-
                clinical_diagnosis(Pt, aml ),
                test_result(Pt,Sa, auer_bodies,==,yes ).

suggested_lineage(Pt,Sa, all, 950 ):-
                                test_result(Pt,Sa, tdt,>,20 ),
                                age_group(Pt, child ).
suggested_lineage(Pt,Sa, all, 800 ):-
                                test_result(Pt,Sa, tdt,>,20 ),
                                \+ age_group(Pt, child ).
```

Figure 2 The method of simulating EMYCIN's uncertainty mechanism
The final value for cell_lineage is the candidate value suggested
with the highest associated number, and not ruled out.
The numbers are the EMYCIN certainty factors multiplied by 1000.

but no attempt was made to copy EMYCIN's "black box" method of
combining certainty factors.

2.2 Examination of the PROLOG Rules

After translating the rules, a simple front end
program was written and the PROLOG system was tested. It
delivered exactly the same answer as the EMYCIN system in 98 of
the 100 test cases, so the translation was judged to be
satisfactory. The two others were interesting and unusual cases
and they will be discussed in more detail later.

The uniform format of the top-level rules allowed them
to be drawn up as a contingency table (Table 1) in which the boxes
contain the diagnoses for each of the possible combinations of
"cell lineage" and "cell type". Three notable features were
obvious from this table:

1. There is a large number of combinations of cell lineage and
   cell type for which no diagnosis is provided. These
   combinations would cause the system to conclude "undiagnosable"
   by a default mechanism; this might or might not be an
   appropriate action in each case.
2. The diagnoses that are offered lie mainly in two areas of the
   table. This suggests that combinations in other areas are
   irrelevant or improbable, and that the domain may have a more
   complex structure than that represented by the rules.
3. The profusion of AML diagnoses in the final column, which were
   found to arise from just one rule:

> RULE055   If: 1) Cell-lineage = aml, and
>   2) Cell-type ¬= lymphoid
>   Then: Diagnosis = aml (1.0)

The power of this "blunderbuss" rule is worrying.
Perhaps the system builder wanted this conclusion every time the
cell type could not be shown to be "Lymphoid", but the generation
of positive conclusions from negative or absent information has
potential for producing unpredictable errors.

The contingency table was discussed with the system
builder who confirmed the appropriateness of 43 of the 45 empty
boxes. Twelve were combinations that could not occur in practice;
25 warranted "undiagnosable" as their conclusion; 6 could
conclude "CML-BC-LYMPHOID", but a duplication in the logic allowed
another box to conclude this simultaneously. Only 2 boxes were
erroneously empty, but these were trivial ommissions. Similarly,
the filled boxes contained only 2 trivial errors and 5 boxes that
concluded "AML" instead of "IMPOSSIBLE VALUES".

The PROLOG system was then modified: the errors were
corrected; a separate rule was provided for every combination of
"cell lineage" and "cell type"; the default method for concluding
"undiagnosable" and "AML" was removed; and each impossible
combination was given a rule that concluded "data or rule error".

CELL TYPE	CELL LINEAGE							
	ALL	Burk. Cells	Hairy Cells	CLL	PLL	CML-BC	CML	AML
non-T non-B	non-T non-B ALL / ?	?	?	?	?	+	x	AML
common cell	C- ALL / ?	?	?	x	x	+	x	AML / x
null cell	null ALL / ?	?	?	?	?	+	x	AML / x
non-mono B-cell	B- ALL / ?	?	?	B- CLL	B- PLL	+	x	AML / x
mono B-cell	mono B- ALL	Burk. Lymph	hairy cell leuk.	mono B- CLL	NHL* / mono B- PLL / +		x	AML / x
T-cell	T- ALL / ?	?	?	T- CLL	T- PLL	+	x	AML / x
Lymphoid	+	?	?	?	?	CML- BC-L	CML- BC-L	x
Myeloid	x	?	?	x	x	CML- BC-M	CML	AML
unknown	+	?	?	?	PLL	?	?	AML

Table 1 The Diagnoses Made by The System
The contents of each box indicate the diagnosis that the system
would make for that combination of cell lineage and cell type.
Empty boxes would result in the conclusion "undiagnosable" by a
default mechanism. The character in the bottom left of certain
boxes indicates the appropriate conclusion for that box, as
specified by the system builder on review: ? undiagnosable;
x impossible combination; + positive conclusion missing.

Abbreviations

mono	– monoclonal	leuk.	– leukaemia
CML-BC-M	– CML-BC myeloid	Burk. cells	– Bukitt's cells
CML-BC-L	– CML-BC lymphoid	Burk. Lymph.	– Bukitt's Lymphoma
NHL*	– non-Hodgkin's Lymphoma	(IF clinical diagnosis agrees)	

When the improved system was tested it was found that its diagnostic accuracy had fallen from 70/100 to 63/100. The new system was concluding "data or rule error" for 7 cases, instead of AML. The cause of this embarrassing change was traced to the removal of the "blunderbuss AML rule": the "cell lineage" and "cell type" deduced for these cases had always been an impossible combination but the "blunderbuss AML rule" had given a conclusion of AML - the correct diagnosis for the wrong reason. As soon as the default nature of the AML rule was removed the previously undetected error in one of the "cell type" rules became painfully obvious; its correction was a simple matter.

2.3 Examination of Cases Mis-diagnosed by the System

Examination of the details of the mis-diagnosed cases and the expert's answers prompted two clear-cut observations.

In 4 cases the system gave the answer CLL when the human expert had concluded "undiagnosable". Investigation suggested that the following rule might be at fault, and its deletion rectified the problem.

suggested_lineage(Pt,Sa, cll, 500):- age_group(Pt, elderly).

This could be an accurate reflection of the prior probability of CLL in an elderly person known to have some form of leukaemia, but the human expert may be unwilling to base firm conclusions on such information. The expert subsequently confirmed this, and it has serious implications for the knowledge elicitation process. During the interviews, the expert had doubtless indicated that 50% of elderly people with leukaemia were eventually found to have CLL. But it should not be deduced from this that he would sign a report giving that diagnosis, when there was no stronger evidence available. This item is just an observation about the world; it is not the stuff of which decisions are made, and the attempt to dodge the responsibility of decision making by using a certainty factor of 500 is not an appropriate substitute. It is clearly going to be one of the duties of knowledge engineers to determine which items of elicited knowledge are a substantial basis for decisions and which items are nothing more than general knowledge.

There were 6 cases in which the system concluded some variety of ALL, but the human expert found them "undiagnosable". Each of these cases had a TDT value of 20 or less, and other test results that would otherwise have allowed a definite diagnosis. Thus it was conjectured that perhaps the low TDT was a disturbing feature that inhibited our expert from making a diagnosis, and that a rule such as the following may be missing.

lineage_ruled_out(Pt,Sa, all):- test_result(Pt,Sa,tdt,=<,20).

This was subsequently confirmed and additional rule corrected the erroneous conclusions.

The remaining 27 incorrect cases were discussed with the system builder, who has a fair understanding of the domain, and he identified the following likely causes of error:

1. In 10 cases the expert diagnosed AML only by using knowledge he had obtained since the system was built. At the time of the knowledge elicitation he would have concluded "undiagnosable", so the system should be excused on these cases.
2. Concurrently with the review the expert had revised his diagnoses of the test cases, without reference to his previous opinions made several months earlier. In 5 cases the system's answer was incorrect with respect to the first opinion, but became correct with respect to the second opinion. Thus they should not be regarded as failures.
3. In 7 cases the system failed because of simple rule errors. Most of these were related to the "blunderbuss AML rule".
4. Five incorrectly diagnosed cases were difficult cases for the expert, and required knowledge of rare cases such as "TDT negative common ALL" (most cases of common ALL are TDT positive). The system does not currently have that degree of sophistication and these cases are unavoidable failures.

2.4 Assessment of the Mechanism for Handling Uncertainty

At this stage most questions had been answered, except for the two cases in which the EMYCIN and PROLOG systems gave different answers. EMYCIN's uncertainty mechanism had been at work in both of these and the PROLOG system failed to emulate it.

In one case EMYCIN offered two firm answers with certainty factors of 0.95 and 0.8, respectively; PROLOG offered the lesser of these two. In contrast, the expert found the case "undiagnosable" because of conflicting features, and suggested that the value given for the TDT result might be incorrect.

In the other case EMYCIN offered 4 answers with certainty factors of 0.53, 0.45, 0.36, and 0.36 respectively; PROLOG offered one of the last two. This case turned out to be a difficult one with some features of the uncommon "TDT negative common ALL" - quite beyond the scope of the system.

The message from this is quite clear. Our expert does not use obscure calculations to get rid of surplus embarrassing conclusions: he uses a qualitative logic of his own that may be as complicated as the system itself. These two cases would be much better served by a mechanism along the following lines:

    IF: You have conflicting strong contenders
    THEN: Check your raw data, or your rules

    IF: You have conflicting weak contenders
    THEN: Admit that you are stumped

However, these are only two cases and there may be many others where the numerical mechanism is working to good effect. To test this hypothesis the PROLOG system was modified so that the numbers were completely ignored. Instead of selecting the single most likely value of "cell_lineage" and "cell_type", it was made to offer all possible values, regardless of their numerical likelihoods. This in turn would result in final diagnoses from all the combinations of these values.

When the modified system was run, it produced exactly the same number of correct diagnoses as before and the majority were single diagnoses. In the few cases with more than one conclusion all the conclusions were the same, and were some variety of CLL. The reason was not hard to find: the rules for concluding "Cell Lineage: CLL" are not mutually exclusive once the numerical strengths had been removed (in fact several of them can be removed from the system without any adverse effects).

Thus, in the correctly diagnosed test cases there is none in which a choice between conflicting answers is required for the successful conclusion. It would be quite another matter to suggest that no case requires a mechanism for resolving such conflict, or that the human expert does not use the EMYCIN method.

```
specific_type( Pt,Sa, common_cell, 1000 ):-
        cell_lineage(Pt,Sa, all ),
        \+ generic_cell_type(Pt,Sa, t_cell, _ ),
        \+ generic_cell_type(Pt,Sa, b_cell, _ ),
      ( test_result(Pt,Sa, hla_dr,>,20 )   )
                                 \+ known(Pt,Sa,hla_dr, HLA_DR ) ),
        test_result(Pt,Sa, c_all,>,10 ).

specific_type( Pt,Sa, null_cell, 1000 ):-
        cell_lineage(Pt,Sa, all ),
        \+ generic_cell_type(Pt,Sa, t_cell, _ ),
        \+ generic_cell_type(Pt,Sa, b_cell, _ ),
        test_result(Pt,Sa, hla_dr,>,20 ),
        test_result(Pt,Sa, c_all,<,10 ).

specific_type( Pt,Sa, non_t_non_b, 1000 ):-
        cell_lineage(Pt,Sa, all ),
        \+ generic_cell_type(Pt,Sa, t_cell, _ ),
        \+ generic_cell_type(Pt,Sa, b_cell, _ ),
      ( test_result(Pt,Sa, hla_dr,>,20 )   ;
                                 \+ known(Pt,Sa,hla_dr, HLA_DR ) ),
        \+ known(Pt,Sa,c_all, C_ALL ).
```

Figure 3   Poor Representation of the Domain
The first four subgoals of each rule share an almost identical set of subgoals, and it seemed likely that these represented some clear-cut concept within the domain. By packing all of the conditions into each rule they are made more difficult to understand, and correction of errors has to be done in triplicate.

But when building an expert system it would seem reasonable to ask
the expert how he decides about conflicting features and to copy
his method in preference to an obscure numerical mechanism.

2.5 Summary of the Analysis

Of the 100 test cases the system initially gave a
satisfactory answer in 70. The hidden errors reduced this to
63/100, but allowance for the cases where the expert changed his
mind or used "secret" knowledge raised the score to 68/90 (76%).
After correcting simple errors in the rules the performance became
85/90 (94%), but improvements beyond that would require a
substantial quantity of new knowledge and fundamental changes to
the architecture of the system. At present it only knows about
orthodox cases; it cannot handle the rare exceptions to general
rules. A high quality system must handle rare cases and will
require a more comprehensive representation of the domain. The
current representation is adequate for simple cases but might
prove disastrous in a complex system (see Figures 3 & 4).

```
specific_type(Pt,Sa, common_cell, 1000 ):-
                          pre_B_cells_present(Pt,Sa),
                          test_result(Pt,Sa, c_all,>,10 ).

specific_type(Pt,Sa, null_cell,    1000 ):-
                          pre_B_cells_present(Pt,Sa),
                          test_result(Pt,Sa, c_all,=<,10 ).

specific_type(Pt,Sa, unclassifiable_pre_B, 1000 ):-
                          pre_B_cells_present(Pt,Sa),
                          \+ known(Pt,Sa,c_all, _ ).


pre_B_cells_present(Pt,Sa):- cell_lineage(Pt,Sa, all ),
                          \+ generic_cell_type(Pt,Sa, t_cell, _ ),
                          \+ generic_cell_type(Pt,Sa, b_cell, _ ),
                          test_result(Pt,Sa, hla_dr,>,20 ).
```

Figure 4 An Improved Representation of the Domain
The first four subgoals of each rule in Figure 3 correspond to the
concept of the "pre-B cell", and the the purpose of the rules is
to identify sub-types. The conversion of these rules to the
2-stage format makes the reasoning easier to follow, not only for
the user but also for the domain expert. Subsequent work on the
system has shown that it is vitally important for the expert to be
able to understand the rules and to recognize his own reasoning in
them; when this is achieved he will easily detect errors in the
proposed rules. The specification used in the rules shown in
Figure 3 is not quite correct but the format would hamper the
expert's ability to detect the errors and correct them.

3. Lessons Learned from the Analysis

1. An expert system is not simply a collection of individual
rules. Each rule relates to some concept in the domain and it
must be consistent with, and complementary to, the other rules
relating to the same concept. Rules should be created and revised
as a unit and there should be no gaps or unwarranted duplications
in the logic of the unit. The notion that individual rules can be
added to an expert system without affecting the performance of the
others is far too simplistic in practice.

2. Elicitation of knowledge from the expert in a piecemeal manner
is likely to yield a poorly co-ordinated collection of rules and a
poor representation of the domain. The concepts of the domain
must be well represented because the intelligibility of the system
depends on them, and subsequent modifications to deal with special
cases will not sit happily on a patchwork of poor rules. Our
experience suggests that it is vital to obtain a detailed overview
of the domain from the expert before eliciting knowledge or rules.

3. It is easy to mis-interpret the knowledge obtained from the
expert. It will contain interesting observations of no decision
making value as well as the hard core of facts required for the
system. The expert will probably not indicate which is which and
the system builder must try to distinguish between the two before
he designs his rules. Even then there is no substitute for
reviewing the draft rules with the expert to ensure that they are
an exact representation of his reasoning process.

4. The designing of groups of rules is not a simple process. If
they do not cover all the situations that may occur in practice or
if the contents of individual rules are not correct, a poor system
will be produced. The production rule format confers no immunity
against errors, and the rules of an expert system have to be
checked comprehensively, just like any other computer program.

5. Rules that makes specific conclusions on the basis of the
inability to prove some item should be avoided at all costs -
because they are not fail-safe. If there any errors in the rules
for proving the item, the system is liable to give the wrong
answer, but more importantly, the erroneous rules will escape
detection. It is much better practice to conclude values such as
"undiagnosable" by specifying all the combinations of
circumstances that would make it the appropriate conclusion. Any
gaps in the logic will then cause the system to crash and the
system builder will soon be on the trail of the errors.

6. Mis-diagnosed cases are very useful for checking the system.

7. It is foolhardy to use uncertainty mechanisms that are not
understood by the system builder nor by the domain expert. The
cases on which they will operate are likely to be difficult cases
and the difficulties should be brought out into the open. Firstly

because the ability of the system to give the correct answer needs to be verified, and secondly because the user may need to know that it was a difficult and unusual case. If the surplus candidate answers are eliminated by a "black box" mechanism the user may assume that it was a simple case, and may not consider alternatives if his first line of treatment fails. It is more helpful to give all the possibilities followed by an indication of the preferred choice, using the logic of the domain expert.

4. Subsequent Developments

Having learned the lessons from this analysis, we returned to the knowledge elicitation stage. After detailed discussions with the expert a more appropriate structure has been devised and expressed in simple PROLOG. With an extensive set of new rules it is now possible for the system to handle special cases, analyse conflicting features in the same way as the expert does, and to mimic the qualifications he applies to his conclusions (eg probably, predominantly, compatible with, minor population of). The performance of the new system has already surpassed the initial 70% of the old system, despite a non-benevolent scoring system (ie both the qualification and the diagnosis must match that of the expert). We see no obstacle to reaching the point where the inaccuracy of the system is less than the inconsistency of the expert.

5. Conclusions

Expert systems offer the hope of solving problems in the manner of the human experts. However, our experience suggests that modest success in a small system is unlikely to lead to success in a large system. The important factor appears to be quality control and this applies to all the stages in the development of an expert system, from the initial elicitation of the knowledge to the final checking of the system.

Reference

Myers, C.D., Fox, J.,Pegram, S.M., Greaves, M.F., (1983). Knowledge Acquisition for Expert Systems: Experience Using EMYCIN for Leukaemia Diagnosis. Proceedings of the Third Annual Conference of the British Computer Society Specialist Group on Expert Systems, 277-293.

REASONING ABOUT BELIEF IN THE CONTEXT OF ADVICE-GIVING
SYSTEMS

Peter Jackson,
Department of Artificial Intelligence,
Edinburgh University.

Abstract.

If we wish to apply logic to advice-giving systems, then we
need to be able to reason about knowledge and belief explicitly.
This paper describes a representation language with this
functionality, based upon a game-theoretic approach to logic.

1. Knowledge representation for advice-giving systems.

Experts employ many different kinds of knowledge in the
execution of their duties. In addition to possessing particular
facts and general rules relevant to their domain, they also have
strategies for applying domain knowledge and dealing with clients.
Such skills are particularly important in the context of
interactive advice-giving, where the expert often deals with a
client face to face and attempts to solve problems as they arise.
One aspect of this is that an expert needs to be able to reason
about his client's beliefs as well as his own. This paper
describes the design and implementation of an interpreter for a
logic-based system to achieve this end.

2. Reasoning about knowledge and belief.

Knowledge representation using logic is essentially
propositional. That is to say, a piece of knowledge will be
represented as one or more propositions in a set of propositions
which constitute the knowledge base, K. Thus, if a proposition,
P, is a member of the set K, then P is deemed to be true, and the
expert being modelled, E, is said to know that P. Further, if P
is not a member of K, but is implied by some subset of K, then P
is deemed true and E is said to know that P.
There are several epistemological problems associated with
this simple-minded approach; here are just some of them.

i) Experts have been known to be wrong. Hence K may not be
veridical.
ii) Expert knowledge may not be complete. Thus it is
possible that K does not imply P, although P is, in fact, true.
"Negation as failure" confounds ~(E knows that P) with (E knows
that ~P).
iii) Experts may not be conscious of all the logical
consequences of their beliefs. Thus, K implies P may not be
sufficient for us to say that (E believes that P).

One contributing factor to these confusions is the inability
of the system to represent a proposition without knowing whether
or not it's true. Knowledge-based programs need to be able to
entertain propositions, i.e. represent them to themselves without

having to make up their mind about them on the spot, as Woods (1975) pointed out years ago. The simplest way to do this is to adopt an indexical semantics, whereby propositions are not true or false in themselves, but rather true or false or indeterminate in certain contexts of evaluation (e.g. Montague, 1970).

Before we move on, it has to be acknowledged that terminology is this area is a bit of a mess. I shall assume that (X knows that P) implies

i) that (X believes that P);
ii) that X has some reason for believing that P;
iii) that P is true in W, a veridical model of the world.

(X believes that P) does not imply that P is true in W, and therefore it does not imply that (X knows that P). It does, however, imply that P is consistent with the rest of X's beliefs. Some of these other beliefs may constitute reasons for believing P that fall short of actual proof.

The account of language games given below is more concerned with belief than knowledge. The players attempt to construct a shared model of the world that they can then reason about, and this model may or may not be veridical, although it is assumed to be consistent. For reasons of space, I am forced to skate over a number of interesting problems to do with the relation between knowledge and justified true belief (see e.g. Lehrer, 1974).

3. The syntax, semantics and pragmatics of the representation language.

Although the representation language described herein is logic-based, it does not employ the clausal form of logic with resolution refutation. The surface syntax is closer to that associated with the predicate calculus in traditional logic texts, while the indexical semantics is based on the game-theoretic interpretation of logic. In addition, there are pragmatic rules which decide whether or not sentence tokens of the language are felicitous in a given context of use. (The notion of "felicity" derives from Austin's (1962) work on performatives, and is concerned, roughly speaking, with whether or not a particular speech act is appropriate in a given context, regardless of whether or not it makes a true statement.) The reason for this additional complexity will become apparent.

3.1. The syntax of the representation language.

Rather than formally specify the syntax, let us take a simple example. The English sentence type "Every boy owns a dog." is represented by the following expression in the representation language:

```
> @Person
  (boy Person
   ->
   %Creature
   (dog Creature
    &
    own Person Creature))
```

which, apart from the prettyprinting and the leading ">" (which I shall explain soon), is not too remote from the

$$(x)(Bx \rightarrow (Ey)(Dy \ \& \ Oxy))$$

of the predicate calculus as she is often spoken.

Though a handy notation, the formula isn't too easy to process as it stands, so it gets transformed into

```
(all Person
    (if (boy Person)
        (some Creature
            (and (dog Creature)
                (own Person Creature)))))).
```

"all", "if", "some" and "and" are logical constants; "boy", "dog" and "own" are non-logical constants; while "Person" and "Creature" are mnemonic (not sorted) variable names.

The ">" indicates that the sentence is in the indicative mood. In other words, the sentence, when typed, constitutes an assertion of the proposition "that every boy does own a dog". It should be clear that sentence-tokens are the truth-bearers in this language, and not sentence types, because a sentence could be true when typed in one context and false when typed in another. A sentence token takes the form msP, where "s" denotes the speaker. Thus

```
? usr:
  @Person
  (boy Person
   ->
   %Creature
   (dog Creature
    &
    own Person Creature))
```

would represent the "utterance" of the English sentence "Does every boy own a dog?" by the user of the system.

The proposition given above would be represented by a hierarchy of frames, and look something like this (simplified):

```
(definst complex-node $25
 data-structure (all Person $26)
 semantics ((> sys) (? usr)) ....)

(definst complex-node $26
 data-structure (if $27 $28) ...)

(definst complex-node $27
 data-structure (boy Person) ...)
```

and so on. "Complex-nodes" stand for propositions, which can be nested to any depth; the "data-structure" fields looks down one level in that nesting. The "semantics" field indicates the value of the proposition at that level at various indices (of which more later). Thus the top level proposition "that every boy does own a dog" is tagged as being true in the expert's belief system (sys), but indeterminate in the client's (usr).

"boy", "dog" and so on are "simple-nodes", which are also functional objects represented by records, along the following lines

```
(definst simple-node dog
 search-space (... $25 ...)
 syntactic-category (S N) ...)
```

All simple-nodes are assigned a syntactic identity by the parser that does the transformation described above, according to the rules of a categorial grammar. For example, "dog" is a function from the Name category to the Sentence category, since if you apply it to a name, like "Sacha", you get the sentence "Sacha is a dog". This assignment is done "on the fly" in a fairly obvious manner and then enforced on subsequent inputs; thus predicates like "dog" do not have variable arity.

Note also that the root node of the proposition $25 appears in the "search-space" slot of the record for "dog". The totality of records in existence at any one time resembles a directed recursive labelnode hypergraph as defined by Boley (1977), and each search space is a connected subgraph of this graph. Such structures have some interesting properties which are exploited in the implementation of the different search strategies described below.

3.2. A game-theoretic semantics.

For ease of exposition, I shall begin by restricting myself to a non-indexical interpretation of the propositional calculus, although the system as implemented is for first-order logic (sans functions and identity). The basic idea of this approach to semantics is that the valuation of a proposition, P, in some calculus with respect to some model, K, can usefully be regarded as a two-person, zero-sum, perfect-information game. One player tries to prove that P is true in K, while the other tries to prove it false. If K is not a model, but a model set, i.e. an incomplete state description that could therefore be taken as describing more than one world, then in addition to win or lose there is the possibility of a draw, and one is no longer playing a perfect-information game.

Let P be an atomic proposition, and K just a set of propositions. Let there be two players, S and H (mnemonic for Speaker and Hearer).

Suppose that S and H play the game P. S wins if he can show that K -> P. H wins if he can show that K -> ~P. Otherwise the game is drawn.

3.2.1. The low game.

Suppose that we have an indexing scheme that can retrieve the set of all the expressions containing occurrences of P in K, courtesy of our frame-like representation. Let this set be K/P. Then, for each Q in K/P, there is a subgame $F(P,Q)$, with the following rules:

    i) If Q = P, then S wins.
    ii) If Q = ~R, then S and H swap places and play $F(P,R)$.
    iii) if Q = $(C-1$ & ... & $C-n)$, then the players play $F(P,C-i)$
for each i, $1<=i<=n$, until a winner is found or they draw. If a
winner of $F(P,C-i)$ is found, for some i, this player is the winner
of $F(P,Q)$. Otherwise $F(P,Q)$ is drawn.
    iv) if Q = $(D-1$ v ... v $D-n)$, then, the players play $F(P,D-i)$
for each i, $1<=i<=n$, until a winner is found or they draw. If a
winner of $F(P,D-i)$ is found, for some i, to win $F(P,Q)$, he must
also win the game ~D-j for all j, $1<=j<=n$ and $j/=i$, else $F(P,Q)$ is
drawn.

    This is very much simpler than it looks; let's go through
these rules one at a time.

    i) We are trying to show that P is true. If P is already in
K/P, then the current incumbent of the role S wins. I have to say
"current incumbent" because the players can swap roles, as pointed
out in ii).
    ii) If the next proposition in K/P is a negation, ~R, then
the players swap roles and the game goes on with respect to R.
The role reversal ensures that, if K/P -> ~P by virtue of a stored
negation, the hearer wins and the speaker loses. The recursive
nature of the rules ensures that the correct result is obtained
even if R is an arbitrarily nested expression.
    iii) If the next proposition in K/P is a conjunction, C, we
need to check the conjuncts to see if C -> P. Of course, C -> P
iff one of the conjuncts implies P. Again, the recursive nature
of the rules allows the conjuncts to be nested expressions.
    iv) If the next proposition in K/P is a disjunction, e.g. (P
v R), then for S to win the game P he must lose the game R. This
is because (P v R), ~R -> P. (This is nothing more than the
natural deduction sequent equivalent to the resolution principle
in the propositional calculus.)

    We assume, in playing P, that the game halts if a player wins
a subgame, $F(P,Q)$ in K/P. If K/P is exhausted without a winner
being found, then P is drawn. This is a three-valued logic, since
it is possible that K implies neither P nor ~P. (It has been
pointed out to me that, if K is not consistent, then we have a
four-valued logic, since it is possible that both players could
win, i.e. that K implies both P and ~P. However, I am assuming
that K is consistent, i.e. that it describes a possible world, or
rather a set of such worlds.)
    I call this the "low" game because it is dominated by the
"high" game for compound propositions, in that strategic choices
made during the high game will determine the low games that get
played but not conversely.

3.2.2. The high game.

    Suppose, however, that P is a compound proposition.
Associated with the logical constant that governs P there is a
sub-game courtesy of a function G:

G($\sim$): given $\sim$P, S and H swap places and the game goes on with respect to P.

G(&): Given (P-1 & ... & P-n), H chooses a conjunct and the game goes on with respect to it.

G(v): Given (P-1 v ... v P-n), S chooses a disjunct and the game goes on with respect to it.

In the context of a three-valued logic, these rules have the following force.

i) The winner of P is the loser of $\sim$P and conversely. If P is indeterminate, then the game is drawn. Thus the value of $\sim$P, V($\sim$P), depends on the value of P in the following way:

$$V(\sim P) = \begin{cases} \text{true if } V(P) = \text{false} \\ \text{false if } V(P) = \text{true} \\ \text{else indeterminate.} \end{cases}$$

ii) The value of a conjunction is the value of its worst conjunct, where falsity is worse than indeterminacy is worse than truth. Thus

$$V((P\text{-}1 \ \& \ ... \ \& \ P\text{-}n)) = \min[V(P\text{-}1), ..., V(P\text{-}n)]$$

in other words

$$V((P\text{-}1 \ \& \ ... \ \& \ P\text{-}n)) = \begin{cases} \text{true if } V(P\text{-}1) = ... = V(P\text{-}n) = \text{true} \\ \text{false if } V(P\text{-}i) = \text{false, for some } i, \ 1<=i<=n \\ \text{else indeterminate} \end{cases}$$

so the best strategy for H is therefore to pick the worst-looking conjunct.

iii) The value of a disjunction is the value of its best disjunct, where truth is better than indeterminacy is better than falsity. Thus

$$V((P\text{-}1 \ v \ ... \ v \ P\text{-}n)) = \max[V(P\text{-}1), ..., V(P\text{-}n)]$$

in other words

$$V((P\text{-}1 \ v \ ... \ v \ P\text{-}n)) = \begin{cases} \text{true if } V(P\text{-}i) = \text{true, for some } i, \ 1<=i<=n \\ \text{false if } V(P\text{-}1) = ... = V(P\text{-}n) = \text{false} \\ \text{else indeterminate} \end{cases}$$

so the best strategy for S is to choose the best-looking disjunct.

It should be clear that V is "complete" iff S maximizes his opportunities, in the sense that a proof of P will be found if there is one. It should also be clear that V is "sound" iff H maximizes his opportunities, in the sense that a refutation of P will be found if there is one. The fact that human reasoning is often neither sound nor complete might be of interest in some applications; consequently, it makes little sense to "design it out" altogether. In any case, exhaustive methods can be very expensive, especially when one is trying to show consistency. Allowing the interpreter to use "short cut" strategies when

evaluating new inputs can be very beneficial under certain
circumstances. Of course, if you allow backtracking over bad
decisions, then you end up with a sound and complete strategy in
any case; there are some situations where you might prefer this.
An account of how an interpreter might go about making and undoing
such decisions can be found in Jackson (1984a), but this is not
really material to the present discussion.

The above is a free adaptation of the two-valued game-
theoretic semantics to be found in Hintikka (1973). An account of
quantification games can also be found therein. More recent
developments can be found in Hintikka (1983).

The game-theoretic approach has a number of advantages over
resolution refutation with Horn clauses, from the point of view of
knowledge representation.

i) You get classical negation, instead of negation as
failure. Negative information is important - it enables you to
rule things out. "Closed world" and "completed database"
assumptions are not always justified for real world applications.
I don't believe in omniscient experts, and I have said from the
outset that I am not dealing with models here, but model sets. On
top of that, negation as failure, as commonly implemented, suffers
from severe technical problems.

ii) You get a clean and clear one-to-one correspondance
between the syntactic rules for constructing expressions and the
semantic rules for evaluating them. This is more or less how
Montague grammar works (see Partee, 1975), and it's obviously in
accordance with "Frege's principle", whereby complex expressions
are evaluated as a recursive function of their compound structure.
In addition, you can write pragmatic rules which represent
different game-playing strategies and associate them with semantic
rules to define a meta-level architecture.

iii) Given this correspondance, the code for the interpreter
is extremely modular. Adding a new propositional connective, e.g.
the conditional or biconditional, only involves writing new
syntactic and semantic rules. I have done this by defining
"demons"; pattern-directed modules which wake up when a particular
kind of proposition is encountered. The syntactic demons know how
to parse and prettyprint such propositions, while the semantic
demons know how to evaluate them by playing various language
games. The pragmatic demons choose strategies for playing such
games, depending upon the indices currently associated with the
proposition.

In summary, game-theoretic semantics has the declarative
force of classical logic; it lends itself to non-standard
interpretations of logic for reasoning about belief, possible
worlds, etc; and the underlying interpreter is modular, extensible
and easy to implement using standard artificial intelligence
techniques.

4. A pragmatics for assertions and questions.

If K is a set of functions from indices to truth values, then
the situation is complicated somewhat. Let us assume that there
is only one index, that which stands for the believer. Let S's

belief system be $B(S)$ and H's $B(H)$.

4.1. Pragmatic conditions.

If S asserts to H that P, then three things follow:

i) if S is being sincere in asserting P, then P is true in $B(S)$;

ii) if S is behaving sensibly in asserting P, then he must believe that H does not already know that P.

iii) if H trusts S, then H will believe that P, unless it is false in $B(H)$.

Let us assume that the players play a series of games, and that the results of previous games (win, lose, or draw) are stored in a record, call it R, which is accessible to both players. S and H are only aware of each other's beliefs as a function of R, i.e. a record of who asked, asserted, accepted and rejected what. Let S's knowledge of $B(H)$ courtesy of R be $B(H/R)$; let H's knowledge of $B(S)$ courtesy of R be $B(S/R)$.

However, we do not assume that $B(X) \rightarrow P$ is equivalent to (X believes that P). This is because X may believe that P, $P \rightarrow Q$, but not (consciously) believe that Q, because he has not yet drawn that inference. Thus, if S asserts that Q, H may only realize that he agrees when he reflects upon the value of Q in $B(H)$. Hereafter, let (X believes that P) represent explicit belief, while $B(X) \rightarrow P$ represents logical implication pure and simple. Thus $B(X) \rightarrow P$ is consistent with ~(X believes that P) but inconsistent with (X believes that ~P), assuming that $B(X)$ is "rational" (see Ellis, 1979).

In the general case, then, there is no guarantee that $B(X)$, $B(X/R)$ and {p: X believes that p} will be identical. In other words, we cannot assume that all of X's beliefs are evident, or that X consciously believes all the consequences of his beliefs. However, it has been suggested to me that the following relations will generally hold. $B(X/R)$ will be a subset of {p: X believes that p} if X is sincere, while {p: X believes that p} will be a subset of {p: $B(X) \rightarrow p$} if $B(X)$ is rational. All this doesn't exactly simplify matters, but I think it makes sense.

The conditions can now be sharpened up.

i) The sincerity condition now requires that (S believes that P), and not merely that $B(S) \rightarrow P$. Thus, even though $B(S) \rightarrow P$ through some long and involved chain of reasoning, it wouldn't be sincere to assert P unless S consciously believed it.

ii) The nonrepetition condition requires that ~[(R $\rightarrow$ P) v (R $\rightarrow$ ~P)]. It is not sensible to repeat evident truths or persist in evident falsehoods.

iii) The acceptance condition now requires that H accept P unless he can show that $B(H) \rightarrow$ ~P, regardless of whether $B(H)$ does in fact imply ~P.

It has been pointed out to me that ii) is still somewhat simplistic, since one might repeat an assertion for emphasis, or to remind someone of something they already know as a preamble to telling them something new. This is certainly true. However, in this paper I am deliberately neglecting rhetorical force in favour of illocutionary force. Although the distinction is not hard and fast, the former includes all manner of stylistic considerations, such as emphasis, irony, modesty, etc, while the latter is more concerned with the function of direct speech acts like asserting, requesting and commanding, i.e. what such utterances set out to achieve in a given context. I also deliberately steer clear of psychological factors, relating to the client's short-term memory, attention span, and so on; that is another story.

It has also been pointed out that the $\sim[(R \to P) \lor (R \to \sim P)]$ in the non-repetition condition might be too strong, since this requires a speaker to realise all the consequences of what has been said so far and stored in the record, R. For example, R might contain P, P $\to$ Q, thus rendering the assertion of Q infelicitous. Since we do not insist on players believing all the consequences of their beliefs, this seems intuitively wrong. A weaker formulation would be to insist that neither P nor $\sim$P were explicitly recorded in R. I am inclined to implement this modification.

The next section extends the game-theoretic approach from the semantics of the representation language to its pragmatics.

4.2. Pragmatic games.

Suppose that S asserts that P.

i) H wins if he can show that P is determinate in R.
ii) The game is drawn if P is indeterminate in R but H does not accept that P, because B(H) $\to$ $\sim$P.
iii) S wins if P is indeterminate in R but H accepts that P.

A similar analysis can be applied to questions. If S asks H if P, then three things follow:

i) if S is being sincere, then $\sim[(S$ believes that P$) \lor (S$ believes that $\sim$P$)]$, regardless of whether P is or is not determinate in B(S);
ii) if S is being sensible, then the same non-repetition condition applies here as applies to statements, since it is silly to ask if P when the value of P has already been established as true or false;
iii) if S trusts H, then he will accept H's answer, Q, so long as he cannot show that B(S) $\to$ $\sim$Q.

My account of questions is complicated by the fact that the game has cooperative as well as competitive aspects. After all, a question is a request for information - one is asking for help. Consequently, I distinguish between winning and losing competitively and winning and losing cooperatively.

Suppose that S asks H if P.

i) H wins competitively if he can show that P is determinate in R.
ii) S wins competitively if H cannot answer, because H cannot show that P is determinate in B(H).
iii) S and H win cooperatively if H can show that P is determinate in B(H) and S accepts H's value for P.

iv) S and H lose cooperatively if H can show that P is determinate in B(H) and S does not accept H's value for P.

H and S score obvious competitive points off each other in i) and ii). However, it is iii) and iv) that are important. Cooperative wins and losses can be thought of as competitive draws, because both parties do well or badly out of the transaction.

Such games are clearly more sophisticated than the semantic games outlined earlier. For a philosophical introduction to that branch of pragmatics known as speech act theory, upon which this work is loosely based, the reader is referred to Searle (1965). For a linguist's view, see Leech (1983); for an artificial intelligence approach see e.g. Cohen & Perrault (1979).

The generality of the game-theoretic approach should now be apparent. In addition to providing an interpretation scheme for classical logic, it also provides us with a framework for drawing non-classical inferences, whereby parties reason about each other's conversational goals. This shows that the game-theoretic way of looking at dialogue can be extended from the semantics of propositions to the pragmatics of illocutionary acts (statements, questions, etc) in a fairly natural way.

5. Present implementation: prospects and problems.

The representation language described in this paper is called TAG, which stands for "Topic Analysis Graphs". Conceptually, it is an attempt to develop an approach to knowledge representation that it based upon epistemological principles, rather than computational convenience or partisan preference for various programming languages. Technically, it attempts to combine the clarity of logic, the efficiency of structured objects and the functionality of rule-based systems. The system also contains a fair amount of support software, e.g. a tracer, a break package, and a graph editor. It is implemented in Franz Lisp and runs on the Ed-AI Vax, where the source code takes up 80 KBytes (about half of which is comments).

This formalism lays the foundations for reasoning about knowledge and belief in a manner that may ameliorate some of the epistemological problems noted earlier. Propositions can be entertained and compared across different contexts of belief. In the context of a consultation between an expert (E) and a client (C), one can distinguish between P, (E believes that P), ~(E believes that P), and (E believes that (C believes that P)).

Not all expert systems require this functionality, e.g. contemporary approaches to fault-finding, but I think that future applications will be more sophisticated in this respect. Remote diagnosis systems may well need to reason about the knowledge state of those who report faults, especially if these are owners or users rather than qualified support personnel. But the most obvious applications are in open-ended consultations, e.g. advising about investments or house purchase, and intelligent tutoring systems, where one needs an explicit model of the student.

This kind of representation also constitutes a first step towards being able to reason about the dialogue itself, as well as the domain of discourse; such capabilities are at the heart of the overlap between IKBS and MMI (see Jackson & Lefrere, 1984, for a recent review). Goal-directed dialogue isn't just concerned with truth or falsity according to some logic, but with additional concepts such as acceptability and appropriateness. I have argued elsewhere that automatic facilities for exposition and explanation will neglect pragmatic issues at their peril (Jackson, 1984b); in other words, explanation does not equal proof.

A major shortcoming of the system as currently implemented is that it does not attempt to keep the client to the point. There is no real notion of focus or progression in the conversation at the macro level; it is up to the client to be relevant and to develop the dialogue in the direction that he wants to go. This is a fairly serious omission, due not to lack of insight into the problem, but a paucity of plausible solutions. Over the last year, I have done some preliminary work on this, but more needs to be done. There is a growing literature on this problem in the fields of cognitive science, text linguistics and non-standard logic, which is well worth exploring.

Acknowledgements.

I would like to thank Richard O'Keefe and Tony Urwin for their comments on earlier versions of this paper.

References.

Austin, J.L. (1962). How to do things with words. Harvard University Press.
Cohen, P.R. & Perrault, C.R. (1979). Elements of a plan-based theory of speech acts. Cognitive Science, 3, 177-212.
Ellis, B. (1979). Rational belief systems. Basil Blackwell.
Hintikka, J. (1973). Logic, language games and information. Oxford University Press.
Hintikka, J. (1983). The game of language. Reidel.
Jackson, P. (1984a). Reasoning about control in the context of advice-giving systems. Paper presented at the Alvey IKBS Inference Theme, First Workshop, Imperial College London, Sept 19-20.
Jackson, P. (1984b). Towards a theory of topics. Computer Education, 8, 21-26.
Jackson, P. & Lefrere, P. (1984). On the application of rule based techniques to the design of advice giving systems. International Journal of Man-Machine Studies, 20, 63-86.
Leech, G.N. (1983). Principles of pragmatics. Longman.
Lehrer, K. (1974). Knowledge. Oxford University Press.
Montague, R. (1970). Pragmatics and intensional logic. Synthese, 22, 68-94.
Partee, B.H. (1975). Montague grammar and transformational grammar. Linguistic Inquiry, 6(2), 203-300.
Searle, J. (1965). Speech acts: an essay in the philosophy of language. Cambridge University Press.
Woods, W.A. (1975). What's in a link: Foundations for semantic networks. In Representation and understanding, Bobrow, D.G. & Collins, A., eds., Academic Press.

NATURAL LANGUAGE INTERFACES FOR EXPERT SYSTEMS:
AN INTRODUCTORY NOTE

Karen Sparck Jones
Computer Laboratory, University of Cambridge
Corn Exchange Street, Cambridge CB2 3QG

Abstract

The paper seeks to provide a context for attempts to
build natural language interfaces for expert systems, by considering
the needs such interfaces have to meet, and the extent to which
these needs can be satisfied given the current state of the art in
automatic natural language processing. Natural language interfaces
are required both to allow adequate communication between user and
machine (in either direction), and to facilitate user modelling
aimed at improving system performance. Supporting these interface
functions implies very close coupling between the operations of the
language processor and those of the underlying expert system.
Research workers in natural language processing have made some
progress in providing resources needed for proper interfaces, but so
far, in relation to expert systems, only for very limited systems
where the interface operations do not press heavily on those of the
underlying decision-making apparatus.

In this paper I shall briefly review

1) the issues involved in seeking to use natural language for expert
system purposes; and

2) the implications of any attempt to apply the present state of the
art in natural language processing to current expert system
activities.

1) the issues involved in seeking to use natural language for expert
system purposes.

What do we want to use natural language for?
In the expert system context natural language is seen
primarily as the communication medium between the user and the
machine, i.e. one is dealing with natural language interfaces rather
than natural language systems. Though expert systems essentially
dealing with linguistic material have been proposed, e.g. for
document retrieval purposes, in general expert systems deal with
non-linguistic objects.
The obvious reason for wanting an expert system interface
is user convenience. The user would often find it easier to work
with his own natural language than with some artificial means of
communication which has to be learnt. The wish for convenience is

closely related to a desire for <u>flexibility</u>. Natural language is good for mixed initiative interaction between the user and the system: it provides the resources for the user to ask questions and offer information, in principle at any time, and without binding the user to respond, narrowly, to the system's initiatives.

The convenience and flexibility of natural language are associated with its <u>expressive power</u>. Artificial languages and system driven operations limit communication and may overly restrict the user's view of the system: in the limit this can mean that relevant information is missed, or wrongly presented, which is bad for the system and so, in the end, for the user.

This is not to imply that artificial languages and system driven operation are necessarily tied together, or that either is necessarily unsatisfactory in all expert system contexts. Mixed initiative interaction is possible with artificial languages, and artificial languages can be very powerful. However they still have to be learnt, and attempts to make them less rebarbative by using English words lead to pseudo-English. This is liable to mislead the user into thinking he is working in English, with unpredictable consequences for expert system operation and the user's perception of this. Some system outputs may indeed be in proper (though canned) English, as in ordinary computing systems; but this increases the risk of confusion. Prompt or menu systems are somewhat different, but from the user's point of view they suffer from limitations similar to those of systems explicitly using artificial languages. The system's output may be in proper (though again canned) English, thus providing an interpretive environment for the user's responses, but the user's responses will be restricted to single words or phrases. The user's communication language is thus a very restricted subset of English, or 'sub-English'. Thus while prompt or menu systems can be very useful, they place heavy constraints on the user's freedom of expression and action.

The justification for full natural language interfaces is therefore that it becomes increasingly difficult for the user to work through an artificial or heavily restricted language, especially when he wants to take the initiative, as the system's scope is extended, its operations become more complex, or its reliance on the user increases. The requirement for serious natural language processing thus stems not only from the need to analyse the user's input, but from the need to generate outputs which, to be acceptable, need more flexibility than can be obtained from a set of canned texts, templates, or simple block assembly strategies.

Thus providing a natural language interface is not merely pandering to the user's comfort. A full natural language interface is required to support deeper system operations effectively, i.e. to allow proper access to the system's motivation and behaviour. This is clearly seen with <u>explanation</u>, but equally applies to other forms of interaction. As a system is endowed with more searching and more flexible explanatory capabilities, it becomes increasingly difficult to show the user what the system has been doing by simple procedures invoking prepared text forms or fragments. The explanation for a particular piece of system behaviour has to be dynamically formed from the conceptual structure embodied in the individual sequence of operations and their context. Expressing the explanation properly thus implies true text generation rather than the mere assembly of pre-compiled components.

The same applies to the treatment of user inputs of a more searching kind, for example meta-questions or probing questions like "Why did X have so little influence on the outcome compared with Y?". Especially at finer levels of detail, these may well not fit any specific supplied pattern, and in any case have to be analysed within the local context, implying a need for true text interpretation. Such questions are quite different from 'Help' questions, which may be handled more crudely from a linguistic point of view, for example on a keyword basis.

As these cases imply, it is important to distinguish what the system does from how this is shown to the user. The demand for better interfaces, and specifically for natural language interfaces, is sometimes expressed in terms of a demand for better explanations. This is confusing ends with means. The point is rather that the system itself has to derive better explanations, and that natural language is only the vehicle, albeit a very handy or the only really adequate one, for conveying them to the user.

The reasons for wanting natural language interfaces discussed so far are first order ones. They refer in a neutral way to the system and any of its users. But there are also second order reasons for wanting natural language interfaces. These stem from user modelling.

User models in expert systems can take various forms and can be used for various purposes. Thus we can distinguish patient models from agent models. Patient models refer to the human subject of the expert system's decisions, agent models to the human being conducting the interaction. The term "user" is ambiguous, and can cause confusion where it is necessary to distinguish patient and agent as separate people, or the different roles of a single person. (I shall thus use "user" only where no distinction is required.) We can also distinguish static user models from dynamic models. The former refer to permanent states of the user (though these may not be discovered all at once), the latter to changes of state dependent on interaction with the system. We can further distinguish, in the static case, modelling based on decision properties of the user, i.e. those to which the system is geared, from modelling based on non-decision properties, where it may be useful to separate objective from subjective properties. Dynamic models could in

principle be based on the same three types of property, but
subjective or <u>mental</u> properties are by far the most important here;
they may indeed be conflated, e.g. in teaching systems, with
decision properties.

This apparent plethora of models is justified (as shown
in more detail in Sparck Jones 1984) by the need to motivate system
behaviour in relation to various goals. This involves predictions
depending on coherent views of the people involved in the system and
their roles. Thus the system requires models for <u>effectiveness</u>,
<u>efficiency</u>, and <u>acceptability</u>. It cannot, of course, be effective in
reaching the decisions for which it is primarily designed without a
decision property-based patient model (or in cases like teaching
systems, without a corresponding dynamic model). But this model, and
all the other possible models, can be exploited to increase the
system's efficiency in reaching its decisions, and to enhance its
acceptability to its users.

Given that all these non-decision models may be valuable
adjuncts to the decision model, and assuming that the system has the
resources needed to deploy them, the important question is how the
information required to build them is obtained. It is in principle
possible to get this information without recourse to full natural
language interaction, for example via simple responses to system
prompts and questions; similarly, information for dynamic models can
be obtained via the pattern of responses. However except where, as
in teaching systems, the user's actions are intimately bound into
the system's behaviour, or where, as in graphic design systems, an
alternative language is the means of communication between user and
machine, it is clear that natural language is potentially a much
richer source of modelling data than an artificial language, or even
than the subset of English available in a menu system. The greater
expressive resources of natural language, for both content and form,
means that more, and more discriminating, information can be
supplied, either by design or accident.

The minimal general case for natural language, therefore,
is that it can make an expert system <u>easy</u> to use. But the case
becomes stronger as the system becomes more sophisticated, because
natural language is the only <u>adequate</u> means of communication between
system and user. The case is further reinforced when other aspects
of system performance than those devoted to raw decision-making are
considered, where individual user models become important. Natural
language is the only <u>rich</u> enough source of modelling information.

2) the implications of any attempt to apply the present state of the art in natural language processing to current expert system activities

If natural language interfaces are sought for expert systems, what experience in automatic natural language processing is available for application or exploitation?

Research in automatic language processing has addressed a wide range of issues, both at the surface linguistic level and the related underlying knowledge level. The former is represented by, for example, work on grammars and parsing, the latter by work on network knowledge representation schemes and their manipulation in inference. The way in which the two are linked is well illustrated by work on the determination and use of discourse focus, which requires both linguistic and non-linguistic information.

The most developed area of automatic natural language processing is database query. Systems have been built for practical use that are quite reliable and fairly comprehensive. They demonstrate an effective use of necessary components of natural language understanding systems, namely syntax, semantics and pragmatics, though primarily for handling only well-formed inputs (see, for example, Bates and Bobrow 1983, Martin et al. 1983).

Even so, unless the demands placed on them are very modest, which amounts to operating with sub-English if not pseudo-English, these systems can fail in many ways. In some cases this is simply because the back end database system is extremely limited in its notions and distinctions; in others it is because the linguistic resources are inadequate; but in most cases it is because the conceptual representation of the world of the database is not rich enough to provide an adequate interpretive underpinning for the language processor (see the example in Bates 1984, p.184).

However the experience to be gained from much better database query would still be of limited value for expert system purposes. This is primarily because database systems (in the current sense of this phrase) are essentially single question-answer pair systems. They have little call for the discourse knowledge and procedures required to interpret and respond to larger texts and dialogues.

The natural language processing research community as a whole has, however, been concerned with many of the problems which would require solutions for effective expert system interfaces. These include the treatment of 'ill-formed' input, of discourse and dialogue structure, and of the language user's beliefs, goals, plans, etc. These three problems roughly correspond to the reasons, listed earlier, for wanting natural language interfaces. The current interest in task oriented dialogue has also led to far more emphasis on generation than is required by database systems, where the

primary concern is analysis: this is obviously relevant to the
provision of explanations, justifications, and so forth in the
expert system case.

Techniques for handling ill-formed inputs are illustrated
by, for example, Carbonell and Hayes (1983), Granger (1983), and
Weischedel and Sondheimer (1983); the management of discourse and
dialogue structure by Clancey (1979); and the determination of user
plans, etc by Perrault and Allen (1980). Relatively powerful
integrated task-oriented dialogue systems have already been
implemented, for example CONSUL (Mark 1981), an electronic mail
system interface, and UC (Wilensky 1984), a Unix interface.

These systems are, however, still limited in their
capacities for producing the truly cooperative responses required
for satisfactory task oriented dialogue between the system and the
individual user. The propositional content and linguistic form of
these cooperative and tailored responses has to be derived from both
the actual discourse and the perceived user needs, in the context of
the system's task domain, the specific system operations supplying
the matter for the response, and the expressive resources available
in the language. The complexity of this process is illustrated on
the one hand by the need to formulate responses couched in terms
which prevent the user from drawing false inferences from them
(Joshi et al. 1984); and on the other by the way in which the
linguistic production of the conceptual response has to be mediated
by appropriate large-scale rhetorical strategies, illocutionary
acts, and individual sentence structures (see, for instance, McKeown
1982, 1983).

Experimental systems tackling various aspects of the need
identification and response generation process have been built, for
example HAM-ANS (Hoeppner et al. 1983); see also Wahlster's
forthcoming survey. As they are experimental systems, however, they
tend to be fragile, and also limited in capabilities not the
immediate concern of the research. Even at their best, moreover,
they are some considerable distance from the systems with the
sustained refined dialogue performance their builders are seeking.

The status of these systems is especially important in
relation to any attempt to build expert system interfaces because
many of them are advice and consultation systems, i.e. generically
expert systems. However, though the underlying system operations
required to respond to the user's input, for example constructing a
plan to achieve a user's goal, may not be trivial, the expert system
element of these systems is rudimentary compared with that of many
regular expert systems. Of course in simple advice systems the
extent to which the system needs to conduct massive reasoning
enterprises, once decision data have been acquired, may be fairly
limited. But it is noticeable that in general in the expert system
type programs used as test environments for advanced natural

language processing research, the underlying decision mechanism,
i.e. the application domain knowledge base and reasoning apparatus
used to obtain solutions to the established user problem, may be
fairly elementary. Domain knowledge may be employed to assist, for
example, in identifying user goals, but the subsequent operation of
deciding how to satisfy these goals can be quite simple, as simple,
even, as table lookup. From a strictly expert system point of view,
as opposed to a user interaction point of view, these systems are
very modest. In relation to the use of knowledge in reasoning, all
the effort has gone into providing the substantial and complex
apparatus needed to support interface functions like determining
user goals.

On the other hand, in the work that has so far been done
on providing a natural language interface to an existing,
substantial expert system, of which XCALIBUR (Carbonell et al 1983)
is a conspicuous example, the more sophisticated capabilities that
an interface should support, like individual user modelling, do not
figure. As Kukich (1984) pointed out, there are serious obstacles to
providing an interface with cooperative response capacities if the
interface's access to the underlying expert system's operations is
limited, i.e. the expert system itself functions as a black box.

In fact this experience, and that of the language
processing research workers, point in the same direction: it is
vital to recognise that providing a serious natural language
interface to an expert system is not simply a matter of adding a
front end box, communicating with the back end expert system through
a narrow channel. It is not even a matter of adding a front end
language processor supported by a description of the domain
expressed in a form suited to its exploitation for language
processing purposes. The relatively simple case of database query
shows that the first strategy severely restricts the power of the
natural language interface, and that even the second is sometimes
inadequate. When the functional expectations of the natural language
interface are combined with the much greater behavioural richness of
a sophisticated expert system, a much closer coupling between front
and back ends is required. Indeed it may be only rational to treat
the whole as a single integrated system.

Supplying a natural language interface for an expert
system thus puts considerable pressure on the underlying expert
system. It not only requires detailed access to the expert system's
knowledge and operations, implying that these be exhibited in an
appropriate form. The kinds of user need natural language interfaces
are aimed at satisfying tend to require enhanced capabilities in the
expert system itself. Natural language interfaces, even when meant
only to serve user convenience, are likely to have unfortunate
repercussions because the user's expectations are raised, and he is
liable, without realising it, to produce inputs demanding new system

resources. What is more important, however, is that it must be recognised that satisfying the more demanding needs which are typically thought of as associated primarily with the natural language interface, can require not merely simple additions to, but substantial modification of, the underlying expert system. Ensuring that a tailored explanation can be produced could, for instance, require adaptation of the basic explanation construction mechanism to interact with the characterisation of the user. Even the more modest strategy of restructuring a given basic explanation to meet user constraints could require that the underlying system gather and make available specific trace information.

Further, it should be noted that all the natural language processing systems discussed rely heavily, even in their more purely linguistic operations, on the specific application domain: their lexicon, semantics, and even grammar, may be domain-dependent. This, in itself, means that providing a natural language interface to a particular expert system is a major effort, because rather little can be imported from other implementations. This effort is then further increased by the need to ensure the tight coupling between front end and back end processing required to support cooperative, tailored responses.

Thus while it is true that even the system driven basis of prompt or menu systems, or the user's confinement to sub-English, is compatible with user satisfaction and considerable sophistication in many user support functions; and while, as the database case shows (Harris 1984), the user can quite happily inhabit more powerful but still restricted natural language interfaces, there is a good case for full natural language interfaces for expert systems. The problem is that providing these is not going to be easy. Tackling this problem has nevertheless recently been identified as a high priority research area for the natural language processing community (Sparck Jones and others 1984). Moreover existing natural language interfaces like EXCALIBUR show that, provided their limitations are clearly understood by the user, such interfaces are of value. So there is everything to be said for seeking them in their own right, as well as as mere bases for research on better things, and not discounting them because they do not give us everything we require.

Acknowlededgement

This paper was written during tenure of a GEC Hirst Research Fellowship.

References

Bates, M. (1984) There is still gold in the database mine. Proceedings of COLING 84; 10th International Conference on Computational Linguistics & 22nd Annual Meeting of the Association for Computational Linguistics, 184-185.

Bates, M. and Bobrow, R.J. (1983) Information retrieval using a transportable natural language interface. Proceedings of the Sixth ACM SIGIR Conference, 81-86.

Carbonell, J.G. and Hayes, P.H. (1983) Recovery strategies for parsing extragrammatical language. American Journal of Computational Linguistics, 9, 123-146.

Carbonell, J.G. et al. (1983) The XCALIBUR project. IJCAI 83; Proceedings of the Eighth International Joint Conference on Artificial Intelligence, 653-656.

Clancey, W.F. (1979) Dialogue management for rule-based tutorials. IJCAI 79; Proceedings of the Sixth International Joint Conference on Artificial Intelligence, 155-161.

Granger, R.H. (1983) The NOMAD system: expectation-based detection and correction of errors during understanding of syntactically and semantically ill-formed text. American Journal of Computational Linguistics, 9, 188-196.

Harris, L.R. (1984) Experience with INTELLECT: artificial intelligence technology transfer. The AI Magazine, 5, 43-50.

Hoeppner, W. et al. (1983) Beyond domain independence: experience with the development of a German language access system to highly diverse background systems. IJCAI 83; Proceedings of the Eighth International Joint Conference on Artificial Intelligence, 588-594.

Joshi, A. et al. (1984) Preventing false inferences. Proceedings of COLING 84: 10th International Conference on Computational Linguistics & 22nd Annual Meeting of the Association for Computational Linguistics, 134-138.

Kukich, K. (1984) Presentation at the Generation Workshop, Stanford, July 1984.

McKeown, K.R. (1982) The TEXT system for natural language generation: an overview. Proceedings of the 20th Annual Meeting of the Association for Computational Linguistics, 113-120.

McKeown, K.R. (1983) Focus constraints on language generation. IJCAI 83; Proceedings of the Eighth International Joint Conference on Artificial Intelligence, 582-587.

Perrault, C.R. and Allen, J.F. (1980) A plan-based analysis of indirect speech acts. American Journal of Computational Linguistics, 6, 167-182.

Sparck Jones, K. (1984) User models and expert systems. Technical Report, Computer Laboratory, University of Cambridge.

Sparck Jones, K.; Bates, M.; Carbonell, J.G.; Flickinger, D.P.; McKeown, K.R. (1984) Contributions to the Panel: Natural Language and Databases, Again, Proceedings of COLING 84; 10th International Conference on Computational Linguistics & 22nd Annual Meeting of the Association for Computational Linguistics, 182-193.

Wahlster, W. (forthcoming) User models in dialogue systems; invited talk at COLING 84; to appear in Journal of Computational Linguistics.

Weischedel, R.M. and Sondheimer, N.K. (1983) Meta-rules as a basis for processing ill-formed input. American Journal of Computational Linguistics, 9, 161-177.

Wilensky, R. (1984) Talking to Unix in English: an overview of an on-line Unix consultant. The AI Magazine, 5, 29-39.

SPECTROGRAM ANALYSIS : A KNOWLEDGE-BASED
APPROACH TO AUTOMATIC SPEECH RECOGNITION

S.R. Johnson, J.H. Connolly, and E.A. Edmonds
Human-Computer Interface Research Unit, Leicester Polytechnic

Abstract

An Expert System incorporating phonetic/phonological and
lexical knowledge is being developed by the Speech Group in the
Human-Computer Interface Research Unit at Leicester Polytechnic. The
spectrogram has been chosen as the initial representation of the
acoustic wave-form of speech through which communication of this
knowledge can be achieved. A set of Prolog rules allows the spectrogram reader to define the relationship between acoustic events as
represented in the spectrogram and linguistic units such as phonemes
or words in a natural and easily refinable manner. The paper will
describe the rules and how they were derived, and present some results
of the program's performance on spectrograms of unknown utterances.

1. Introduction

Research into Automatic Speech Recognition (ASR) has been
actively pursued throughout the world for the last thirty years..the
first system having been produced in the Bell Laboratories in 1952
(Davis, Biddulph and Balashek, 1952). However, although there exist
a number of current systems which can perform restricted speech
recognition tasks, use of such systems is still limited to highly
artificial conditions. The majority of speech recognition systems
today are capable of recognising a limited number of words or phrases,
spoken in isolation in a controlled environment, by a co-operative
speaker whose voice the system has been trained to recognise. These
systems generally rely on conventional pattern, or template, matching
methods, using dynamic programming techniques to perform informed
matching between the input utterance (typically a single word) and a
set of stored reference templates. For a comprehensive review of the
state of the art see Baker (1981) and White (1984).
While these techniques perform well for isolated word
recognition over restricted vocabularies, any realistic system for the
automatic recognition of speech must not only cope with more natural
continuous speech over a potentially unrestricted vocabulary, but
also adapt easily to the speech of more than one speaker without the
need for training, and not be over-sensitive to environmental conditions. A thorough description of current techniques and their problems
for continuous speech can be found in Vaissiere (1983).
The root of the problem lies in the inherent variability
of speech. Put simply, this means that the "same" word or phoneme is
pronounced differently by different speakers, and even by the same
speaker on different occasions. It has therefore been argued(Isard,
1983;Zue, 1983) that template matching techniques are not capable of
dealing with arbitrarily large vocabularies, or of achieving true
speaker independence.
Continuous speech poses additional problems, however.
Boundaries between words are not normally detectable, the effects of
co-articulation alter the realisation of each sound according to its
context, even across word boundaries, and many types of elision and
insertion may occur. Thus in fluent speech the acoustic signal may
not in itself contain sufficient information so as to enable its

unambiguous decoding. It is therefore not possible to achieve continuous speech recognition simply by concatenating templates for individual words.

It is generally accepted that human listeners solve these problems by drawing heavily on both linguistic and non-linguistic knowledge sources in order to extract the linguistic message from the acoustic signal. If ASR is to be extended beyond current capabilities, it is argued that it will be necessary to incorporate at least some of these knowledge sources into the machine.

A number of questions arise from these assumptions. Firstly, what is the relevant knowledge, and secondly, how can it best be formalised and represented for use in a machine? Our approach has been to tackle these questions and to build a system to test the answers we arrive at.

2. The Approach

The first question is not difficult to answer. Speech scientists and psychologists have studied the roles of acoustic phonetic, lexical, syntactic, semantic, and pragmatic knowledge in speech understanding, and there is no lack of knowledge about these areas, even if their exact mechanisms and interactions are not yet fully understood. What is needed is an ASR system which incorporates these knowledge sources and uses them intelligently .. a knowledge-based system.

A general answer to the second question ..how to express this knowledge in a formalism which can be implemented on a computer.. has not yet been found. The main problem is of finding a means by which the linguist can express his knowledge in a way which is both natural for him and also sufficently formalised for the computer. In order for the linguist to be able to communicate with the machine it is necessary to find a representation of the speech signal which is familiar to him, and hence easy for him to talk about. The spectrogram is a visual representation of speech which is widely used by linguists in the study of the segmental acoustic cues of speech and their relationship to its production and perception. In the light of the demonstration by Zue (Zue and Cole, 1979; Cole et al., 1980) that a human can learn to read spectrograms, we have chosen to use that representation of speech as our main vehicle of communication with the machine in respect of phonetic/phonological and lexical knowledge. We are, of course, aware that this will not be the only representation of speech necessary for future research. The point is that we are attempting to establish a framework within which specialised knowledge about all aspects of speech can be expressed in a natural and coherent manner. The spectrogram seems to be a reasonable starting point in this research, but additional representations will be used as they become necessary, and the knowledge gained from them encoded within the same rule-base.

An Expert System which uses Prolog rules to interpret the spectrogram in terms of both phonemes and words is being developed by the multi-disciplinary team, as part of their long-term goal of speaker-independent, unrestricted continuous speech recognition. Other researchers in the USA (Johannsen et al., 1983) and in France (Memmi et al., 1983) have also investigated this approach, but have not yet, to our knowledge, published any results. This paper presents the

results of the program's performance on spectrograms of continuous
utterances   both sentences and continuous digit strings.   But first,
the processes involved in formulating the rules are described and some
simple examples given.

3. Rule Encoding

          The spectrogram provides a visual representation of the
acoustic wave in terms of the intensity of energy present at each
frequency over a period of time.   An example spectrogram of the utterance "pineapple juice is smooth" is given. Before knowledge of how to
interpret the patterns on the spectrogram can be encoded, that knowledge must first be acquired.   This involves both the discovery of
the relevant visual features and the definition of the realtionship
of these to phonetic events ...in other words it involves learning
to read spectrograms.   Therefore one of the members of the team (SRJ)
attempted to do this, and then to encode the expertise thus gained.
          Six hundred reference spectrograms containing exponents
of the English phonemes, covering the phonotactic possibilities of
the language were produced by a male and a female speaker.   These
were used as a basis from which a set of visual features which appeared
to be relevant to the decoding process was established.   This set was
then tested using spectrograms of unknown utterances recorded by the
male speaker of the reference set.   These spectrograms were not
labelled in any way, and the reader was told only that they represented
syntactically and semantically well-formed examples of English.   Since
the purpose of this was both to test the feature set and to discover
how the reader uses those features to build up a phonetic description
of the utterance, a careful record of the processes involved in the
interpretation of these spectrograms was kept.
          The feature set eventually arrived at was defined in terms
of subjective visual patterns, starting with a description of the
general type of pattern.   This is usually one of three main types:
areas where there are broad horizontal bands of darkness, called
formants, correspond to the sonorant sounds of English (the vowels,
nasals and liquids); while areas of random fuzzy-looking pattern are
the visual correlates of the fricatives; and short periods with no
markings in the spectrogram are generally indicative of the silent
closure interval of the plosives. Attributes of these patterns such
as their relative length and intensity, the position of the two lowest
formants, and the direction and extent of their movement, if any, are
also used.   In addition, features such as an area of very low frequency energy(voice bar) and fine vertical striations were included,
as were the rate and direction of formant transitions and a rapid rise
and fall of F3 and/or F4,which was named a "chevron" because of its
appearance.   For the fuzzy areas the point on the vertical axis where
most of the noise stopped was found to be an important feature, and
was therefore included in the feature set under the title "cut-off".
Absolute measurements of length, intensity, and formant height were
deliberately avoided in the hope that by using relative values for
these features a degree of speaker independence could be achieved.
          The spectrogram reader achieved 88% correct phoneme re-
cognition accuracy on these utterances,(the total number of phonemes
in the sample was 1038) and this rate remained relatively constant,
even when spectrograms from two completely new speakers were introduced. Sentence recognition was 60% over 60 sentences, while word

KAY ELEMETRICS CO. TYPE B/65 SONAGRAM ® – WESSEX ELECTRONICS LTD. BRISTOL BS16 5SE (0272) 571404.

"Pineapple juice is smooth"

p aɪ n ʌ p l̩ dʒ u s ɪ z s m u: ð

recognition was 66% over 281 words. These results were encouraging enough to suggest that if the knowledge just gained could be expressed in the machine, it would form a sound basis for the phonetic part of an unrestricted recognition system.

The notes made during the learning phase were used to build up a description of the interpretation procedure. It was found that the first stage involved the classification of the spectrogram into areas representing the three major pattern types described above, using rules such as:

If the area has formants it is a sonorant.

If the area contains a fuzzy pattern it is a fricative.

If the area has little or no marking it is a plosive.

These classes were then divided into sub-classes, according to the presence or absence of certain features. The fricatives were the easiest class to divide in this way and the decisions were more clear-cut. For this reason and for the purposes of clarity, the details which follow concern this class. The principle, however, is the same for the other classes.

There are eight fricatives in English, and these can be sub-divided into strident(sibilant)(i.e. /s/ as in seed, /z/ as in zoo,/ʃ/ as in short, and /ʒ/ as in pleasure), and non-strident, (i.e. /f/ as in fin, /v/ as in vine, /θ/ as in thin, and /ð/ as in then), on the basis of intensity. For example:

If the area is a fricative, and it has a high intensity, it is strident.

Otherwise it is non-strident.

The strident fricatives can be further divided according to place of articulation, indicated by the cut-off point.
If the event is strident and the cut-off is around 2700Hz it is alveolar.(/s/ or /z/)

If the event is strident and the cut-off is around 1500Hz it is palatal-alveolar.(/ʃ/ or /ʒ/)

The place of articulation of non-stridents is not so easy to identify in this way, and indeed, without the aid of lip-reading, a human listener can find it hard to distinguish between labio-dental /f/ and dental /θ/ or between their voiced counterparts /v/ and /ð/.

Phonemes are in turn defined in terms of combinations of these event types.
If the event is alveolar and unvoiced it is /s/.

If the event is palatal-alveolar and unvoiced it is /ʃ/.

If the event is non-strident and unvoiced it is either /f/ or /θ/.

Context can be important too. For example, the phonotactics of English dictate that a voiced palatal-alveolar fricative, the /ʒ/ in pleasure, can not occur in an initial position:
If the event is palatal-alveolar and voiced and not in initial position it is /ʒ/.

Having thus defined the rules informally, the next important step was to find a suitable formalism for this knowledge. It was decided to use Prolog for this, as it provides a useful tool for the easy implementation of rules in a format that conforms with the spectrogram reader's perception of the situation. This naturalness of rule formulation is an important factor of the Expert System, as it enables a non computer specialist to encode and test rules easily and rapidly. And because the resulting program will therefore correspond closely with the linguist's way of thinking about the problem, it will be easier for him to refine.

In actual fact the informal rules needed little translation into Prolog, so once started, the initial encoding procedure was completed quite rapidly, thus allowing testing and refining at an early stage. The Prolog rules for the fricative examples given above are given in Figure 1, where the symbol ":-" can be read roughly as "if", and the commas signify logical "and". The T1 refers to the area along the time axis that is being examined. For the purposes of brevity in the rules the description palatal has been used for palatal-alveolar throughout.

Input to the program consists of description of the spectrogram in terms of the visual features present in each area, expressed as Prolog facts. Work on the extraction of these features is currently underway in the team, and will be documented elsewhere. In the meantime, the description is done manually with the help of a Prolog interface which asks questions about each area of the spectrogram and asserts the appropriate facts, according to the response.

```
event(fricative, T1)   :- type-of-pattern(fuzzy, T1),
                          not(length('<9',T1)).

event(strident, T1)    :- event(fricative, T1),
                          intensity(high, T1).

event(alveolar, T1)    :- event(strident, T1),
                          cut-off('2700',T1).

event(unvoiced, T1)    :- event(fricative, T1),
                          not(length(short, T1)),
                          not(feature(voice-bar, T1)),
                          not(feature(stripes, T1)).

phoneme('s',T1)        :- event(alveolar, T1),
                          event(unvoiced, T1).

phoneme('ʒ',T1)        :- event(palatal, T1,
                          event(voiced, T1),
                          not(context(initial, T1)).
```

Figure 1. Example spectrogram reading rules.

Output from the program consists of strings of the possible phonemes for each time slot in the spectrogram. The putput from a spectrogram of the utterance "pineapple juice is smooth" is:

```
* P aI N ⁻ p  P∫ IU s i s N u v *
      I      dʒ     @         ᶑ
      E
      @
```

Figure 2. Example output from the rules.

The symbols in this output should be interpreted as follows:
aI as the sound in w̲i̲n̲e̲, / / as in h̲u̲t̲, /I/ as in h̲i̲t̲, /E/ as in h̲e̲a̲d̲,
/@/ as in a̲b̲o̲u̲t̲, /dʒ/ as in j̲u̲d̲g̲e̲, /IU/ as in h̲u̲e̲, /i/ as in h̲e̲a̲t̲,
and /u/ as in w̲h̲o̲'̲d̲. The upper case "P" and "N" are used for a
special purpose, described below. The asterisks denote word boundaries, in this case only at the beginning and end of the utterance.
The hierarchial structure of the rules, where event types are classified first, then phonemes defined in terms of these, means that a
linguistic description of the event is always available at any level
of analysis. This is important because although the plosives are relatively easy to identify as a class, it can sometimes be impossible
to discriminate between individual phonemes within the class, between
/b/ and /d/ or /k/ and /p/, for example. The same is true for the
nasals. Therefore whenever it can not identify a particular phoneme,
the program puts out an indication of the class it belongs to, as it
has done in this example for the initial 'p' in "Pineapple" and for
the nasals, represented by "P" for plosive, and "N" for nasal,
respectively.

Although the rules are still being refined, the basic shell
and structure of the program remain the same so as to provide a
constant base from which adaptations can be made. The next section
presents some results of the program's performance on a number of
spectrograms of unknown utterances.

4.   Results and Discussion

The program has so far been tested on twenty spectrograms
of continuous speech from four different speakers, two of each sex.
They were all produced on a standard Kay Sonagraph under normal
environmental conditions, without undue attention to enunciation.

The results are analysed in terms of the percentages of
phonemes correctly identified, those confused with other phonemes,
and those simply missed. Figure 3 presents a summary of the performance for all the phonemes.

percent phonemes correct	63
percent phonemes confused	16
percent phonemes missed	21

Figure 3. Recognition rate of the rule program.

Figure 4 presents a more detailed breakdown of the
results of the fricatives. It should be noted that the relative
infrequency of some phonemes may affect the results, and for this
reason the total number of times each fricative appeared in the
initial test data is also shown.

phoneme	% correct	%confused	%missed	total
s	94.7	5.5	0	19
z	100	0	0	16
ʃ	100	0	0	3
ʒ	100	0	0	2
f	71.4	14.3	14.3	7
v	25	50	25	8
θ	66.6	33.3	0	3
ð	33.3	33.3	33.3	6

Figure 4. Results of the rule program for the fricative phonemes.

The most frequent errors occurred between items belonging to the same natural class. For example, there was a high rate of confusion among the plosives. In general, the program's discrimination between the natural classes was good....The overall error rate between natural class being less than 10%.

These results show that although the overall phoneme recognition rate of 62% is reasonable for the first evaluation of the program, it is expected that this will improve as the rules are refined and more experience gained. However, the low error rate for natural class discrimination suggests that this may be a more reliable criterion on which to base lexical access. This idea has been tried with considerable success by Huttenlocher and Zue(1983), and we are proposing to adopt a similar strategy.

To test the feasibility of this, strings of continuous digits are being used. The digit lexicon consists of rules which are very similar to those for phonemes or any of the other events in the spectrogram. It is not within the scope of this paper to discuss the exact structure of the lexicon, but briefly, instead of containing the phonemic transcriptions of the words, the rules encode knowledge of their broad phonetic structure. It is too early to give statistically significant results of this experiment, but initial tests on nine spectrograms of digit strings spoken by five new speakers have shown that the correct digit can be identified around 90% of the time. This is a very encouraging result and suggest that the above may be a viable approach to lexical access.

5. Summary

If the capabilities of current ASR systems are to be extended to anything approaching normal, fluent speech, it will be necessary to make use of a great deal of linguistic and non-linguistic knowledge. How this knowledge is to be represented in the machine is therefore a key issue. An Expert System for the capture and encoding of a part of the large body of relevent knowledge ...the segmental phonetic/phonological...has been described. The spectrogram was chosen as the initial medium through which communication of this knowledge is made, and expertise was accumulated about how this visual respresentation of speech may be interpreted. Prolog rules are used to define the relationships between the visual features and linguistic units such a phonemes or words, and a knowledge-based system which produces a phonetic description of the spectrogram has been set up. As this knowledge is in a format which the linguist himself has specified, it is easy for him to add to and refine. The program can achieve more than 60% correctly recognised phonemes from unknown utterances on a speaker-independent basis. The low error rate for natural class recognition has prompted the team to investigate the idea of lexical access based on such classes and preliminary attempts to recognise strings of continuous digits have had extremely encouraging results. This success seems to indicate that our approach is worth pursuing as part of our research into speaker-independent unrestricted automatic speech recognition.

References

Baker, J.M. (1981). How to achieve recognition: a tutorial/status report on Automatic Speech Recognition. Speech Technology(USA), Vol.1, No.1, pp.30-31, 36-43.

Cole, R.A., Rudnicky, A.I., Zue, V.W. & Reddy, D.R. (1980). Speech as patterns on paper. In Perception and Production of Fluent Speech, ed. R.A. Cole, pp.33-50. New York: Hillsdale.

Davis, K.H., Biddulph, & Balaskhek, S. (1952). Automatic Recognition of Spoken Digits, JASA., Vol.24, No.6, p.637.

Huttenlocher, D.P. & Zue, V.W. (1983). Phonotactic and Lexical Constraints in Speech Recognition. Speech Communication Group Working Papers, Vol.III, MIT.

Isard, S. (1982). Speech Recognition and Understanding, Synthesis and Generation. (1st.Workshop Tutorial), prepared for SERC Study Project on Architectures for Knowledge-based Systems.

Johanssen, J., Macallister, J., Michalele, T., & Ross, S. (1983). A Speech Spectrogram Expert. Proc. Int. Conf. on Acoustics, Speech and Signal Processing, pp.746-9.

Memmi, D., Eskenazi, M., Mariani, J., & Nguyen-Xuan, A. (1983). Un systeme expert pour la lecture de sonagrammes. Speech Communication, Vol.2, Nos.2-3. Special Issue, pp. 234-6. North Holland.

Vaissiere,J. (1983). Speech Recognition. In Computer Speech Processing, SERC/CREST-ITG Advanced Course. Corpus Christi College, Cambridge. 11-22 July.

White, G.M. (1984). Speech Recognition: an idea whose time is coming. Byte, Vol.9, No.1, pp.213-22.

Zue, V.W. & Cole, R.A. (1979). Experiments in spectrogram reading. Proc. IEEE Int.Conf. on Acoustics, Speech and Signal Processing, pp.116-9.

Zue, Z.W. (1984). The use of phonetic rules in automatic speech recognition. Speech Communication. Vol.2, Nos.2-3, Special Issue, pp.181-186. North Holland.

PSYCHOLOGICAL TECHNIQUES
FOR ELICITING EXPERT KNOWLEDGE

John G. Gammack and Richard M. Young
MRC Applied Psychology Unit, Cambridge

ABSTRACT

        Present techniques for eliciting expert knowledge tend
to rely upon informal interviews combined with the coding of the
knowledge into empirical rules. This approach has two shortcomings: (1) expert knowledge is of more than one kind, not all kinds
being conveniently expressed as rules; (2) informal interviews are
not suitable for eliciting many of these kinds. Established techniques from psychology are available for eliciting some of these
other kinds of knowledge: in particular we discuss the methods of
protocol analysis, multidimensional scaling and concept sorting.
We argue that an appropriate way to elicit knowledge in even a
single domain is to use a variety of techniques, matched to the
different kinds of knowledge in the domain.

1. INTRODUCTION

        It is often stated that the bottleneck in building
expert systems is knowledge acquisition (e.g. Hayes-Roth, Waterman
& Lenat, 1983), especially the kind known as knowledge elicitation
(KE) for which the source of information is a human expert. While
one can dispute whether this really is the case - for example,
Young (1984) argues that the bottleneck lies instead in the weakness of available knowledge representation techniques - it is easy
to see how the belief has arisen. Present KE techniques rely
heavily upon informal interviews with the expert, coupled with an
attempt to code the information obtained into empirical rules in a
pre-determined format. (If, for example, one is using the EMYCIN
shell (van Melle, 1979), one has no choice but to try to code the
information into EMYCIN rules.) This is followed by a protracted
stage of feedback-driven refinement, in which the behaviour of the
prototype system is compared with that of the human expert working
on the same problem, and the discrepancies used to suggest additions and modifications to the rules. It is this latter stage
that gives rise to the familiar complaints about the slowness of
KE and the inability of experts to express their knowledge in the
required form (e.g. McDermott, 1982).
        We argue that the shortcomings of current techniques
are due primarily to two factors. Firstly, expertise in a technical domain comprises knowledge of more than one kind, not all of
which can reasonably be represented in the form of empirical
rules. Secondly, not all of these kinds are suitable for elicitation by informal interview. Fortunately a number of techniques
are available from psychology for eliciting these other kinds of
knowledge, and the task then becomes to match up types of
knowledge with appropriate techniques. This paper, after briefly

sketching some of the different types of expert knowledge, will describe three psychological techniques, those of protocol analysis, multidimensional scaling, and concept sorting, and discuss their suitability for expert system KE.

It might be objected that if all this "psychological" knowledge cannot be coded into empirical rules, then it has no place in an expert system. While this is perhaps true as an observation about the limitations of current expert systems and the weakness of their knowledge representations, it reflects far too narrow a view of their requirements. The extra, more structural knowledge is needed as soon as the expert system has to make use of knowledge deeper than empirical connections, for example to engage in causal reasoning. It is needed for communicating with the user and providing intelligible explanations, and perhaps for supplying semantic support to a Natural Language interface. It is needed for indexing over large knowledge bases, for allowing more flexible use of knowledge, and in general for moving the capabilities of the expert system closer to those of the human expert.

2. DIFFERENT KINDS OF KNOWLEDGE

The dissatisfaction with current practice usually leads to suggestions that what is needed is a large-scale study to find "good" KE techniques, or a comparative evaluation to probe the "strengths and weaknesses" of several of them. We argue that a better way to look at the problem is to recognise from the start that even in a single domain of expertise, the expert's knowledge is of several different kinds. These different kinds of knowledge almost certainly will demand different KE techniques to capture them most effectively. Accordingly, the problem becomes transformed from that of finding one (or several) "good" techniques to that of amassing a suitable battery of techniques and knowing how best to match them to the different kinds of knowledge.

Finding a way to taxonomise knowledge on a principled basis is a difficult and ambitious task that has eluded philosophers for thousands of years. However, given a restricted domain, it is not too hard to make an attempt at identifying some broad categories. For example, in a small technical domain such as maintenance and fault-finding on a mechanical plant, we can reasonably distinguish between:

(a)   knowledge of concepts and relations: Perhaps taking the form of a glossary ranging across the whole domain, this describes the main items involved in the construction and operation of the plant, and the relations between them. This knowledge can be thought of as being akin to a large scale road map, showing the major cities and the main roads connecting them.

(b)   knowledge of routine procedures: standard techniques
                and procedures, e.g. for starting up the plant. In
                fault-finding, checking and diagnostic sequences come
                into this category. Some of these procedures might not
                be in manuals, yet form an important part of the
                expert's knowledge.

(c)   facts and heuristics: particular facts, e.g. about
                the components of the plant, and a collection of
                short-cuts and rules of thumb for getting various
                tasks done. This might include knowledge about the
                obsolescence of components, and makeshift repair
                tricks, supplementing and fleshing out the conceptual
                skeleton of (a).

(d)   classificatory knowledge: making fine distinctions
                among a number of similar items (for example,
                squeaky-rumbly noises from the steam generator) or
                knowing about when various tests (e.g. diagnostic
                tests) are best deployed. In fault diagnosis for
                instance, having homed in on one area of the domain,
                knowledge of a finer grain will become appropriate. To
                continue the map analogy, it is the difference between
                a nationwide road map, and the street plan for a par-
                ticular city.

These categories may not be the only or best breakdown of domain
knowledge (cf. Wielinga and Breuker, 1984), but this is not critical. The point is rather that recognising the existence of different types of knowledge helps with the process of knowledge elicitation. The problem is that not all of these different kinds of
knowledge are suitable for elicitation by the currently favoured
informal interview technique. In the next section, after discussing briefly the cases where interviews are appropriate, we
describe some techniques developed within psychology and report on
preliminary studies exploring their suitability for KE aimed at
building expert systems.

3. PSYCHOLOGICAL TECHNIQUES

3.1 Interviews

                Interviewing is the most familar method of elicita-
tion. In a relatively simple way it quickly generates a lot of
knowledge that indicates the terminology and main components of
the domain. Thus it has an important role to play early in the
process of KE, in order to get some basic concepts and information
established as a framework for what comes later. Interviews can
be "structured" to various degrees and in various ways. One of
the simplest is to ask the expert to prepare and deliver a one-
hour introductory lecture, aiming to lay out the main themes and
ideas of the domain. Later systematic probing interviews can pursue the relevant areas to a greater depth. Here methods for prob-

ing memory, abundant in the cognitive psychological literature may
prove useful. Generalised checklists (e.g. Osborn, 1953), critical
incidents (Flanagan, 1955) and autobiographical memory procedures
(Bahrick and Karis, 1982) may provide a systematic methodology
here.

Interviews however have serious limitations. These
appear when they are subsequently used to try to refine early versions of an expert system, in an attempt to elicit the essential
expertise that differentiates the human expert from an inferior
performance program. One aspect of this problem is trying to capture in the form of rules knowledge that is not suitable for such
a representation, leading to the familiar problems with rule
modification reported throughout the literature. This is not
merely a problem of representation, but also has implications for
elicitation. Although the expert clearly <u>has</u> the knowledge, this
may not be directly communicable in the interview situation, and
must be inferred using other techniques.

3.2 Protocol analysis

Protocol analysis leading directly to a production
system model of problem solving was first described by Newell and
Simon (1972), and more recently by Ericsson and Simon (1984). In
the classical method, behaviour (verbal or otherwise) is recorded
as an expert works through a problem, and this protocol is transcribed and analysed, by (ultimately) converting it to a set of
productions that transform one solution state to the next. It has
been used in industrial settings (Bainbridge, 1979) and as part of
a systematic knowledge acquisition methodology (Breuker & Wielinga, 1983). Its merit is that it goes beyond what experts can
explicitly <u>tell</u> you in a problem solving situation, to permit
inference of what knowledge they must be using, but either cannot
verbalise or are unaware of. By reconstructing the solution using
inferred production system rules, the expert's knowledge can be
modelled. Such a method is particularly useful for eliciting procedures that experts use in problem solving, which they may not be
able to articulate.

Closely related to protocol analysis is task analysis,
which is applied before protocol analysis proper. In this the
constraints imposed by the nature of the task are determined. When
we analysed one subject solving a logic problem, the protocol suggested that she was thrashing haphazardly, and only by chance hit
on the solution. However, a task analysis showed that the problem
had a strong underlying structure and that the subject was in fact
taking advantage of this property to guide the solution. Having
identified this task-imposed constraint her behaviour became much
more predictable. Current practice might benefit from such a
technique.

A variant of the classical method, not involving
reconstructive inferences, has been successfully used by Myers,
Fox, Pegram & Greaves (1983). Their method is to take transcripts
of tape-recorded protocols and to "highlight" (using a text
editor) what they take to be substantive content. This content is

then coded directly into rules. Such a method is less time con-
suming and produces performance acceptable for an initial prototype system, and thus can be used in place of, or as a supplement
to interviews.

Protocols can be taken concurrently with experimental
as well as with real world tasks. These 'incidental' protocols may
provide useful heuristics or facts which a knowledge engineer can
use, either directly as domain knowledge, or indirectly as metaknowledge. In pilot experiments where we have taken such incidental
protocols, remarks by the expert have provided a wealth of information which has made subsequent interpretation easier. Throwaway
remarks, provoked by the nature of the knowledge elicitation procedure, may provide key insights into the expert's thinking that
would not have emerged in an interview.

3.3 Multidimensional scaling

A number of multidimensional scaling techniques have
been used in psychology to show how a particular set of concepts
are structured. These techniques identify similarities among
objects and group them conceptually. One such is the repertory
grid method arising from Personal Construct Theory (Kelly, 1955;
Fransella & Bannister, 1977; Shaw, 1981). For expert knowledge
elicitation this technique seems appropriate when there are a
number of closely related concepts, typically not well differen-
tiated by novices, and expertise consists in being able to make
discriminations. In addition there may be no specialised vocabulary to describe such subtle distinctions and relationships, for
example noises made by malfunctioning mechanical components. In
such cases repertory grid can elicit finer-grain criteria than can
the interview method.

The method yields a set of dimensions defining the
space containing the domain objects. Clustering on these dimensions gives the structure that differentiates these domain objects
from one another. That the method can uncover an independently-
agreed structure is shown by Shaw and Gaines (1983) who used it to
elicit constructs known to describe a real-world domain.

We have used the method to illuminate the sub-area of
statistics concerned with probability distributions (binomial,
Poisson, normal, etc.) by asking an expert to differentiate among
15 such distributions. The method first produced the "objective"
distinctions one might expect to find in textbooks, with such
dimensions as "continuous vs discrete". However, it also gave
more subjective, experientially-based criteria such as the dimension "useful-in-modelling vs common-test-statistic". An hierarchical cluster analysis applied to the data yielded known families
of distributions, such as the closely related F, gamma and log
gamma distributions which were highly matched. (The discrepancy
from a perfect match reflects the fact that the expert is indeed
able to distinguish one distribution from another.)

3.4 Concept sorting

Apart from the detailed knowledge which experts bring to bear on specialised areas, they are likely also to have a more global structuring of the domain and such metaknowledge will prove useful when there is a lot of information to be organised. A familiar paradigm in cognitive psychology, that of concept sorting (e.g. Chi, Feltovich & Glaser, 1981), is a helpful technique for getting this organisational knowledge. A simple version of the technique is to obtain a set of concepts that broadly cover the domain. They can be derived from a glossary or text, or can be gleaned from an introductory tutorial talk. The next step is to transfer each concept to a card, and ask the expert to sort the cards into a number of groups, describing what each group has in common. The groups can then iteratively be combined to form a hierarchy.

The method is applicable when there is a large set of concepts, ranging across the whole domain, which require a suitable structuring to become manageable. We have used the technique to decompose the technical domain of central heating systems into a conceptual organisation of subsystems. This revealed a tree of related concepts with the bottom level being 75 basic components of the domain, progressing through 5 different levels of abstraction, to the higher order concepts relating them. The resulting hierarchy clearly demonstrated, for example, the expert's subjective organisation of the domain into major subsystems dealing with the flow and regulation of, respectively, gas, water, electricity, and heat.

4. DISCUSSION AND CONCLUSIONS

Whether or not these techniques alone are sufficient for capturing the knowledge that an expert uses, the whole endeavour of KE becomes more tractable by realising that expertise, even in a single domain, comprises knowledge of several different types, and that different techniques are needed to elicit them. A first attempt to characterise these types and match them to appropriate techniques is summarised in Table 1.

The table shows examples of some of the different kinds of knowledge in the domain of statistics, and suggests how different techniques can be deployed to elicit them. According to the table, the main concepts can be generated by asking the expert informant to present an introductory lecture, the text of which can be sifted to extract a glossary of terms. Repertory grid or other multidimensional scaling techniques can be used to identify the key concepts and the relations between them, and sorting tasks can be used to provide a structure for the larger set of concepts. Procedural knowledge is best provided by protocol analysis.

The problems for KE are to construct a pragmatic classification of the different types of knowledge (perhaps guided by a taxonomy of domain properties), to find ways of matching techniques to knowledge types, and to devise new techniques where none of the existing ones is appropriate. Although the case is far from proven, the results of the pilot studies just described indicate that these psychological techniques for KE are sufficiently promising to deserve further attention.

Table 1. Different types of knowledge in the domain of statistics, and possible elicitation techniques.

TYPE OF KNOWLEDGE	ILLUSTRATIVE EXAMPLES	POSSIBLE ELICITATION TECHNIQUES
CONCEPTS AND RELATIONS	hypothesis testing, significance, families of distributions, degrees of freedom, modelling	tutorial or lecture, repertory grid
ROUTINE PROCEDURES	calculation of means & variance, statistical tests, e.g. t-test, checking assumptions are met	protocol analysis, task analysis
FACTS AND HEURISTICS	powers of 2 yield simple designs, data transformations, what to do if assumptions are violated	incidental protocols, memory probe techniques, structured interview
CLASSIFIC-ATORY KNOWLEDGE	choosing among candidate tests, levels of description, classes of related domain objects	sorting tasks, multidimensional scaling

REFERENCES

Bahrick,H.P. & Karis, D. (1982) Long-Term Ecological Memory. In Puff, C.R., Handbook of Research Methods in Human Memory and Cognition. Academic Press.

Bainbridge, L. (1979) Verbal reports as evidence of the process operator's knowledge. International Journal of Man-Machine Studies, 11, 411-436.   .

Breuker, J.A. & Wielinga, B.J. (1983) Analysis techniques for knowledge based systems. ESPRIT project 12, memoranda nos. 10 & 13. University of Amsterdam.

Chi, M.T.H., Feltovich, P.J. & Glaser, R. (1981) Categorisation and representation of physics problems by experts and novices. Cognitive Science, 5, 121-152.

Ericsson, K.A. & Simon, H.A. (1984) Protocol Analysis: Verbal Reports as Data. Bradford Books/MIT Press.

Flanagan,J.C. (1954) The Critical Incident Technique. Psychological Bulletin, 51, 327-358.

Fransella, F. & Bannister, D. (1977) A Manual For Repertory Grid Technique. London: Academic Press.

Hayes-Roth, F., Waterman, D.A. & Lenat, D.B. (Eds.) (1983) Building Expert Systems. Addison-Wesley.

Kelly, G.A. (1955) The Psychology of Personal Constructs. New York: Norton.

McDermott, J. (1982) R1: A rule-based configurer of computer systems. Artificial Intelligence, 19, 39-88.

Myers, C.D., Fox, J., Pegram, S.M. & Greaves, M.F. (1983) Knowledge acquisition for expert systems: Experience using EMYCIN for leukemia diagnosis. In J. Fox (Ed.), Proceedings of the Third BCS Conference on Expert Systems, 277-283 Cambridge.

Newell, A. & Simon, H.A. (1972) Human Problem Solving. Prentice-Hall.

Osborn, A.F. (1953) Applied Imagination. New York: Scribner.

Shaw, M.L.G. (Ed.) (1981) Recent Advances in Personal Construct Technology. New York: Academic Press.

Shaw, M.L.G. & Gaines, B.R. (1983) A computer aid to knowledge engineering. In J. Fox (Ed.), Proceedings of the Third BCS Conference on Expert Systems, 263-271. Cambridge.

van Melle, W. (1979) A domain-independent production rule system for consultation programs. In B.G.Buchanan (Ed.), Proceedings of the Sixth International Joint Conference on Artificial Intelligence, 923-925. Stanford, California.

Wielinga, B.J. & Breuker, J.A. (1984) Interpretation of Verbal Data for Knowledge Acquisition. In T.O'Shea (Ed.), ECAI-84: Advances in Artificial Intelligence, 41-50. Elsevier.

Young, R.M. (1984) Human interface aspects of expert systems. In J. Fox (Ed.), Expert Systems. Pergamon Infotech, in press.

Knowledge acquisition for medical expert systems:
A system for eliciting diagnostic decision making histories.

M. J. Cookson, J. G. Holman and D. G. Thompson
The London Hospital Medical College
Turner Street
LONDON   E1 2AD

Abstract

Knowledge acquisition is a major problem in the development of medical expert systems. One approach is to present clinical diagnosticians cases using actual or simulated patients and record the history of the diagnostic process. A system is described which elicits and records histories of decision making of experimental subjects practicing diagnostic skills on clinical case studies stored on a computer system. This data is applicable to the problems of developing expert systems in the area of medical diagnosis.

1. Introduction

A central problem in the successful application of expert systems is the difficulty of acquiring the knowledge which forms the knowledge base (Gotts 1981).

In some domains, such as fault diagnosis for electronic circuits or oil-rig platforms, acquiring the necessary knowledge is comparatively straightforward. The knowledge can relatively easily be made explicit, therefore can be obtained by interviewing experts, consulting textbooks, etc. Systems have been developed, e.g. Teiresias, to partially automate this process (Davis 1983).

Most of the present generation of medical expert systems adopt a similar approach to knowledge acquisition, and also deal with areas in which the diagnostic process is reasonably well understood. However, these areas are probably the exception in medicine. Indeed, most clinical teaching imparts diagnostic skill, not through the explicit presentation of factual information or strategic knowledge, but by providing extensive practical experience of working with patients. It is thus hardly surprising that clinicians often find it difficult to express their knowledge verbally, at least in the particular form prescribed by the expert systems, and that such accounts as can be obtained may be inaccurate or at variance with actual practice (Nisbett & Wilson 1977). The 'strategic' knowledge (Buchanan et al 1983) vital to effective and reliable decision making proves particularly difficult to verbalise, yet it may well be important to capture this kind of knowledge, especially when the primary purpose of the system is to assist in the teaching of diagnostic skills.

In view of these difficulties, a more promising method for acquiring expert knowledge may be to study the clinician's performance in the context in which diagnostic expertise is normally both acquired and exercised, namely, while working with a patient. However, an obvious difficulty with recording practitioners in their usual clinical practice is that they are challenged by different cases presenting widely different diagnostic problems. Moreover, the transcription and analysis of the resulting dialogues is labour intensive, limiting the amount of information that can be obtained.

A computer-based system under development at the London
Hospital Medical College may go some way towards overcoming these
problems. The system uses data-bases derived from actual clinical cases
to simulate a patient, allowing clinicians to conduct interviews and
examinations much as they would in real life. The decision-making
history is recorded automatically, allowing data from a large number of
subjects to be collected in a standard form. Moreover, many subjects can
work with the same 'patient', who can be relied upon to respond in the
same manner every time, removing an important source of variability in
the study of doctor-patient interaction.

2. Project Description

The area of clinical diagnosis is one in which it is possible
to automate the process of recording the performance of practitioners.
Since the interaction between clinician and patient is fairly standard,
there is a limited number of questions that can be asked, a limited
number of examinations that can be performed, and a limited number of
tests which can be applied. This property can be exploited in recording
the decision history of a diagnostician.

At the Department of Medical Education, Southern Illinois
University School of Medicine, Barrows has produced a set of programmed
learning texts to teach clinical diagnostic skills using case studies
(Barrows & Tamblyn 1980). These have been widely used in medical
education. From experience of this approach at the London Hospital
Medical College, the following specification for a computer based system
was devised.

1) The presenting situation.

The computer provides the subject with a description of the
patient as he or she first presents themselves. In this is included such
data as may be provided by the family general practitioner etc.

2) Consultation.

During the consultation with the patient, the subject chooses
questions to ask and examinations to perform from the standard list.
This list contains over 200 questions and 120 examinations. The subject
types in the code number of the question or examination and the results
for this patient are displayed on the screen. The questions and
examinations requested are stored in the computer for later analysis.
The consultation is terminated by the subject when he decides that
sufficient information has been obtained.

3) Provisional diagnosis and tests.

After the consultation the subject writes his formulation of
the patient's problem. Then he selects from a standard list the
laboratory tests or diagnostic procedures he would like done on the
patient in the order he wishes them to be done. Once these are recorded
the system goes into the actual patient management history.

4) Patient Management History.

The history tells what actually happened at the time the
patient was treated, the tests which were done, and the results. The
actual management does not necessarily represent the optimal management
of the patient but the real life history. The results of the tests the
subject requested are displayed at the appropriate times. It was
considered important for user acceptability that the system should not
simply record the subjects decision history, but also give feedback about

the actual management of the case. The subject can then compare what he
has done with what the real manager of the case did.
        As part of the normal diagnostic procedure the subject
produces written case notes. It was considered that to require subjects
to type the case notes directly into the computer would have created
considerable user resistance. Consequently, the recorded decision
history consists of the case notes written by the subject together with
the stored list of requested questions, examinations and tests.

3. Implementation

        The database for a complete case is approximately 200K. This
makes it feasible to implement the system on a microcomputer.
        In the initial experimental phase it was decided to place
supplementary pictorial data such as CAT scans, X-rays, etc. into sealed
envelopes. At a later date it is intended to use a digitising system
connected to a T.V. camera for the storage of pictures.
        The requirement that the system should be available on a wide
range of computers necessitated using a language and operating system
with a high degree of portability. There are two operating systems with
the required characteristics, UNIX and UCSD p-System. As successful use
of UNIX requires high processing power and large disc capacities it was
decided to use the UCSD p-System version IV, on the Sirius microcomputer
using Pascal with the turtlegraphics package which is standardised across
machines running version IV.
        At present, the first two parts of the system have been
implemented, and are undergoing user trials. In view of the difficulties
experienced in getting user acceptance of medical expert systems,
considerable emphasis is placed upon acceptability to potential subjects.
In addition, the sets of questions, examinations and tests are being
reviewed to check that they are comprehensive and clear.

4. Discussion

        One possible criticism of this system is that by constraining
the diagnosticians to use standardised questions, a structure is being
imposed on the dialogue which is dissimilar from that which exists in
real life. However, Barrows has shown that normal clinical dialogues
can easily be translated into the standard form of questions and
examinations employed in the system.
        Shortliffe (Shortliffe 1982) found that good diagnostic
performance of an expert system does not in itself preclude user
resistance. It may also be important that the system reaches a diagnosis
in a similar way to a human practitioner. This project, by providing
information about the way diagnosticians work in practice, should assist
in the design of expert systems acceptable to the medical profession.
        Experts and novices are said to be distinguished by two
differences in expertise. Firstly experts know more, and secondly they
use their knowledge more effectively. This project is concerned with
clarifying these differences, by examining the clinical decision making
of a wide range of subjects from first year medical students to senior
consultants and professorial staff. In addition, it is of interest to
determine whether clinicians in different medical specialisations use the
same diagnostic skills in the same way.

A second major aim of the project is to study how the novice becomes an expert, what the relationship is between the amount of experience the user has and the growth of his expertise. It is intended to examine in detail how diagnostic skills develop through the students career.

The knowledge bases of most current expert systems consist largely of factual knowledge. However, continued addition of factual knowledge does not ensure enhanced diagnostic performance. Strategic knowledge is likely also to play an important role. By looking at the performance of human subjects as they develop from novice to expert diagnosticians, we hope to illuminate the contributions of increased factual and strategic knowledge to problem solving performance.

5. References

Gotts, N.M. (1984). Knowledge acquisition for medical expert systems - a review. Report AIMG-5, University of Sussex.

Davis, R. (1983). TEIRESIAS: Experiments in communicating with a knowledge-based system. In Designing for human-computer communication, eds. M.E. Sime and M.J. Coombs. London: Academic Press.

Nisbett, R.E. & Wilson, T.D. (1977). Telling more than we can know: verbal reports on mental processes. Psychological Review, 84, pp. 231-59.

Buchanan, B.G., Barstow, D.R., Bechtel, R., Bennett, J., Clancey, C., Kulikowski, C., Mitchell, T., & Waterman, D.A. (1983). Constructing an expert system. In Building expert systems, eds. F. Hayes-Roth, D.A. Waterman & D.B. Lenat. Addison-Wesley.

Barrows, H.S. & Tamblyn, R.M. (1980). Problem-based learning. Springer, New York.

Shortliffe, E.H. (1982). The computer and medical decision making: good advice is not enough. IEEE Engineering in Medicine and Biology Magazine, 1(2), pp. 16-18.

EXPERIENCE IN THE USE OF AN INDUCTIVE
SYSTEM IN KNOWLEDGE ENGINEERING

Anna E.Hart,
School of Computing,
Lancashire Polytechnic, Preston PR1 2TQ

Abstract

Knowledge acquisition from people is known to be a
problem. An experiment was carried out to investigate the use of
a computer-based inductive system, in which an implementation of
Quinlan's ID3 algorithm was used to deduce rules from a training
set. The performance of the ensuing system was evaluated by
comparing its results with further examples, and also by comparison
with the expert's own view of what he did. The expert was
willing to take part in tape-recorded interviews.
This gave an insight into the manual system
identifying problems and inconsistencies. It also highlighted
the relative merits of inductive systems. In particular there
are shortcomings in the algorithm where data are incomplete and
uncertain.
Using established statistical techniques it is
possible to enhance ID3 to overcome these problems. Results from
numerical taxonomy assist in the selection of examples and
attributes for such an algorithm. A new methodology is
proposed, using the enhanced inductive system as an "intelligent"
advisor in knowledge acquisition.

1. Background

This work arose out of research on knowledge exchange
and in particular interview skills. Some papers have been
published about interview skills in medical training (Tanner and
Silverman, 1981) but as Welbank comments (1983) the systems
analyst's skill in asking questions has not been formalized.
Many of the results in this paper agree with the findings of
Welbank.
Knowledge acquisition for expert systems has been
acknowledged as an area for research (Grover 1983; Smith and
Baker 1983), and the possible role of inductive systems has not
been explored fully. These results are based on findings from
the use of an implementation of Quinlan's ID3 algorithm (Quinlan
1979), and interviewing a "friendly" expert. In each case a
simple rule-based system was derived.
Details of the application area are given in Section
11. It was chosen carefully so that there was a large set of
examples available which could be used on ID3 before interviewing
the expert. Also I was familiar with the general principles of
the procedure, but not the details of how the expert worked.

2. Problems with ID3

The choice of examples and **attributes** for a training
set is a non-trivial problem. If examples are selected badly
then the resulting decision tree may be very good at dealing with
certain types of cases, but very poor with others. A poor
choice of attributes will yield a decision tree which is
unnecessarily obscure, and different from the expert's view of
what he does. These problems are well discussed in statistical
literature, and outlined later.

ID3 itself has short-comings. The main ones are
listed below:

(i)   it needs a complete set of examples
(ii)   the rule cannot be probabilistic,
(iii)   each example has equal weighting; two identical
         examples have the same effect as one,
(iv)   it cannot deal with contradictory examples,
(v)   the results can be highly sensitive to changes in
         the example set.

3. Proposed enhancement to ID3

The accuracy of the induced tree is likely to improve
as the size of the training set is increased, so it would be
difficult to eliminate (i). However, (ii) - (v) can be improved
by a slight modification to the algorithm.

Quinlan's algorithm uses information content,
described as an heuristic. Kullback (1967) has shown that the
information statistic is asymptotically equivalent to a
chi-squared variable. At each stage ID3 measures the information
content of each remaining attribute, and selects the one which
gives largest increase in information content. However, it does
not distinguish between a substantial increase and a negligible
increase in this choice, and it ignores the degrees of freedom
associated with the attributes.

4. The χ^2 -statistic

The algorithm would be improved by considering the
chi-squared value χ^2 instead of the information statistic.

Consider attribute A with possible values
$A_1, A_2, \ldots A_{\alpha+1}$, and classes $C_1, C_2, \ldots C_{\gamma+1}$. Let the total number
of examples in the current subset of the training set be N. A
is not a good discriminator if the values of A are randomly
distributed within the C_j's. Any apparent clumping or deviation
from randomness will suggest that A is a good discriminator
between classes.

If our null hypothesis is:

Prob(example is in class C_i|value of attribute is A_j)
= Prob(example is in class C_i) for all i,j.

then the corresponding χ^2 -value is

$$\sum_{i,j} \frac{(E_{ij} - O_{ij})^2}{E_{ij}} \qquad \text{----------(1)}$$

where O_{ij} is the number of examples with value A_j in class C_i, and

$$E_{ij} = \frac{\sum_k O_{ik} \sum_\ell O_{\ell j}}{N} \quad . \qquad \text{(summation over the current example sub-set)}$$

The number of degrees of freedom is $\alpha\gamma$. Using a statistical test the null hypothesis would be rejected if the χ^2 value were sufficiently high. This would suggest that the corresponding attribute did discriminate between classes. The attribute selected as the best discriminator should be that with the highest significant χ^2 -value i.e that with the pattern which is least likely to occur by chance.

5. Use and advantages

        Algebra similar to that in Kullback (1967) shows that (1)is equivalent to N times ID3's information statistic. However, use of the χ^2 -value has very important differences. An attribute which has a large number of values may discriminate well by chance. The higher number of degrees of freedom means that the χ^2 value has to be correspondingly larger in order to be sufficiently significant. It is possible for the algorithm to stop when no χ^2 value is significant at, say, 10% level. This reduces the "guess-work" and makes the resulting tree less sensitive to small changes in the training set.
        Any terminal node will, in general, have probability estimates. At a node where no attribute has been selected as good enough these estimates will be relative frequencies, independent of attribute value, and given by

$$\text{Prob(class } C_i) \; = \; \frac{\text{no. of examples in } C_i}{\text{no. of remaining examples}}$$

If the last attribute is significant (at the designated level) then
the probabilities will be conditional on the attribute values and
given by

$$\text{Prob}(\text{class } C_i \,|\, \text{attribute } A_j) = \frac{0_{ij}}{\sum\limits_{k} 0_{kj}}$$

using the previous notation.

6. Example

The method is illustrated with the example in Table 1,
where attributes are code and colour, and classes are + and -.
The induced tree is shown in Figure 1.

Table 1.

colour code	I	II	III	IV
blue	3+ 5-	6+ 8-	4+ 7-	6+ 6-
black	10+	6+ 2-	4+ 4-	6-

Example data set

Figure 1

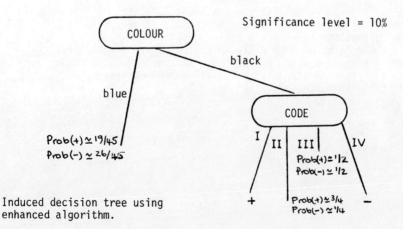

Significance level = 10%

$\text{Prob}(+) \simeq 19/45$
$\text{Prob}(-) \simeq 26/45$

$\text{Prob}(+) \simeq 1/2$
$\text{Prob}(-) \simeq 1/2$

$\text{Prob}(+) \simeq 3/4$
$\text{Prob}(-) \simeq 1/4$

Induced decision tree using
enhanced algorithm.

7. Critical Assessment

One of the ID3's merits is that it is computationally efficient. I believe that the modification to the algorithm would not reduce the efficiency substantially, although this has not been investigated. The induced decision tree may still be hard to understand (Corlett, 1983) as the overall working of the algorithm is unchanged. Also both algorithms have the deficiency of only considering one attribute at a time. A joint pair of attributes may be an excellent discriminator while each individual attribute may be poor. The best solution to this seems to be a careful choice of attributes prior to using the algorithm.

Use of a χ^2 -statistic does present some problems. Results are not reliable if a value of O_{ij} is less than 5. This demands a large training set which might be difficult to obtain. Nonetheless the amended algorithm is an enhancement and useful for dealing with incomplete or uncertain data.

In taxonomy where attributes are often referred to as "characteristics" the information statistic and χ^2 have been suggested as an aid in selecting suitable characteristics for taxonomic classification (Bonham-Carter 1967; Bisby 1970). The application here is similar. The relationship between information and fuzzy logic is described by Xie and Bedrosian (1984) and extension to a χ^2 -variable may be applicable in this area too.

8. Selection of examples and attributes

It is tempting to take a random sample from all available examples, if a choice is feasible. In the case where a large proportion of examples are very similar then this would result in a very good rule for straightforward cases, but little information about difficult or rarer cases. This would yield elementary information, enabling further discussions with the expert. An alternative procedure would be to select examples (randomly if appropriate) from the different classes, thereby getting a better picture of the rule. Such decisions would be based on the original information obtained from the expert, and an early question should be about the distribution of different types of cases he encounters.

The choice of attributes is very similar to the taxonomist's task of selecting characteristics. This subject is still under discussion, but well-documented. Johnson (1970) warns that the grouping of attributes as well as their choice can influence the results. Writers warn against bias, the selection of inadmissible attributes (e.g. codes or names given to items) or redundant (e.g. invariant or irrelevant) attributes. Attributes can be correlated in many ways. These include logical correlation (where an attribute is conditionally defined on the value of a different attribute), functional correlation, and statistical correlation (Jardine & Sibson, 1973).

It is generally accepted that careful choice of
attributes is preferable to addition of attributes in an
unmethodical manner.   Sneath and Sokal (1973) recommend that
several people independently select attributes, as people will
view things differently.   In general, redundant attributes should
be ignored, and those chosen should be relevant and homologous.
In my work I encountered problems very similar to these, and my
findings endorse the taxonomists' conclusions.

9. Methodology

Welbank (1983) suggests the use of an inductive system
as an aid rather than a replacement for an interview.   The
question which arises is when it should be used.   Ideally I feel
that the initial contact with the expert should be minimal, and
that the algorithm should be used extensively in the early stages.
However, it will probably be impossible to procure examples and
select attributes without lengthy discussion with the expert.   I
propose the approach represented in Figure 2.
The knowledge engineer should always approach the
expert with specific questions, and preferably talk about types
of examples.   Testing the rule-based system is difficult.
Merely testing the decision tree on a further set of examples
derived in a similar manner to the training set has logical
problems (Ehrenberg 1982).   This is an area for further work.

Figure 2

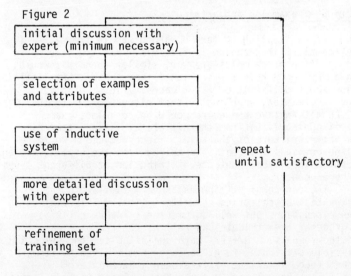

Use of an inductive system

10. Conclusion

Traditional data analysis in statistics is complex for
the non-expert, and results are often difficult to interpret.   All
the same there has been criticism of neglect of well-established
statistical techniques in expert system work (Spiegelhalter &
Knil-Jones 1984). This paper attempts to identify results in
statistics which are of immediate benefit to knowledge engineering.
Gordon (1981) describes advantages of computer-based
taxonomy. The ability to reduce large amounts of data to
manageable form, operate without bias, and deal simultaneously with
large number of items is a great advantage. Talking about
ecological applications, he says that invariably the program gives
information which a trained ecologist would derive from factors
not in the data, and also detects something in the data which the
ecologist, despite his extra knowledge, would miss. This
summarizes the potential of an inductive system as an intelligent
adviser.

11. Details of the experiment

The expert was the admissions tutor for a course in
Higher Education.   I was familiar with the application forms, but
not the way in which the tutor made his decisions.   He is able to
decide quickly how to deal with an application, but other staff
find the process difficult.   This area was chosen because it is
relatively simple; this enabled me to assess the role of the
program Expert-Ease (then marketed by Export Software
International).   Also all the application forms were available
from the previous 2 years .
A training set was selected from a previous year's
application forms.   The set was refined until a reasonable tree
was produced.   The training set consisted of 50 examples from a
population of over 300.   The rule was then tested on remaining
examples from that year and the successive year.   The success
rate was over 93%.   (This may be misleading because many
examples are very similar).   The main problems were in the
choice of attributes as discussed in 8, and contradictory examples.
At this stage it was easy to identify the 'problem-cases'.   All
this was achieved without talking to the expert.
The expert agreed to participate in a tape-recorded
interview.   After two interviews a flow chart was drawn up,
which he approved.   This was subsequently found to contain a
serious error.   This represented the first traverse of the loop
in Figure 2.   It was clear that the way to proceed was to try to
remove any apparent contradictions in the two sets of results.   I
did not pursue this as the aim was the evaluation of the inductive
system, not the production of an expert system.

Acknowledgements

This work was carried out at the Department of Mathematics, Liverpool Polytechnic.   I am indebted to Alan Price for many hours of stimulating discussion, and to Joe Higgins for his encouragement and help.

I thank the referees for pointing out similar work by Kass, (1980).

References

Bisby F.A. (1970). The evaluation and selection of characters in Angiosperm Taxonomy: an example from Crotalaria. New Phytologist 69, 1149-1160.

Bonham-Carter G.F. (1967). An example of the analysis of semi-quantitative petrographic data. Proc. 7th World Petroleum Congress 2.

Corlett R.A. (1983). Explaining induced decision trees. Proc. Expert Systems 1983.

Ehrenberg A.S.C. (1982). Comments on a paper, JRSS B 44, no.3 311-312.

Gordon A.D. (1981). Classification: Methods for the Exploratory Analysis of Multivariate Data, Chapman & Hall.

Grover M.D. (1983). A pragmatic knowledge acquisition methodology. Proc.8th Joint Conference on Artificial Intelligence, 436-438.

Jardine N,Sibson R. (1973). Mathematical Taxonomy, J.Wiley.

Johnson L.A.S. (1970). Rainbow's end: the quest for an optimal taxonomy. Systematic Zoology 19, 204-239.

Kass G.V. (1980). An exploratory technique for investigating large quantities of categorical data. Applied statistics 29 no.2 119-127.

Kullback S. (1967). Information Theory and Statistics. Dover.

Quinlan J.R.(1979). Discovering rules by induction from large collections of examples. In Expert Systems in the Microelectronic Age, ed., Michie D., pp 168-201. Edinburgh: Edinburgh University Press.

Smith R.G. and Baker J.D. (1983). A dipmeter advisor system: a case study in commercial Expert Systems development. Proc. IJCAI-8. 122-129.

Sneath P.H,Sokal R.R. (1973). Numerical Taxonomy, W.H.Freeman and Co. San Francisco.

Spiegelhalter D.J. and Knil- Jones R.P. (1984). Statistical and knowledge-based approaches to clinical decision-support systems, with an application in Gastroenterology. JRSS A 147 Part 1 35-77

Tanner L.A., Silverman G. (1981).   A teacher's guide to teaching
medical interviewing.   Medical Education 15 no.2   100-105

Welbank M. (1983).   A review of knowledge acquisition techniques
for expert systems.   Martlesham Consultancy Services, British
Telecommunications.

Xie W.X.,Bedrosian S.D(1984).An information measure for fuzzy sets.
IEEE Transactions on Systems, Man, and Cybernetics, Smc-14,
no.1.   151-156.

ACCI - AN EXPERT SYSTEM FOR THE APPORTIONMENT
OF CLOSE COMPANIES' INCOME

A.E. Roycroft & P. Loucopoulos
Department of Computation,
University of Manchester
Institute of Science and Technology
P.O. Box 88, Manchester M60 1QD.

Abstract

The complexity of tax legislation coupled to the
large number of different cases that tax inspectors must
consider in any financial year makes it difficult if not
impossible for many inspectors to be familiar with all
relevant regulations.

This paper describes the development of ACCI, a
prototype expert system which can be used in one area of
taxation known as the "apportionment of close companies'
income". Its use greatly alleviates the problem of a lack
of experts in this area.

Legal reasoning is fundamentally different to
medical reasoning. Legal reasoning is characterised by its
deterministic nature and logical structure. This paper
discusses the implications of these characteristics with
regard to the development of ACCI.

The paper addresses itself to the issues relating
to:
   (a) The analysis of the domain of expertise.
   (b) The conceptual modelling of the domain and
   (c) The building of the knowledge base.

1. Introduction

It is a well established principle of English law
that legislation which imposes a charge to tax will be
interpreted by the courts in such a way as to give the
taxpayer the benefit of any doubt there may be over the
meaning of the legislation (Pinson, 1982). This provides
the draftsman of the legislation with a considerable
incentive to ensure that the tax statutes are drafted as
precisely as possible. However, precision is gained only at
the expense of clarity and brevity. Tax legislation is both
lengthy and complex.

This complexity causes problems not only for the
taxpayer but also for the tax inspector, who needs to
understand and be familiar with a mass of legislation. It is
inevitable that even the most experienced tax inspector will
sometimes consider and use legislation which is irrelevant
or, conversely, overlook that which is relevant to the
particular problem.

Tax legislation may therefore be seen as having
two characteristics. It is well defined so that ambiguity
in its interpretation may be avoided but it is also very
complex.

These characteristics have attracted several authors to attempt to use computers to solve some of the problems associated with tax legislation (Foundos 1971; Bellord 1980; Hellawell 1980). In the past traditional programming languages have been used but, they have been found to have serious limitations with regard to legislation.

An alternative to these methods is the use of expert systems. This paper describes the development of ACCI, a prototype expert system for use by the Inland Revenue in a small area of its work relating to Corporation Tax. ACCI was implemented with the use of an expert systems shell under VME on an ICL 2900 computer.

This expert system incorporates tax legislation explicitly, together with the control structures relating to the interdependency of the statutes. A tax inspector therefore can obtain advice about apportionment of a company's income in an accurate, cost-effective and natural manner. The main benefits accrued from using ACCI are that speed and accuracy are enhanced but most importantly the use of the system greatly alleviates the problem of a lack of human experts in this area of taxation.

2. The Application Area

When a company distributes its profits amongst its shareholders by paying a dividend, the amount received by each shareholder forms part of his income and is subject to income tax. Dividends are, in effect, paid after deduction of tax at the basic rate so that a shareholder who pays tax only at the basic rate is not required to pay any further tax on the dividends he receives.

Wealthier shareholders, however, who pay tax at the higher rates, must pay an additional amount of income tax on the dividends they receive, and they may also be liable to pay investment income surcharge. Wealthy shareholders who control a company may therefore decide that the company should not pay a dividend, but should instead accumulate its profits, so that they will not have to pay this additional tax.

Since 1922 there have been statutory provisions designed to counteract the avoidance of tax in this way. The current provisions are contained in Schedule 16 to the Finance Act 1972 and these empower the Inland Revenue to apportion the income of certain companies, called close companies, amongst the companies' shareholders.

Exercise of the power to apportion a company's income results in the amount apportioned to a shareholder being treated as income received by him. Thus, although the company has not distributed its profits, it is deemed to have done so and the shareholders are charged to income tax and investment income surcharge accordingly.

The legislation contained in Schedule 16, Finance
Act 1972 determines whether the Inland Revenue may apportion
a company's income in given circumstances and defines the
method of calculating the amounts, if any, which may be
apportioned. The Inland Revenue issues its inspectors with
a manual, hundreds of pages long, which contains detailed
explanations of the statutory provisions.

The problems faced by the tax inspector in
deciding whether to apportion a company's income are no
different from those presented by much legislation. These
problems were outlined in the introduction. However, the
problems with regard to Scedule 16 are exacerbated by the
fact that this legislation is used only infrequently, with
the result that it is difficult for the inspector to become
familiar with its provisions.

Another difficulty is the sheer volume of the
inspector's work. Although 90% of the cases with which the
inspector has to deal for the purpose of apportionment can
be eliminated very quickly , the remaining 10% can occupy
the inspector for a considerable amount of time. An
inspector who specialises in apportionment may be able to
deal with each case in a little more than a quarter of an
hour. The average tax inspector however, may be occupied
for many hours in dealing with each case.

3. A Solution Through Expert Systems

The Inland Revenue's problem is therefore one of a
lack of a sufficient number of experts to deal with the
apportionment of close companies' income.

The application area is characterised by the fact
that the tax inspector deals with cases which may result in
a multitude of solution possibilities. To examine all valid
solutions is an often difficult undertaking. The same task
carried out by an expert system in a systematic way will
ensure that all possible solution paths are explored.

3.1 Expert Systems

An expert system is a computer system which
possesses a set of facts about a specific domain of human
expertise and by manipulating these facts intelligently, it
is able to make useful inferences for the user of the
system. These systems use rules of inference to draw
conclusions or make decisions within defined areas, making
use of techniques such as search and knowledge
representation. Their power comes from the presence of
facts and procedures which have been identified by human
experts as the key components in the problem solving
process.

An expert system should manifest the following
characteristics (Lane & Loucopoulos 1983) :
(a) Be able to embody domain-specific knowledge from one
    or more specialists.
(b) Represent this knowledge in a form condusive to
    meaningful interpretation and manipulation by a
    computer.
(c) Provide a facility for updating and refining its
    underlying knowledge.   .
(d) Interact with a user in an easy and "natural" manner.
(e) Provide the domain expert with explanations as to its
    line of reasoning.
        The knowledge embodied in an expert system
represents the knowledge of one or more human specialists as
viewed by the system builder and verified by the specialist.
The process of building a domain-specific knowledge base is
an iterative process involving the domain expert and the
computer scientist working together to build a system which
is relevant and bears no ambiguity or redundancy. The tools
that may be used in building an expert system fall into two
broad categories.
        Firstly, a general purpose programming language
can be used. When this is the case the expert system is
tailored made in all its apects, for the application in
hand.   Secondly, an expert system may be built using a shell
system. A shell is a package which can provide the means of
building, using and maintaining a system without the need
for developing it from scratch. Most shell systems are
domain-independent and can be used for a wide range of
applications. Their use provides great savings in
development time but performance usually suffers.
        The choice of tool is a compromise decision by
taking into consideration a number of often conflicting
factors such as performance, maintenance, cost, development
effort etc. ACCI was to be developed over a relatively short
period of time and this in effect dictated the use of a
shell rather than a more special purpose tool.

3.2 ADVISER - A Shell System

        ADVISER is an expert system shell supported on the
ICL 2900 series under VME and since its use in building a
system that could satisfy the five criteria outlined in 3.1
was found to be adequate, it was chosen as a tool for the
development of ACCI. Use of ADVISER meant that the
inference engine of the system was already provided, thus
reducing the problem of implementation to the problem of
defining the rules necessary to make up the system's
knowledge base and building the appropriate interface.
        Domain-specific knowledge is represented in the
form of production rules written in the ADVISER language.   A
feature of this language is its resemblance to ordinary
English ; this, together with the fact that rules may be
written using the jargon with which the expert is familiar,

results in code which is highly readable, easily checked for
correctness and easily maintained. An example of an ADVISER
rule is given in section 4.

The ADVISER software consists of two parts, the
knowledge base builder and the knowledge base interpreter.

The ADVISER Knowledge Base Builder produces the
knowledge base from the rules specified using the ADVISER
language. A consultation is managed by the Knowledge Base
Interpreter, the system's inference engine. This accesses
the knowledge base, asks questions of the user in order to
elicit the information which will enable it to reach
specified goals, and advises the user of the results. Using
text contained within the knowledge base, the Interpreter is
able to explain to the user the meaning of its questions,
and also to explain the reasons why those questions have
been asked.

4. Developing The System

The task of constructing the knowledge base of the
expert system has two aspects. Firstly, there is the problem
of knowledge acquisition; discovering how a human expert
carries out his work. Secondly, rule formulation takes
place from the facts collected during knowledge acquisition.
This is not simply a two stage process, rather it is
iterative, so that after formulating one set of rules one
returns to the task of acquiring further knowledge as well
as refining the existing rules. It is, however, convenient
to consider these two proceses separately.

A third process, that of conceptual modelling
was found to be necessary in developing ACCI.

4.1 Knowledge Acquisition

Before any attempt could be made to begin to
formulate the rules which were to be included in the
knowledge base, it was necessary to have a general
understanding of the domain. In fact, one of the authors
was already familiar with some of the statutory provisions,
and so it was possible to gain this general understanding
relatively quickly using standard text books (Pinson 1982).

Once this stage had been reached, there were four
sources of information : Statutes; Inland Revenue training
notes; the tax inspector's "field manual"; and interviews
with an expert.

Of these, perhaps the most important was the set
of notes used by the Inland Revenue in training its
inspectors. Although, as explained below, it was possible
in many cases to derive rules directly from the legislation,
it is difficult to understand from the legislation alone how
the various rules are linked together or what their combined
effect is. The training notes provide a clear explanation
of the meaning of the legislation, with examples of how the
rules are to be applied in practice.

From the training notes and field manual, the various stages of the tax inspector's work and the main statutory provisions associated with each stage were identified.

The starting point in each case was the description of the relevant statutory provisions given in the training notes. The cross references in these notes were used to refer both to the detailed and comprehensive instructions contained in the field manual and to the legislation itself. In this way, it was possible firstly to come to an understanding of the domain and secondly, using this understanding, to formulate the rules relevant to each stage to be included in the knowledge base.

Most of the rules could be derived in this way, working solely from the written sources. However, interviews with an expert from the Inland Revenue were also necessary. The purpose of these interviews was fourfold.

Firstly, it was necessary to decide at the very beginning what and how much expertise was to be contained within the system. Secondly, there were inevitably parts of the legislation which were difficult to understand and questions which were not answered by the written sources ; these difficulties had to be resolved. Thirdly, where assumptions were made in the course of developing the system in order to simplify the task of building the knowledge base, it was necessary to confirm that such assumptions were valid and acceptable to the Inland Revenue. Finally, it was necessary to check that the questioning used in the consultation and the form of the advice given by the system was acceptable.

4.2 Modelling the Domain

It is often quoted in the literature by developers of expert systems that a knowledge base can be constructed directly from the facts collected during the knowledge acquisition process. In developing ACCI we found that an intermediate step was necessary, namely that of conceptual modelling.

By conceptual modelling we mean the process of organising the mass of facts about the domain into a model which represents the system developer's understanding of the domain. Such a model should be rich enough to encompass all relevant parts but abstract enough to suppress any details which may be irrelevant to the development process. An analogy may be drawn with a database conceptual model.

In developing ACCI it was possible to build a model of the rules at a global level before the knowledge base was built. Legal reasoning is in many ways different to medical reasoning (McCarty, 1984). The rules are deterministic rather than probabilistic, they are logical in structure rather than associative and they apply individually rather than cummulatively. This precision aided the construction of the conceptual model.

The conceptual model for ACCI was constructed mainly by analysing the legislation. Since the tax inspector's work is defined precisely by legislation, the legislation itself becomes the source of information for the model. Another possible way of building the model is by observing the inspector's work, in which case there is no need for the developer to become involved with all of the intricacies of the legislation. However, because this method involves a high degree of innacuracy at the early stages, necessitating lengthy 'debugging' sessions, and because there is a need for constant contact with the expert, the former method was chosen.

The conceptual model consists of three parts, each major part representing a characteristic of the relevant legislation.

(a) The statutory provisions.

The main statutory provisions relevant to each aspect of the tax inspectors work are identified. These are shown in table 1.

These statutory provisions form the basis of the conceptual model. They are however complex. Much complexity is caused by the fact that the various monetary amounts with which the inspector is concerned are defined by the legislation by reference to other amounts which are themselves further defined.

Amounts apportionable	Main relevant statutory provisions
Excess of relevant income over distributions	sections 177, 238, 239, 248 Income and Corporation Taxes Act 1970; section 93, 95 Finance Act 1972; Paragraphs 1, 8, 9, 10 Schedule 16 Finance Act 1972.
Whole relevant income	as above plus paragraph 2 Schedule 16 Finance Act 1972.
Annual payments	paragraph 3 Schedule 16 Finance Act 1972.
Interest payable	paragraph 3A Schedule 16 Finance Act 1972.

Table 1

(b) The entity interdependency.

This part of the conceptual model defines the dependencies between the different entities (amounts). These are represented diagramatically in figure 1. For each node there exist one or more statutory provisions associated with that node.

Each node is numbered and the appropriate
statutory provision(s) is cross referenced by an entry in
table 2.

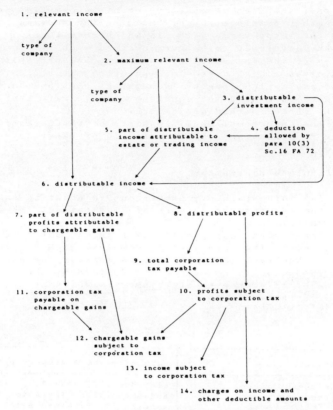

Figure 1

1.	paragraph 8(1) Schedule 16 FA 1972
2.	" 9 "
3.	" 10(3) "
4.	" 10(3) "
5.	" 10(4) "
6.	" 10(2) "
7.	" 10(2)(b) "
8.	" 10(2)(a) "
9.	s 238 et seq ICTA 1970; ss 93, 95 FA 1972
10.	s 238(4)(a) ICTA 1970
11.	s 265 ICTA 1970
12.	s 93 FA 1972
13.	s 250 ICTA 1970
14.	s 248 ICTA; para 10(8) Schedule 16 FA 1972
	s 177 ICTA

Table 2

(c) The type of company.

        Underlying all of the legislation relating to
apportionment, is an understanding of the different types of
company with which the inspector must deal. This part of
the model is a representation of this understanding and is
represented as a hierarchical structure (Roycroft 1984).

4.3 Building the Knowledge Base

        Having reached an initial understanding of the
legislation from the training notes and field manual, it was
possible to derive many of the required rules through a
careful consideration of the legislation itself.
        Building the knowledge base for ACCI was a process
of stepwise refinement. First, a piece of legislation is
considered. This in turn is translated into English-like
rules which are subsequently transformed into ADVISER rules.
Finally the rules are ordered in a structure relevant to the
application in hand.
        For example, one of the key statutory provisions
Scheduis paragraph 9 of le 16, Finance Act 1972, which
provides that:

9(1) - Subject to paragraph 13 below, the relevant income of
a company shall in no case be taken to exceed the company's
distributable investment income for the accounting period
plus 50% of the estate or trading income for the period.

(2) - In the application of sub-paragraph (1) above to a
company which is a trading company or a member of a trading
group, the trading income shall be disregarded; and in the
application of that sub-paragraph to a trading company the
estate income -
        (a) if it is less than the appropriate fraction of the
relevant maximum amount, shall be treated as reduced by one
half of the amount required to make it up to that fraction
of the relevant maximum amount; or
        (b) if it is less than the appropriate fraction of the
relevant minimum amount, shall be disregarded ....

        Paragraph 9 above is translated into four rules
which define maximum relevant income. Firstly, there is the
general rule in sub-paragraph 9(1) :

maximum relevant income = distributable investment income +
50% of estate or trading income.
        Secondly, in the case of trading companies and
members of trading groups:

maximum relevant income = distributable investment income +
50% of estate income.
        Thirdly, in the case of trading companies whose
estate income is less than a certain fraction of the
"relevant maximum amount":

maximum relevant income = distributable investment income +
50% of (estate income - abatement), where abatement = 1/2 *
((appropriate fraction * relevant maximum amount) - estate
income).

    Finally, in the case of trading companies whose
estate income is less than a certain fraction of the
"relevant minimum amount":
maximum relevant income = distributable investment income.

    If we ignore, for the moment, the need to know
what the relevant minimum and maximum amounts are, and what
the appropriate fraction is, the above rules can be
expressed directly in the ADVISER language as shown below.


```
First, maximum_relevant_income IS distributable_investment_income
                    + (50/100 * estate_or_trading_income)

Second, maximum_relevant_income IS distributable_investment_income
                    + (50/100 * estate_income)
         PROVIDED trading_company OR member_of_trading_group

Third, maximum_relevant_income IS distributable_investment_income
                    + (50/100 * (estate_income - abatement))
         PROVIDED trading-company AND
             (estate_income < (appropriate_fraction * relevant_
             maximum_amount))
         ALSO abatement IS 0.5 * ((appropriate_fraction * relevant_
             maximum_amount) - estate_income)

Fourth, maximum_relevant_income is distributable_investment_income
         PROVIDED trading_company AND
             (estate_income < (appropriate_fraction * relevant_
             minimum_amount)
```


    The terms "relevant minimum amount", "relevant
maximum amount" and "appropriate fraction" are defined in
paragraph 9 and it is a simple matter to derive further
rules from these definitions. Thus, it has been possible to
construct four rules which define maximum relevant income.
    However, the rules cannot simply be added to the
knowledge base. Consider the case of a trading company
whose estate income is less than the appropriate fraction of
the relevant minimum amount. In such a case, the conditions
attached to each of the rules is satisfied. Thus there are
four conflicting rules as to what constitutes the company's
maximum relevant income.
    Reading paragraph 9, it is possible to identify
the fourth rule as being the correct rule to apply to the
case postulated above. The general rule is by implication
subject to the other three and, in the same way, the second
rule is subject to the third (and fourth), and the third
rule is subject to the fourth.
    ADVISER chooses amongst conflicting rules within
the knowledge base by selecting the rule which appears
first. Therefore, in order to make rule (a) subject to rule
(b), rule (b) must appear before rule (a) in the knowledge

base. The final version of the rules is represented
therefore in the structure shown below.

```
    RULE  calculate_maximum_relevant_income :
          "see para 9 Schedule 16 FA 1972"

maximum_relevant_income IS distributable_investment_income
PROVIDED trading_company AND (estate_income < (appropriate_fraction
                                     * relevant_minimum_amount))

ALSO maximum_relevant_income IS distributable_investment_income
                    + (50/100 * (estate_income - abatement))
PROVIDED trading_company AND (estate_income < appropriate_fraction
                                     * relevant_maximum_amount))

ALSO abatement is 1/2 * ((appropriate_fraction * relevant_maximum_
                    amount) - estate_income)

ALSO maximum_relevant_income IS distributable_investment_income
                    + 50/100 * estate_income)
PROVIDED trading_company OR member_of_trading_group

ALSO maximum_relevant_income IS distributable_investment_income
                    + (50/1000 * estate_or_trading_income)
```

5. Results

An example of a consultation can be found in
(Roycroft 1984).
During a consultation period a concise style of
questioning is adopted, using terminology familiar to the
inspector so as to allow the consultation to be conducted
quickly and easily. The time taken for each consultation
depends on how much explanation the inspector requires the
system to give of its reasoning. The one extreme is where
the inspector accepts the advice unconditionally, whereas
the other extreme is where a detailed explanation may be
required. In any event, each case can be dealt with in a
few minutes. This compares very favourably with half a day
taken by an inspector to carry out the examination of a
company's accounts manually, and with fifteen or twenty
minutes which may take a senior tax inspector who
specialises in apportionment.

6. Conclusions

ACCI relieves the tax inspector of the need to
refer constantly to a manual and is able to provide accurate
advice concerning the apportionment of close companies'
income quickly and easily. ACCI therefore demonstrates the
effective use of expert systems technology in solving the
very real problems which can occur wherever there is a
shortage of human experts.
One of the characteristics of early expert systems
such as MYCIN (Shortliffe, 1976) and PROSPECTOR (Duda et al,
1979) is their ability to use vague or uncertain

information. In contrast, ACCI requires the tax inspector to
give exact information, and there is a corresponding
precision in the advice given.

This difference between ACCI and systems such as
MYCIN reflects the difference noted by (McCarty, 1984)
between legal reasoning and the type of reasoning used in
medical diagnosis. In view of the precision required by
ACCI, it is arguable that the system ought to have been
implemented by using traditional programming techniques. The
authors do not doubt that ACCI could have been implemented
in this way. However, this would have had certain
disadvantages.

Use of a traditional programming language would
obscure the representation of the legal rules. The rules
would be embedded in the program code and as a result it
would be difficult to check for correctness. Equally
important is the fact that it would be very difficult to
change the rules when, as is inevitable, the law changes.
The legal rules used in ACCI on the other hand are
represented explicitly and declaratively, very much the same
as they appear in the legislation . It is possible to
identify and check each rule for correctness and it is a
simple matter to modify any rule in the knowledge base.

In its present version, ACCI is designed to deal
with the cases that an inspector considers for detailed
examination. Inspectors currently disregard a large number
of cases by simple examination of some key characteristics
on the companies' return accounts. A possible extension of
ACCI would be to consider including the rules of thumb used
by the inspector to eliminate these cases, thus emulating
the inspector's work in its every aspect.

Acknowledgments
        Work on ACCI could not have been carried out
without the assistance of Knowledge Engineering Business
Centre of ICL and of Mr. John Morris and Mr. Mike
Templeman of the Inland Revenue Technical Division. Their
help is gratefully acknowledged.

References
Bellord, N.J. (1980) 'Tax Planning by Computer', In
Computer Science and Law, ed. B. Niblett. Cambridge
University Press.

Duda, R. et al. (1979) 'Model Design in the PROSPECTOR
Consultant System for Mineral Exploration', In Expert
Systems in the Micro-Electronic Age, ed. D. Michie,
Edinburgh University Press.

Foundos, S. (1971) 'Cybernetics and Tax Law',
Association of Certified Accountants.

Hellawell, R. (1980) 'A Computer Program for Legal planning
and Analysis: Taxation of Stock Redemptions', Columbia Law
Review.

Lane, V.P. & Loucopoulos P. (1983) 'Knowledge based
Systems as a mechanism for Optimization of Conceptual Design
in Civil Engineering projects' In Proc.   IFIP WG 5.2 Working
Conference, Optimization in CAD, Lyon 24-26 Oct. 1983.

McCarty, T.L (1984) 'Intelligent Legal Information Systems:
Problems and Prospects' In Data processing and the Law, ed.
C. Campell, Sweet & Maxwell.

Pinson, B. (1982) 'Pinson on Revenue Law', Sweet & Maxwell.

Roycroft A.E. (1984) 'The Development of an Expert System
for the Apportionment of Close Companies' Income', M.Sc.
Dissertation, Department of Computation, UMIST.

Shortliffe, E.H.   (1976) 'Computer Medical Consultations:
MYCIN', Elsevier.

EXPERT SYSTEMS AND VIDEOTEX: AN APPLICATION IN THE
MARKETING OF AGROCHEMICALS
M J Jones and D T Crates
ICI PLC Plant Protection Division, Farnham, Surrey

ABSTRACT

The Development of a Computer based Agricultural Advisory system
is described bringing together the technologies of Expert Systems
and Videotex. The factors leading to the choice of these media
are discussed in the context of the role of the system as a
marketing aid.

1   INTRODUCTION

The use of agrochemicals plays an increasingly more important
part in ensuring the world's food supplies. ICI Plant Protection
Division is a major supplier both in the UK and in almost every
other country in the world. Information is a vital ingredient
in any business and never more so than with agrochemicals both
for effective management and to ensure correct and effective
usage of the products. Information technology is increasingly
being used and this paper sets out details of just one
development concerned with helping farmers make better management
decisions on correct agrochemical use.

2   BACKGROUND

ICI Plant Protection Division set up a videotex operation in
October 1982 initially to provide a better form of communication
with it's sales force of 80+ working from home in the rural areas
of the UK. The videotex software is IVS-3 from Aregon and
currently the host machine is a DEC PDP 11/44 sited at Fernhurst
in Sussex. The system has since been considerably expanded to
also include a number of interactive program modules providing
business management information to 40 of ICI's top distributors
at many of their branches. Some of the modules have involved
interactions between the PDP 11 and a Burroughs 7900 which
supports the main commercial systems for the Division.

3   THE PROBLEM

Correct and rational decision-making on agrochemical usage is
fundamental to the continuing success of the farmer and
agrochemical industry. For the farmer it is essential that money
invested in agrochemicals is cost effective and a continuing
viable agrochemical market depends upon this. Rational chemical
usage also minimises possible adverse environmental effects and
helps create a public atmosphere more conducive to efficient use
of all available resources for maintenance and improvement of
profitable crop yields.

The main problem is having the right information available at the
right time in order to make the right decisions. The weather in
the UK ensures that no 2 seasons are ever the same. The complex
geology means that every field has to be treated differently.
Advances in plant breeding mean that crop varieties constantly
change. New products are continuously being evolved in the
battle against weeds, pests and diseases and the timing of
application of these products for maximum effect can be critical.
All these factors and many more need to be taken into account
constantly throughout the growing season and action taken where
appropriate. A vast amount of valuable information is
continually being produced and is being used as effectively as
possible by farmers and advisors. As this information filters
down, so the number of crops, the number of times at which
decisions are being made and advice sought is increasing. Yet
sheer economics means that the number of people with sufficient
expertise to be able to sift and utilise the information at the
same rate does not exist. At peak periods at least, the ratio
of advice seekers to advice givers is out of balance and the
quality of many of the decisions could be questioned.

Computers have for some time been used as an aid in this area
but have been hampered by their lack of ability to provide
reasoning to back up the advice and recommendations given,
normally done by the scarce and expensive human expert. In
addition the cost involved of a true multi-user system would have
been enormous and also the presentation of data unacceptable to
the non-computer specialist. A cheap and simple-to-use system
was therefore required, which was available over a long period
and gave results which were not only readily understandable but
could be questioned and backed up with reasoning. The system
needed to be flexible and capable of rapid incorporation of new
information.

4   A SOLUTION

At least partial answers to these problems have been provided by
recent software developments and have been utilised by ICI Plant
Protection Division to devise a crop management program,
initially concentrating on wheat disease control. The program
is registered as Counsellor and is an Expert System running on
videotex. The big break through with Counsellor is the
interfacing of videotex to an Expert System which is at the
leading edge of software development. Expert Systems add a new
dimension to the way a program is set up and in its presentation
to the user. Videotex's use of colour and very simple commands
makes it a truly 'user-friendly' system.

5   WHY VIDEOTEX

ICI Plant Protection's use of videotex with its own staff had
demonstrated its flexibility and ease of use even by the layman.
Videotex is now becoming widely used both in the UK and the rest
of the world. It is best known in the UK as Prestel, the public
system, but over 200 private systems are also in use, primarily
in the holiday and motor trade. ICI Plant Protection Division
has a private system, code-named Grapevine, which is regularly
accessed by its field staff in the UK and a number of
distributors. The great virtue of Videotex is that it has the
potential of bringing the power of the main frame computer into
every home at relatively low cost. Using the ordinary telephone
and, at the lowest level an adapted television set, access can
be made to a videotex system. While most videotex systems allow
you to look at static pages of text, connection can be made to
interactive programs. Our experience of running interactive
programs through videotex bringing the power of the mainframe to
the end user led us to believe that interfacing with an Expert
System was the next logical step. All of these factors together
with the widely acknowledged 'user-friendly' features of videotex
led to the use of videotex for Counsellor.

6   WHY EXPERT SYSTEMS

There are many types of Expert Systems e.g. Prolog, Lisp, Frames,
and Plausible inference etc. and we had to find the one best
suited to our needs. Availability of certain types of software
i.e. frames, blackboards, narrowed the choice initially. To meet
our requirements we had to find software that was able to
accumulate evidence, (as a human expert would), interface with
videotex, be flexible in its display to the user, be able to
perform certain basic arithmetic, retrieve information from a
central database, and of course be commercially available. This
pointed to the Plausible inference type of Expert System. The
particular software that was adopted has now been released as
SAVOIR (ISI 1984). At the time Counsellor was being developed
Savoir was also under development and by working very closely
with ISI the interface between videotex and Savoir was evolved.
The ability of Savoir to perform external functions provided a
possible link with a database.

The features offered by this type of Expert System gives
rise to a number of advantages over conventional computer systems
which were found particularly relevant in the construction of
Counsellor. In general the Savoir type of Expert System offers:

    a. Ease of expressing knowledge. The language used
for expressing knowledge, although still a computer language, is
more comprehensible to the non-computer person. This means that
an Expert System can be built more quickly than a conventional
program to do the same job, and that subsequent modification is
easier. This is particularly important in areas like fungal
disease, where the knowledge is continually changing due to
scientific innovation or practical changes in the field e.g.
introduction of new crop varieties or a change in their
resistance to disease.

    b. Flexibility of expression. While conventional
scientific programs often work at a level of great detail, Expert
Systems offer the flexibility of working at several levels, from
the deep science of fungi to the rules-of-thumb that rarely get
written down in textbooks but which farmers never-the-less use
on a day-to-day basis.

    c. Explanation of reasoning. While conventional programs
give an answer, Expert Systems can additionally explain how they
arrived at that answer or why they are asking a particular
question. This is particularly useful where unexpected advice
is given and the response may be "no computer is going to tell
me what to do". In addition, such explanations can have an
educational side effect.

    d. Human-like reasoning. In real life we often reason thus
"because this field has heavy soil the crop is likely to suffer
from damp conditions and so eyespot is more likely", which is a
long way from the precise calculations performed by conventional
computers. Expert Systems, because they operate with items and
relationships, and can handle uncertainty, can perform reasoning
very similar to this.

In short, it offers a more human-like type of computing. They
are thus more able to tackle some areas of real life where more
judgement is required than conventional programs.

7   THE KNOWLEDGE BASE DESIGN

As previously stated Counsellor is based on Expert System
software known as 'Savoir' (ISI 1984) which works by using an
'Evidence Net' consisting of boxes and arrows. Figure 1 shows
part of the net which is used to predict the risk of powdery
mildew.

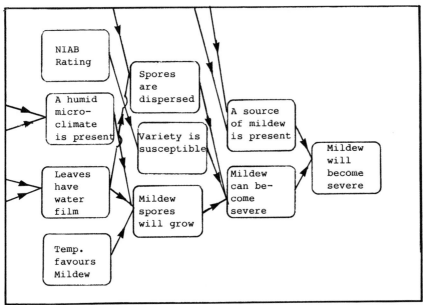

Figure 1. Part of 'COUNSELLOR' Evidence Net for Wheat Powdery
          Mildew

The evidence nets for other diseases are similar but incorporate
different factors. The boxes represent meaningful concepts which
must be clearly defined and understood. Each box represents the
risk of something occurring, e.g. "mildew will become severe"
which is dependant on the other boxes within the evidence net.
The arrows indicate the causual links. For instance "spores are
dispersed" is one of the evidence factors for "mildew can become
severe". That is, if spore dispersal is likely, we can increase
our belief that "mildew can become severe" which in turn
increases our belief that "mildew will become severe".

Counsellor investigates each disease in turn by tracing the paths from right to left until it finds a box without any arrows feeding into it. Such a box is derived, not from other evidence, but by putting a question to the farmer. This ensures that only relevant questions are asked. The answers thus received are propagated through all the appropriate causual links. The result is that after all the relevant questions have been answered the right-most boxes attain a degree of belief in the facts they represent being true, i.e. that disease will be severe. Propagation of evidence is carried out in accordance with Bayesian updating mechanisms. (Duda et al 1979)

Whilst Figure 1 is part of an evidence net for predicting the risk of disease, Counsellor also has evidence nets which are used for optimising treatment recommendations.

The evidence for each box is weighted according to its importance and each starts with an initial degree of belief. Both the weights and initial degrees of belief are based on probabilities calculated from research work and expert judgement. Sources used so far include MAFF Surveys of Foliar and Stem Base Diseases, NIAB Guides to Cereal Varieties, Gair et al (1983), Cook (1982) and ICI experience from development work.

The risk of each disease is firstly determined independently of the other diseases. They are then combined to estimate a resultant yield loss.

As the knowledge in this type of Expert System is held as meaningful boxes, it is also easy to provide the farmer with information to support the main recommendations by displaying some of the boxes in the middle of the net. It is the ability to give supporting information that is so important in aiding decision-making, particularly where judgement or prediction is involved. The art of constructing Expert Systems is still in its infancy. During the construction of Counsellor a number of issues were encountered which are discussed by Attarwala and Basden (1984). A major issue was the level of detail to which the evidence nets should be taken. At one extreme we could go down to the minutest biological mechanisms of fungi but this level of detail is unnecessary for most farmers. At the other extreme there is no detail at all but this does not allow the generation of supporting information. The most appropriate level of detail was considered to be one level deeper than that with which most farmers are fully familiar. Expert System software like Savoir allows us to choose our level of detail.

8   WHAT WHEAT COUNSELLOR DOES

Counsellor can operate in two modes. Firstly, it can help to
plan the fungicide programme for the season ahead based on
knowledge of the farm/field situation and past history.
Secondly, immediate in-season problems can be identified and
recommendations offered for the rest of the season. This may
seem fairly conventional but much more in-depth information is
available to explain the reasoning behind the recommendations.
A typical consultation could take the following form:

1. Identification of user, farm and field.
2. Retrieve available information from a database, e.g.
   field history, wheat variety susceptibility.
3. Ask the farmer relevant questions concerning information
   not already in the database, e.g. seed rate, fertiliser
   usage.
4. Evaluate the risks from the diseases. Justify the
   evaluation if required by displaying some of the more
   in-depth information and reasoning (Fig. 2).
5. Make treatment recommendations (including no treatment
   if this is appropriate).
6. Display cost/benefit analysis for treatment
   recommendations.
7. If required display cost benefit analysis of alternative
   treatments.

```
              ICI PPD WHEAT COUNSELLOR
        Phase 3: Report Disease Assessment
        Farm 1: Field 2: Variety 2: Aut. Plan

          The Risk factors and variety
        susceptibility (based on NIAB) are on
        the scale (0 to 1)

        Risk of Mildew becoming severe
            and causing Yield loss........ 0.88
        Due to:-
        .Risk of Source................. 0.65
        .Risk of Spore dispersal........ 1.0
        .Risk of Suitable conditions.... 0.86
        .Variety Susceptibility......... 0.30

     Key # to continue

        COMMAND  <              >
```

Figure 2. COUNSELLOR Example Display of Mildew Risk Assessment

The whole consultation is carried out in the form of a dialogue
close to the situation in real life with both the computer and
user asking and answering questions and challenging statements
made. Counsellor is able to recall previous consultations and,
therefore, will only ask for information that may have changed
e.g. observed level of disease in the crop, crop growth stage.

9   PROGRESS TO DATE

The decision to mount a full scale project to develop a wheat
management aid was taken in July 1983, work in earnest started
in September 1983. The first public viewing in videotex form
took place in February 1984 in front of a group of influential
agrochemical distributors. Its advantages were immediately
obvious to those present.
Further development and viewings to a considerable number of
people occurred in the following months. It was formally
launched at the Royal Agricultural Society Show in July 1984.
Over four days it was demonstrated live to farmers, consultants,
government officials and members of the agricultural trade with
great success.

10   WHERE NEXT

The first program on cereal disease control is being made
available to farmers through ICI's agrochemical distributors in
the UK in the Autumn of 1984. It will be available at "clinics"
on distributors premises and possibly eventually on the farm desk
through portable videotex terminals or modified microcomputers.

The system now running on a DEC VAX will be further developed to
deal with further crop/pest problems. A possible development at
this stage is the interfacing of Counsellor with videodisc so
that in addition to textural questions being displayed actual
photographs or film can be shown to help elaborate certain points
where required.

11 CONCLUSION

Videotex has brought the power of the computer within the reach
of millions of people. It can be used to add value to products
and as such becomes a marketing tool. Conventional videotex is
limited in what it can do but linked up to more powerful programs
the scope is considerably widened. With the type of Expert
System used in Counsellor a dialogue is encouraged between user
and computer. This is likely to lead to a much wider acceptance
of the computer on the farm as an advisory tool rather than
purely for use with farm accounts etc. In the agrochemical
industry the link between Expert Systems and Videotex is being
used as a marketing aid in an ever more complex business area.
Developments of the type outlined in this paper could lead to a
much wider acceptance of computers in this role.

REFERENCES

Duda, R.O.; Hart, P.E.; Konolige, K.; Reboth, R. (1979) A
Computer-based consultant for mineral exploration. Project Report
6415 S.R.I. International, Menlo Park, California.
ISI Ltd (1984) Savoir. ISI Ltd, Redhill, Surrey.
Attawala, F.T.; Basden, A. (1984) An emerging methodology for
constructing Expert Systems. R & D Management (In Press).

ARTIFACT: A REAL-TIME SHELL FOR
INTELLIGENT FEEDBACK CONTROL

J.C. Francis and R.R. Leitch
Department of Electrical and Electronic Engineering,
Heriot-Watt University, Edinburgh.

Abstract

        A PROLOG shell suitable for real-time feedback control
applications is described. The shell utilises domain specific
knowledge consisting of a set of conditional goal/subgoal pairs.
These are used to represent subsystem relationships within a complex system and taken together form a relational model.
        Uncertain inference is used to deduce applicable rela-
tions consisting of goal/subgoal pairs with associated truth
values. These are combined by a planning routine to deduce paths
involving changes in the control inputs of the system that satisfy
a prescribed control objective.
        The method described is illustrated by considering an
example from process control involving fluid level control in two
coupled tanks. An extension to n-coupled tanks is used to illustrate the considerable reduction in the number of heuristics
achieved with the use of a relational model.

1. Introduction

        With the current resurgence of interest in the methods
of Artificial Intelligence no area appears to be safe. Here is
yet another area - but one with an enormous economic potential for
manufacturing industry in general, and the process industry in
particular. First some fundamental and challenging problems will
have to be solved.
        The conventional analytic methods of control neces-
sarily assume a description of a process in terms of differential
or difference equations. For complex systems such as those found
in the process industries, the essential modelling assumptions are
seldom valid under the normal range of operating conditions. In
practice this leads to a deterioration in control and can lead to
unsatisfactory performance or possibly to dangerous conditions.
Furthermore, the human understanding of a system and its mathematical description are often alien, resulting in a lack of
comprehension and loss of confidence in the control decisions.
This lack of communication between man and machine can also
prevent effective control adjustments being made in the light of
operational experience. Knowledge based control offers considerable advantages when contrasted with analytic methods.

The ARTIFACT shell was developed as a research tool
for real-time knowledge based process control. It uses domain
dependent knowledge to model [1] the process under control and a
continuous inference mechanism to deduce an appropriate control
action such that a prescribed objective is satisfied. The PROLOG
language has been used to implement a large part of the shell,
with the real-time aspects being handled by the language C. The
case for using a logic formalism in expert systems has been argued
by Kowalski [2]. A diagram of the shell showing the principle
components and relationships is given in figure 1.

2. Data acquisition

The data from a suitable dynamic system is acquired at
successive intervals using an iterative "C" based process running
concurrently with PROLOG. This second process takes care of the
real-time aspects of the shell, as well as overcoming stack space
problems associated with indefinite recursion and continual iteration through backtracking.

Data acquisition takes place synchronously with the
time between samples being determined by a clock pulse. The clock
rate is constrained both by the Nyquist sampling criterion and by
the decision time of the shell. The data items are typically
numerical quantities obtained from sensors and transducers,
although more generally they can be any PROLOG structure
representing qualitative attributes of the system. At each sample
period a list of current data items is written to a pipe communicating with PROLOG. The nth list, augmented by the current values
assigned to the control inputs of the system, forms a data tuple
denoted by d_n. The set consisting of all possible data tuples
will be denoted by D.

3. State representation

A list of the most recent data tuples forms a
representation of the state of the system. After each sample
period the old state is retracted from the PROLOG data base and
the new data appended. The state length, h, is given by a domain
specific heuristic referred to as the time history number. The
state at the nth sample, denoted by s_n, is thus defined to be

$$s_n = (d_n, \ldots, d_{(n-h+1)}).$$

The set of all possible states, S, is therefore given by $S = D^h$.

If the system can be modelled by differential or
difference equations, then a comparison can be made with analytic
theory. In such a case s_n is analogous to the observation matrix

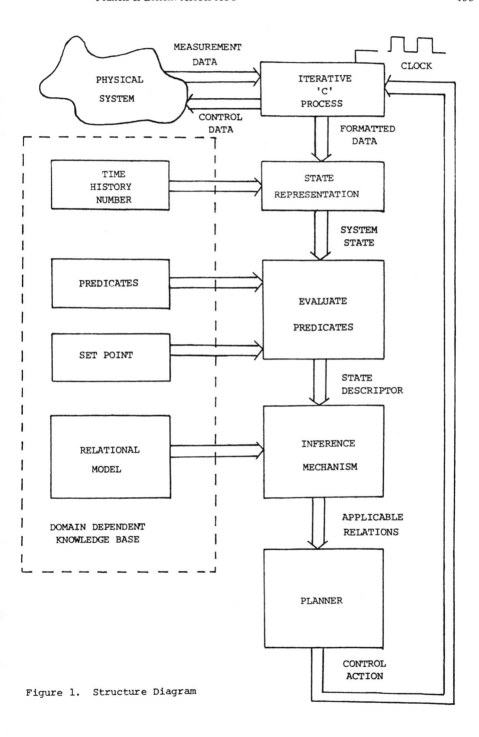

Figure 1. Structure Diagram

and forms a non-canonical representation of the system state. In
analytic theory the term "set-point" is used to denote the desired
steady state value of a dynamic system. This notion can be linked
to that of a state error, where a metric defines the distance of a
state from the desired state. An analytic controller attempts to
minimise a function of this error by assigning appropriate values
to the control inputs of the system. The shell allows the user to
specify a set-point denoting a subset of the state set S containing the desired steady state.

4. State attributes

After each sample period predicates operate on the new
state and the current set-point. The list of predicate images
(truth values) forms the state descriptor. Each predicate
corresponds to a state attribute and the truth value returned by a
(multivalued) predicate can be variously interpreted as the extent
to which some attribute is present in the state; or the probability of the attribute being present given noisy data etc..

The shell determines the state descriptor by evaluating all domain specific predicates once, the computation time is
therefore linearly related to the number of predicates provided.
In practice, because many predicates are mutually exclusive, a
large proportion will evaluate to false. To aid computational
efficiency the shell makes a closed world assumption so that a
predicate failure is taken to imply falsity and this information
is omited from the descriptor.

All domain specific predicates used by the shell are
of the form predicate(Attribute,State,Set_point,Truth_value),
where Attribute is instantiated to a PROLOG structure denoting a
state attribute, State denotes the current system state, Set_point
denotes a subset of S and Truth_value is returned by the predicate
definition. Normally the predicates are evaluated using an indexing routine that operates on the state and set-point to produce a
key which is used to access the truth value from an appropriate
list of ordered pairs. If, however, Attribute is instantiated to
one of the forms

1)   at_time_minus(n,X),
2)   since_time_minus(n,X),

where n is a natural number and X is a PROLOG structure denoting a
state attribute, then shell procedures modify the state to give a
Substate and make calls of the form

                predicate(X,Substate,Set_point,Truth_value).

In case 2, the conjunction of each recursive call is taken to
determine the overall truth value.

5. Knowledge representation

5.1. Condition/action rules

The term condition/action rule will be used to denote
a rule of the form

Condition => Control_action,

where the condition is some conjunction of state attributes and
the control action is a modification to the control inputs of the
system. This type of rule has been used by Mamdani in work on
fuzzy logic controllers [3].

In analytic theory each modification to the control
inputs is intended to drive the system towards the set-point (i.e.
to minimise an error metric). In knowledge based control an error
metric is not necessarily defined and the notion of moving towards
the set-point is replaced by that of achieving a subgoal leading
to a desired state. Thus, a rule of the above type could be
reformulated in teleological terms as

Condition => (Control_action,correct)

where the ordered pair (Control_action,correct) denotes that the
control action is a subgoal leading eventually to the goal of a
state having the attribute 'correct'.

5.2. Relational models

The teleological form above can be generalised to

Condition => (Subgoal,Goal),

where Subgoal and Goal are arbitrary state attributes. The
interpretation of this is that if the specified condition occurs
at time t and the goal is to be true of the system at time $t + t2$,
then the subgoal should occur at time $t + t1$, where $0 < t1 < t2$.
This formalism can be used to describe relations holding between
the subsystems of complex systems. These can be combined to
deduce a control action. A collection of subsystem relations
allowing all condition/action rules to be deduced forms a relational model. Some of the main advantages of such models are:-

1) The number of heuristics is linearly proportional to the
   number of subsystems, whereas the number of condition/action
   rules rises exponentially as the number of subsystems is
   increased.

2) Heuristics describing subsystem relations are generally much
more obvious than condition/action rules.

3) The explanation of control decisions can be in terms of the
structure of the system.

4) Analogy between subsystems can generate heuristics [4].

5.3. Knowledge representation within the shell

The formalism described above is supported by the
shell. All heuristics are ordered pairs of the form
(Antecedent,Consequent), where Antecedent is instantiated to a
list of state attributes and Consequent denotes an ordered pair of
the form (Subgoal,Goal). The terms Subgoal and Goal are both
state attributes.

The shell determines the truth value of each element
of the antecedent by finding the associated truth value within the
state descriptor. The conjunction of the truth value of each element is taken to give an overall value, v. Any required definition of conjunction (e.g. possibilistic, probabilistic, definition
in terms of a lattice etc.) can be included.

The ordered pair (Consequent,v) will be referred to as
an applicable relation. The shell generates all applicable relations and asserts them in the PROLOG data base. The computation
time for this operation is proportional to the number of heuristics.

The applicable relations are combined by a planning
routine, which attempts to find all paths from the goal of being
in a state specified by the set-point, to subgoals involving
modification of the control inputs. The truth value of each applicable relation is taken into account to arrive at the overall
truth of a path. The planner must to be sophisticated enough to
resolve any conflicts between goals, and if multiple paths are
present a unique modification to a control input must be deduced.
The planner should preferentially choose paths containing subgoals
that are attributes of the steady states. This ensures that
steady state conditions are achieved.

At the present time there would not appear to be one
planning algorithm suitable for all system structures, and the
planning routine is currently domain dependent. It does appear,
however, that a given routine will be suitable for all systems
having the same feedback and feed-forward structure. It is to be
hoped that eventually a suitable planner may be generated using an
inductive definition, from a specification of the system structure
in terms of feedback and feed-forward connections.

6. Examples from process control

6.1. Two coupled tanks

The following example illustrates some of the ideas
discussed above. Two tanks containing fluid are coupled as shown
in figure 2. A pump supplies fluid to the left hand tank (tank1)
at a rate determined by a control voltage (the control input). The
pressure caused by the head of fluid in tank1 causes liquid to
flow into the right hand tank (tank2). When the level in tank2
rises, a proportion of the fluid escapes through a drain. The control problem is to bring the level in tank2 up to a value specified by the set-point, with the minimum of overshoot, and to keep
the level constant at this value (the steady state condition).

At each sample period a data tuple is formed by augmenting sensor measurements with the pump control voltage. A list
of the most recent data tuples represents the state of the coupled
tanks. The following state attributes are defined:-

1)   pump_control(increasing),

2)   pump_control(steady),

3)   pump_control(decreasing),

4)   tank1(increasing),

5)   tank1(steady),

6)   tank1(decreasing),

7)   tank2(increasing),

8)   tank2(steady),

9)   tank2(decreasing),

10)   tank2(too_high),

11)   tank2(correct),

12)   tank2(too_low).

Attributes 1-3 refer to the control input of the system and
reflect entries in the state that are set by the controller.
Attributes 4-12 have corresponding predicate definitions. In this
example all the predicates are two-valued and return the atom
'true' if the call succeeds. The predicates 7-12 have obvious
definitions in terms of the level of tank2 and the set-point.
Predicates 4-6 can be defined directly in terms of the fluid level
in tank1 or alternatively they can be inferred from tank2

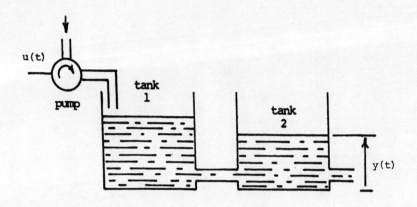

Figure 2.   Two Coupled Tanks

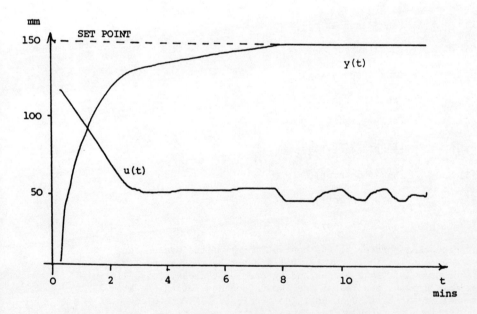

Figure 3.   Response of Feedback Control System

measurements using the following definitions:-

tank1(increasing)   if $y_n - y_{(n-1)} > y_{(n-1)} - y_{(n-2)}$,

tank1(steady)   if $y_n - y_{(n-1)} = y_{(n-1)} - y_{(n-2)}$,

tank1(decreasing)   if $y_n - y_{(n-1)} < y_{(n-1)} - y_{(n-2)}$.

Table 1 gives a list of 21 subsystem relations that form a relational model of the coupled tanks described above. Each relation is of the form

[[Antecedent],[Subgoal,Goal]].

It will be noticed that in this particular example the antecedent of each relation consists of only one attribute. In general, however, any number of attributes can be given.

Since some of the state attributes are mutually exclusive there are only 27 possible descriptors. The 21 heuristics allow a control action to be deduced for each of these. To find the action associated with a given descriptor the shell first determines all the applicable relations, which are then combined to give a control action. For example, if the state descriptor indicates that the following attributes are true of the current state:-

a)   tank1(increasing),

b)   tank2(steady),

c)   tank2(correct),

then the applicable relations are:-

1)   [tank2(steady),tank2(correct)],

2)   [tank1(increasing),tank2(increasing)],

3)   [tank1(steady),tank2(steady)],

4)   [tank1(decreasing),tank2(decreasing)],

5)   [pump_control(steady),tank1(increasing)],

6)   [pump_control(decreasing),tank1(steady)],

7)   [pump_control(decreasing),tank1(decreasing)].

It is readily seen that relations 1, 3 and 6 give a path from the subgoal of pump_control(decreasing), to the goal of tank2(correct). The shell therefore decreases the pump control

```
[[[tank2(too_high)]],[tank2(decreasing),tank2(correct)]],
[[tank2(correct)]],[tank2(steady),tank2(correct)]],
[[tank2(too_low)]],[tank2(increasing),tank2(correct)]],

[[tank2(increasing)]],[tank1(steady),tank2(increasing)]],
[[tank2(steady)]],[tank1(increasing),tank2(increasing)]],
[[tank2(decreasing)]],[tank1(increasing),tank2(increasing)]],

[[tank2(increasing)]],[tank1(decreasing),tank2(steady)]],
[[tank2(steady)]],[tank1(steady),tank2(steady)]],
[[tank2(decreasing)]],[tank1(increasing),tank2(steady)]],

[[tank2(increasing)]],[tank1(decreasing),tank2(decreasing)]],
[[tank2(steady)]],[tank1(decreasing),tank2(decreasing)]],
[[tank2(decreasing)]],[tank1(steady),tank2(decreasing)]],

[[tank1(increasing)]],[pump_control(steady),tank1(increasing)]],
[[tank1(steady)]],[pump_control(increasing),tank1(increasing)]],
[[tank1(decreasing)]],[pump_control(increasing),tank1(increasing)]],

[[tank1(increasing)]],[pump_control(decreasing),tank1(steady)]],
[[tank1(steady)]],[pump_control(steady),tank1(steady)]],
[[tank1(decreasing)]],[pump_control(increasing),tank1(steady)]],

[[tank1(increasing)]],[pump_control(decreasing),tank1(decreasing)]],
[[tank1(steady)]],[pump_control(decreasing),tank1(decreasing)]],
[[tank1(decreasing)]],[pump_control(steady),tank1(decreasing)]]]
```

Table 1 - Relational model of coupled tanks.

voltage before it's next sample period, which gives the new state
the required attribute.

The above rules have been successfully used to control
a laboratory scale coupled tank apparatus. A performance graph
obtained using the relational model is shown in figure 3.

6.2. An extension to n-coupled tanks

If the above system is extended to n-coupled tanks,
where the pth tank has three associated state attributes:-

tankp(increasing),

tankp(steady),

tankp(decreasing),

then the reduction in the number of heuristics achieved using a
relational model is evident. After allowing for mutual exclusion
of attributes, the number of descriptors is

$$3(n+1).$$

Since each descriptor has an associated control action, this is
also the number of condition/action rules needed to control the
system. However, if a relational model is used, then the number
of heuristics required to allow all possible condition/action
rules to be deduced is $3 + 9n$. By way of example, if a system
consisting of 20 coupled tanks is controlled in the above manner,
then 3^{21} heuristics representing condition/action rules are
required and the control scheme is clearly impracticable. If a
relational model is used, then only 183 heuristics are needed.
Furthermore, since any two adjacent tanks have analogous relations, heuristics can be written down directly.

7. Conclusion

The results obtained by applying ARTIFACT to the above
example are very encouraging. The performance achieved compares
well with that of a conventional analytic controller and should be
much superior for more complex systems.

The use of a relational model can significantly reduce
the number of heuristics required to describe a process. Furthermore, relations between subsystems are relatively easy to obtain
and do not depend on the system complexity. The applicability of
the method to more complex systems is currently under investigation.

Acknowledgement

        J.C. Francis was supported by a SERC research student-
ship during the work described above.

References

[1]   Francis, J.C., Leitch, R.R., Intelligent Knowledge
          Based Process Control. Proc. IEE International
          Conference Control 85. To appear.

[2]   Kowalski, R., Logic for Expert Systems. Proc. 3rd BCS
          Expert Systems Conference (1983).

[3]   Mamdani, E.H., Sembi, B.S., Process Control using
          Fuzzy Logic. In Fuzzy Sets: Theory and Application to
          Policy Analysis and Information Systems, Wang/Chang,
          Plenum Press, New York (1980).

[4]   Munyer, J.C., Towards the use of Analogy in Deductive
          tasks. Board of Studies in Information Sciences,
          University of California, Santa Cruz.

WHY WE NEED MANY KNOWLEDGE REPRESENTATION FORMALISMS

Aaron Sloman
Cognitive Studies Programme
University of Sussex, Brighton, England

Abstract

Against advocates of particular formalisms for representing all
kinds of knowledge, this paper argues that different formalisms are
useful for different purposes. Different formalisms imply different
inference methods. The history of human science and culture illustrates the point that very often progress in some field depends on
the creation of a specific new formalism, with the right epistemological and heuristic power. The same has to be said about formalisms for use in artificial intelligent systems. We need criteria for
evaluating formalisms in the light of the uses to which they are to
be put. The same subject matter may be best represented using different formalisms for different purposes, e.g. simulation vs explanation. If different notations and inference methods are good for
different purposes, this has implications for the design of expert
systems.

1. Introduction

It is sometimes a good strategy to adopt an extreme position
and explore the ramifications, for instance choosing a particular
language, or method, and acting as if it is best for everything.
This can have two consequences. First, by striving to use only one
approach one is forced to investigate ways in which that approach
can be extended and applied to new problems. Secondly if the
approach does have limitations we will be in a better position to
know exactly what those limitations are and why they exist.

For example, it is a good thing that some people should
think, rightly or wrongly, that the methods of AI can be used to
simulate and explain every aspect of human mentality, and try to
establish this by doing it. If they are wrong, their efforts will
give us new insights into both why they are wrong, and what the AI
methods can achieve.

Similarly, it is good that some people pin all their hopes
on first order predicate logic (FOPL) as the language to be used for
all purposes, as recommended by Bob Kowalski, in characteristically
forceful style:

> "There is only one language for representing information --
> whether declarative or procedural -- and that is first-order
> predicate logic. There is only one intelligent way to pro-
> cess information -- and that is by applying deductive infer-
> ence methods.
>
> (Kowalski 1980)

Many people have been inspired by this idea, and as a result excellent work has been done, and will be done, exploring the power of logic-based programming languages. It is, perhaps, sad that without the motivation provided by a mistaken ideal, such work might not be done.

Anyway, my present purpose is neither to praise nor to bury logic but to understand its limitations and assess some alternatives. Predicate logic needs no praise from me, for it is clear that there is no other formalism which is simultaneously so well understood, so widely applicable, and so clear in its semantics. It must therefore play an important role in theorising about intelligent systems, and perhaps also in modelling them.

Nevertheless, logic is not all-embracing. It may be best for the largest range of uses, without being best for everything. FOPL is an example of an 'applicative' formalism (defined below). I have previously argued (Sloman 1971, 1978) that for some purposes analogical representations may be better than applicative formalisms, including logic. Bobrow (1975) suggests, more generally, that there are several dimensions along which the utility of representations may be compared. Logic does not always win. Goodman (1969) has also compared different schemes of representation. (He makes more distinctions than I shall discuss here.)

It is evident that many different representational systems are used by ordinary people, by scientists and by engineers, including maps, models, diagrams, flow-charts, etc. And there is plenty of evidence that logical thinking is not always what people use most naturally or effectively (Johnson-Laird, 1983), though that in itself does not prove that logical thinking should not be used for all tasks.

2. Terminology

In this general survey of issues, I shall not be very precise in my terminology, switching between expressions like 'symbolism', 'language', 'notation', 'representational system' and the like. In all cases I am talking about a set of possible structures which can be used in a systematic way for one or more of the following: storing information, communicating information, comparing information, formulating questions or problems, making inferences, formulating plans, controlling actions, etc. It does not matter whether the structures are within the mind, brain, or computer, or external structures, e.g. marks on paper. Neither does it matter whether they are concrete physical structures or abstract "virtual" structures (explained below).

I shall say very little about notations used for communication between intelligent systems as I regard the "internal" functions as more basic (for reasons given in (Sloman 1979)). A more complete discussion would need to analyse the problems and constraints involved in various forms of communication, showing which features of a notation make it more or less useful. For instance, redundancy will assist the cognitive processes in a receiver. Even for internal reasoning, within a single intelligent system, we shall see that different notations will be best for different purposes. Compare Brown and Burton (1975).

3. Why notations are important

In designing or describing an intelligent system, we can consider its knowledge at varying depths.

(1) The actual content of the knowledge base will be unique to that individual and be able to explain only its actual behaviour.

(2) The system of concepts used explains how that knowledge can be grasped, and would account equally well for many alternative contents. It also explains the range of questions which can be asked, problems formulated, instruction understood, etc.

(3) The formalism or notation used, toether with relevant procedures, explains how that set of concepts, and the knowledge or questions expressed with their aid, may be stored, communicated, manipulated in reasoning, etc. But the same notation might be used for a quite different range of concepts, and thus the notation explains a wider range of possible belief states.

So the notation used has a deep explanatory role. What gives a notation or formalism its power is not just the static structure of the various symbols or representations, but the procedures available to operate on it, e.g. matching, parsing, substituting, etc. Logical inference procedures are a special case.

4. Some alternative notations

A survey of notations, formalisms, symbolisms, representational systems, used by mathematicians, scientists, engineers, musicians, programmers, choreographers, cartographers, and even some logicians will show that there is a very wide variety of types. It is very unlikely that all of these, or even a majority, have grown out of arbitrary whims. Rather there are cultural and evolutionary pressures provided both by the nature of the domain of application and the purposes for which they are used, which have shaped their development. Some of the pressures include the perceptual and cognitive problems involved in parsing and interpreting structures. Some include the requirements of cognitive processes making use of the structures for such varied purposes as inference (e.g. calculation), planning, searching and problem solving, and detailed control of actions.

For example, it seems that for many purposes of control of actions, the two-dimensional structure of the visual field plays an important role, as it does in discerning what somebody is looking at, by following the line of sight across the scene.

Even within logic, geometrical representations and geometrical procedures play a role. For instance the unification algorithm used in logic programming is a 'geometrical' inference procedure, operating on the syntactic structure of symbols to infer whether one can be transformed into another by a suitable geometric substitution. If instead of representing logical formulas geometrically, and performing geometric operations on them, we tried to use only logical descriptions of their structure, and logical deduction, then we should have an infinite regress.

If it is true that different sorts of representations and inference procedures should be used for different sorts of tasks, then the implications for Expert System design are profound.

5. Applicative and other notations

What is special about logic? We shall answer this in terms of the type of syntax (or geometry) used, the semantic presuppositions and the inference procedures. FOPL uses an 'applicative' notation. This means:

a. Applicative syntax.
   All composite formulas are constructed from simpler formulas by a combination of function symbols and argument symbols, so as to represent the application of a function to its arguments.

b. Applicative semantics.
   The denotation of any complex symbol depends on the individuals denoted by its arguments and the function denoted by the function symbol. (How it depends on them needs to be defined more precisely.)

(b) Is sometimes referred to as the principle of compositionality, probably first understood and analysed by Frege (which is why in (Sloman 1971, 1978) I previously used the label 'Fregean' for applicative representations). Using an applicative representation presupposes that there are individuals and functions (mappings from individuals to individuals). We later show this to be a restrictive presupposition.

Together, (a) and (b) imply the principle of substitutivity: in an applicative formalism, symbols and well-formed combinations of symbols will be divided into syntactic types, such that in a complex well-formed formula, any well-formed sub-formula can be replaced by another (simple or complex) of the same type and the result will still be well-formed. Morever this will not affect the significance of any other symbol in the formula. For example, in "3 + 2", "2" can be replaced by "(5 x 99)" and "+" can be replaced by "-", and in either case the remaining symbols and their denotations will not be altered, although the denotation of the whole expression is changed.

Thus, "3 + 5" uses an applicative notation, with "+" as function symbol, "3" and "5" as arguments. Similarly, in its obvious interpretation, "between(3,2,4)" is applicative, though here the function is from triples of numbers to truth-values.

Pictures generally violate the principle of substitutivity. E.g. in a picture of animals in a field, there is no way that a picture of an elephant can be replaced by a picture of a giraffe, without it also making a difference to how much of the background is depicted.

The substitution property is one of the features which gives logic its generality. Assertions made about one class of objects, or inference principles discovered in relation to one class of objects, may be sensibly transferred to others by substituting appropriate sub-expressions. This encourages the formulation of new conjectures and various kinds of analogical and metaphorical reasoning. So applicative notations underpin some of the most powerful and creative reasoning processes.

First order logic uses an applicative notation, since, as
Frege noticed, predicates are functions from n-tuples of objects of
any kind to truth-values. Moreover, quantifiers (e.g. "for all x",
"for some x") can be construed as 'second level' functions from
predicates to truth-values. (I.e. 'for all x P(x)' is true if every
meaningful substitution of an argument in 'P( )' produces a true
result.
      (c) The principle of extensionality, is also a feature of
applicative notations. It states that if F1 is a well-formed formula, and S1 is a subformula of F1, then if S1 is replaced by
another formula S2 with the same denotation, transforming F1 into
F2, then F2 will have the same denotation as F1. Extensionality is a
feature of FOPL. (This definition needs to be relativised to a
situation or possible world. See Sloman (1965))
      As Frege first pointed out, it seems that natural languages
do not satisfy this condition, and in particular that sentences
about the mental state of an intelligent system will not always
retain their truth-value if a component is replaced by another with
the same denotation. E.g. if 'Bill Bloggs' and 'The mayor of Mares-
ville' denote the same individual, then replacing the former with
the latter will not alter the truth-value of an extensional assertion like:
      'Bill Bloggs hit Harry Holmes'
whereas it may alter truth value in an intensional context, like:
      'Fred Fikes believes Bill Bloggs hit Harry Holmes'

      Various attempts have been made to show how such assertions
can be translated into FOPL, preserving extensionality, e.g. using a
metalinguistic extensional language. For instance,
      'Fred believes the evening star is the morning star'
might translate into something like:
      sentence(s1) & believes(Fred,s1) & identity(s1)
      & arg(1, s1, 'the evening star')
      & arg(2, s1, 'the morning star')

I.e. there is an identity statment which Fred believes whose arguments are: 'the evening star' and 'the morning star'. More complex
translations would be required for other sorts of beliefs. There are
problems with this sort of suggestion. An acceptable translation
must not assume that Fred is an English speaker, for example.
Attempting to get round this by avoiding literal English strings,
and instead using a representation of the meaning common to them and
their translations in other languages, might re-create intensional
contexts. For an alternative attempt to rescue FOPL see McCarthy
1979. Frege's own means of rescuing the principle of extensionality
was to allow an embedded expression to denote an abstract entity
called the "sense" or "intension" of the expression. The debate will
no doubt continue for a long time.
      For now we may merely note that it is not obvious that an
extensional notation like FOPL is adequate for describing intelligent systems. Expert systems which reason about intelligent agents
may therefore need a richer formalism.

6. The importance of truth-values

One of the reasons for the generality of logic is that it postulates in its ontology (i.e. its implicit theory about what exists) a class of entities called booleans, i.e. the truth-values TRUE and FALSE. What these entities actually are is irrelevant, since all that is important is their role in defining logical operations.

The same expression (e.g. 'P or Q') may evaluate to TRUE in a variety of ways. So simply indicating that the expression is true is a convenient way of conveying very non-specific information, which is often useful when further details are either irrelevant or unknown. For instance if the predicate 'is red' is defined suitably, then 'the ball is red' conveys information about the colour of the ball without being at all specific about the precise shade of red, etc. By contrast, a painting of the ball would not normally be able to do this. Similarly 'There is a table in front of me' is totally non-committal about which table it is, what sort of table, and how it is spatially related to the speaker. A painting cannot be so non-committal, though some styles attempt to overcome this.

Paradoxically, almost, we can say therefore that part of the power of logic is its ability to express various kinds of imprecise information, including negative, disjunctive and existentially quantified assertions. However, we shall see that it may nevertheless be limited by specific sorts of ontological committments.

To sum up, FOPL uses applicative notations, with a compositional denotative (i.e. extensional) semantics. It uses the principle of substitutivity for its generality and the principle of extensionality to achieve its semantic simplicity. It presupposes the existence of individuals of some kind, including booleans, and (situation relative) mappings from individuals or sets of individuals to booleans -- i.e. properties and relations.

7. Logic presupposes a meta-ontology

We have seen that logic (or the use of logic) presupposes that the world can be construed as made up of:
1. objects (including booleans)
2. functions (which subsume properties and relations.)

It is arguable that this is too restrictive for some purposes. Consider a human body. We do have names for many parts, but there are few natural boundaries: the names refer to portions which are not necessarily precisely demarcated from the rest, causing difficulties in deciding whether a particular object has a property or stands in some relation to another object. Deciding whether a forefinger is or is not longer than a thumb depends on what the boundaries are: compare the views of a hand from the palm side and the knuckle side.

More importantly, a physical object appears to be a continuum, and at least at the resolution at which we can perceive or think about it, seems to be indefinitely divisible in many different ways, rather than made up of a fixed hierarchy of objects. Different kinds of properties and relationships will be relevant to different modes of subdivision. For some actions, such as touching an object, little or no decomposition may be required.

So, to represent the way we perceive a body, or even the way
we think about what we perceive, or the action of running a finger
smoothly along the surface of a torso, we require a representation
which does not presuppose some decomposition into well-defined
objects. Sculptures and paintings are examples of such representations. They are examples of what I call 'analogical' representations. Instead of explicitly naming individuals, properties and
relations, they represent complex wholes by allowing properties and
relations to be represented implicitly by properties and relations,
including shapes, colours, etc.

8. Analogical representations and continuity

The concept of an 'analogical representation' does not
require the representation or what it denotes to be continuous or
ontologically uncommitted. For example, a list of names of people
might be a discrete analogical representaton of the order in which
the people were born, or the chain of command in a military unit.
Similarly, in a Prolog program, the order of portions of the text
analogically represents the order in which subgoals (at a certain
level) are attempted. This is Prolog's procedural aspect.
        An analogical notation may or may not be capable of
representing some continuous reality. A discrete analogical or logical notation may be used to describe a continuous object to any
desired degree of resolution if there is some means of decomposing
that reality into small enough individuals. Does that presuppose the
use of some other notation to represent the continuous reality prior
to finding a good decomposition?
        Computer vision systems use a quantized approximation to
continuous representations e.g. 2-D arrays. These may be thought of
as providing a sample of data in a continuous optic array. The same
sample could be represented in a database of logical assertions,
though, in the array, unlike a logical database, neighbourhood and
other relationships are represented analogically, possibly at a
'virtual' level (explained below).
        The array is committed to a particular ontology for the sam-
ple, i.e. a finite set of measurements, but not for the domain of
structures represented. Procedures which search for evidence of
edges may be thought of as helping the search for a good decomposition.
        So a finite discrete machine can embody representations of a
continuous, unarticulated, reality in an ontologically uncommitted
fashion. (This requires further analysis.)

9. "Analogical" does not imply "similar" or "isomorphic".

People often fall into the trap of assuming that an analogical representation must be isomorphic with or similar to what it
represents. But this is not necessary. For instance, in a flat picture of a three dimensional scene, relations between things in the
picture represent relations between things in the scene, yet picture
and scene have quite different structures - one is two dimensional
and the other three dimensional. Moreover the relation between what
is represented and how it is represented may vary according to context. In a picture of a room, the relation 'higher' in the picture
may represent any of 'higher', 'further', 'nearer', depending on

which portion of the picture is involved (Sloman 1971, 1978). Similarly, a flow chart may represent a linear computer process in which
many sub-processes are represented by one loop. Despite the lack of
isomorphism between chart and process, this is an analogical
representation, though, like a map, it may also include other notations. Finally, as we have seen, a discrete, finite, structure may
be an anological representation of a continuous structure.

10. Uncommitted ontologies

More importantly, an analogical representation need not be
composed of parts with properties and relations in any determinate
way. Like the portion of the world it depicts, a picture or sculp-
ture or map may be decomposed into parts, with mutual relationships,
in many different ways, which may be significant for different purposes. This can give such representations great flexibility and
power. By contrast, a logical formula wears its syntactic decomposition on its face: you cannot understand it at all without knowing
how it is to be parsed.

This need not be true of a very large collection of logical
formulae, even though it is true of individual formulae. A massive
database needs some organisation in order to be useful, and different organisations (at a high level) may be useful for different
purposes, even though individual formulae may be uniquely parsed.
The clean simplicity of logic may be irrelevant to such global complexity, just as knowing everything about the structure of individual circular dots may be irrelevant to making sense of a newspaper
picture composed of dots.

One reason why this sort of ontologically (comparatively)
uncommitted representation may be important is that it provides a
framework in which learning can take place. A learning system not
yet sure of the best way to decompose the world may need to have
some way of representing it which is not yet committed to any particular decomposition into objects properties and relations.

'Low level' representations created by visual and other perceptual systems may have this important property. How exactly they
are used, how the learning takes place, how a new ontology is formed
and represented are all important unanswered questions. Recent work
by G.L. Scott at Sussex University (unpublished apart from (Scott
1984)), involves attempting to discover how structure can be imposed
on unarticulated data by very general processes which simply attempt
to maximise aesthetic qualities. Goodman (1978) also discusses the
construction of alternative world-views, suggesting that aesthetic
criteria play a significant role. We have yet to understand the
trade-offs between totally general ontologically uncommitted learning processes and various kinds of comparatively domain-specific,
partly committed learning. Perhaps the former type, like biological
evolution, requires millions of years to achieve what the latter can
do quickly, at the cost of more stored prior information and restricted generality.

Learning systems and theories which assume the kind of
decomposition required by an applicative representation cannot
explain how that decomposition is learnt. This applies to many
psychological learning theories, to philosophical theories about
inductive inference, and to most AI learning theories. In many cases
the 'learning' consists simply in trying to find a set of rules

which best fits some data where the set of possible rules is constrained by a definite formalism and ontology. For a survey see
(Bundy Silver and Plummer 1983).

The crucial feature of an analogical representation is that
instead of using explicit names (predicate symbols, relation symbols) to represent properties and relations of things it uses properties of and relations between parts of the representation itself.
This does not require all analogical representations to be totally
ontologically uncommitted. For instance, a London underground map is
committed to the existence of railway routes, stations along those
routes, and to relations of ordering and connectivity. The map also
gives a very vague indication of other spatial relations. Maps with
dots and other symbols representing named towns, roads, rivers, distances, etc. may also contain a mixture of ontological commitments
and uncommitted representation. For instance, there need be no com-
mitment to a particular decomposition of a winding river into parts.
An aerial photograph of the same terrain would be even less committed.

Expert systems concerned with diagnosis and repair of equipment may need to use spatial representations which allow different
decompositions to be explored in tracking down unusual problems. I
once saw a mechanic attempting to divide the engine compartment into
regions more and less likely to be affected by the temperature
change as the engine warmed up, in tracking down an elusive fault
which appeared only after running for a few minutes.

An important task for AI is to study such mixed representations, to understand how they are created, how they are used, and
how a learning system can move between different levels of ontological awareness.

11. Perception and ontology

The same issues arise in perceptual systems. The physical
world is not intrinsically articulated in any particular way. A perceptual system may have to deliver some sort of articulated, perhaps
even logical, representation that can be used as a basis for planning, monitoring actions, forming generalisations, testing
hypotheses, communicating with others, etc. As we have seen, in
order to derive such cognitively useful representations the system
has to have some way of representing and processing information
about the unarticulated starting point.

Similar remarks may be made about the need for representations which can guide the behaviour of external objects - arms,
legs, wheels, grippers, etc. Many actions, such as catching a ball,
throwing a stone at a moving target, tracking an object with one's
eyes, drawing or painting a scene, dancing to music, require both
perceptions and actions which involve continuous variation and are
closely matched to each other. In simple devices this can easily be
achieved by means of mechanical or electronic feedback loops. In
humans and other animals there seem to be far more sophisticated and
powerful processes, which can improve themselves qualitatively as
well as quantitatively. I shall not speculate about the sorts of
internal representations required, or the inference, retrieval and
matching processes. We understand very little of these matters.
Designers of expert systems for real-time control will have to
address the problems.

All this raises the question whether there can also be more and less ontologically committed representations of more abstract domains, such as number theory, set theory, computing science, etc. If so, do we need a variety of types of representations to account for learning in these domains, or are the different kinds of knowledge all expressible in FOPL because of the structure of the domain?

Notice that even if everything can be expressed in FOPL, this may be of little use in relation to the task of imposing an organisation on the massive database of fragmentary information. For example, the power of logic would be of little use to a visual system which translated all its image arrays into logical assertions. The major problems would remain unchanged.

Our discussion suggests that we need to qualify the claim in (Woods 1975) that we need a representation that will precisely, formally, and unambiguously represent any particular interpretation. It depends what you want to use the representation for, and how far your learning has progressed.

12. Explanation and representation

Usually philosophers of science who discuss explanation (e.g. (Nagel 1961)) assume that an explanation is composed of a series of assertions expressed in a verbal or logical formalism. Yet if we examine the cognitive function of explanations, namely their role in producing new insights, a deeper ability to make plans and predictions, to diagnose faults, to form new questions and hypotheses, we find that often an explanation is most usefully expressed in a non-verbal, non-logical form. For instance, seeing a diagram showing the workings of a mechanical clock, or even opening up the clock and looking directly at the cogs and levers, can yield a deeper understanding of how it works and the many ways it can go wrong, than a purely verbal description. Why and how this is so, and what abstract knowledge is presupposed, requires further analysis. I offer it now as yet another familiar example of the power of analogical representations, including the use of something to represent its own structure.

13. Numerical notation

Besides applicative and analogical notations, there are many special-purpose notations. To illustrate further the claim that different sorts of notations may be best for different purposes, we may consider how our ordinary arithmetical notation deviates from being purely applicative.

Ever since the heroic, but unsuccessful, attempts of Frege, Russell and Whitehead to reduce arithmetic to logic it has been clear that there are deep relationships between the two. So it may seem surprising that the notation we regularly use for arithmetic is not predicate logic, but a special purpose formalism, with features specifically designed for their heuristic power in this domain.

Numerals, like "999" are composite formulas whose denotation depends on the denotations of the parts in a systematic way. But instead of having one or more symbols to represent the functions being applied, we use relative positions of the digits. So being n

steps from the right (or to the left of a decimal point) represents
being multiplied by the (n-1)th power of 10 and added to the running
total. This not an applicative notation: the principle of substitutivity is violated. In this notation, you cannot replace an arbitrary argument symbol (e.g. the middle '9' in '999' with any other
arbitrary symbol denoting a number (e.g. '65' or '3 + 77'), and
leave the rest of the expression with the same function-argument
relations as before. Moreover, the functions being applied to get
the total are not explicitly represented by symbols which can be
replaced by other symbols representing different functions. Hence
this is not a pure applicative notation.

The invention of the place notation, including a special
symbol for zero, was a major intellectual achievement. It enables
the notation to do a lot of work for us, when we do additions, mul-
tiplications, and divisions. In particular it enables us to use
position of a digit, at intermediate stages of a calculation, to
carry useful information in a very economical form, and it enables
us to get by with a small set of primitive numerals in representing
all possible integers.

We could, of course, extend our notation using parentheses
so that, for example "9(65)9" denoted the same number as

9 x 100 + 65 x 10 + 9

but that would lose some of the economy and power of our existing
system, although it might have other advantages. It would still not
be a completely applicative system, insofar as some functions and
relations were not represented by explicit names, but by syntactic
relations. Our existing notation has 'heuristic power' because of
the particular properties of its domain, and the operations we wish
to perform in that domain. There are many different kinds of notations which have special features, tailored to the structure of a
domain and our purposes.

Diagrams, models, simulations, etc. can play heuristic roles
in controlling the search for a formal proof. E.g. don't try to
prove subgoals false in the model.

Some of these representations can also be used more con-
structively -- suggesting a good strategy. For example, if you
need the shortest route from A to B, then a good heuristic is to
draw a straight line beween A and B on a map of the available roads,
and then investigate only nearby roads. This heuristic assumes
that closeness along roads is represented by closeness on the
map. This is not always true, when roads have to go round a large
river, for instance.

This method works only because fragments of roads are implicitly indexed by their geometrical relationships, so that one can
use geometrical relationships in the map to control the search for
roads satisfying a geometrical relationship: being close to the
shortest line joining start and end points. This is one of many
ways in which a relation of 'nearness' in a representation can be
used to represent nearness in the world, to great effect.

14. Intelligence and notations

Intelligence has different dimensions. One is the type or
level of competence achieved. Another can be defined as productive
laziness. It is not only what a system can do that determines
whether we think of it as intelligent, but·also how it is done. If

methods of blind exhaustive search are used, for example, then that
may be useful if the searching is fast enough, but it is not as
intelligent as finding a way to avoid the search.

Sometimes finding the right representation for information
and problems is a crucial first step -- for instance mapping the
well-known chess-board and dominoes problem into a representation
involving numbers, in order to prove that a set of dominoes covering
adjacent squares cannot cover the board with a pair of diagonally
opposite corners removed. Discovering the mapping is made much
easier with the aid of a geometric analogical representation of the
board in which neighbouring squares are given different colours.
(Proving that this can always be done with a rectangular grid is not
as easy as always seeing how to do it with a particular grid. The
general proof requires something like an abstract logical representation.)

Whether it is intelligent to use a particular method may
depend on context. For a simple problem with a small search space,
the lazy, and therefore the intelligent, strategy may be blind
exhaustive search, for instance selecting the right key in a bunch
to fit a given lock. When there are many thousands of keys distributed over a variety of shops, it may be intelligent to do some
preliminary detailed study of the lock and its properties in order
to delimit the search space.

15. Subject matter does not determine best notation.

The uses are important, since a domain in itself may be usefully representable in many different ways. For example the London
underground railway system may be represented for most users of the
system in a fashion which indicates connectivity very accurately,
but distances and directions only very loosely. But for the
engineers working on the system, and time-table planners, it is
important to have a representation which conveys more detailed
information.

16. Illustrating the power of diagrams - internal and external

Because they help to control the search space, diagrams are
often used in mathematical and logical reasoning, in planning, in
design, etc.

Layout planning (Eastman 1971) often uses a map of the
situation, to constrain the set of possibilities to be explored in
searching for a configuration satisfying some constraints. Because
the representational medium is closely related to what is
represented all sorts of possibilities are pruned from the search
space simply because they cannot be represented. If a logical or
verbal representation were used, there would be nothing in the syntax of the formalism to prevent the impossible situations being
described. We now know, from 2-D pictures of impossible 3-D scenes,
that Wittgenstein was wrong when he claimed (1922) that it is impossible to represent geometrically the geometrically impossible.

Consider the following problem. In how many points will a
'perfect' circle and a 'perfect' triangle intersect if one corner of
the triangle is inside the circle and two outside? How did you solve
that problem? If the triangle is entirely inside or entirely outside

the circle the number of intersection points is zero. If exactly one
corner lies on the circle and the other two outside the circle, the
number of intersections is one? (How can you be sure?). How many
different numbers of intersection points are possible? Don't read on
until you have worked out your answer, and then thought again about
whether you have considered all possibilities.

Most people seem to explore a 'space' of possible configura-
tions of the circle and triangle. But hardly anyone does so simply
by manipulating verbal or logical descriptions of possible confi-
gurations and checking them against axioms for geometry. Instead
they seem mentally to construct something which functions like a two
dimensional diagram on which they impose geometrical transforma-
tions, like sliding the triangle around, making it larger or
smaller, changing its shape, etc. It takes most people some time to
do this exploration, and not all do it thoroughly enough to find all
seven possible numbers of intersections.

Having used a (real or imagined) diagram to explore the
problem and identify a likely solution, we may use logic to demonstrate its correctness. But it would not be intelligent to start
with a logical representation alone. The burden of constantly referring to explicit geometrical axioms is removed by using a representational medium in which the axioms cannot be violated. This enor-
mously constrains the search space, enabling us to be lazy and productive.

Of course, this does point to a problem of the sort of
'meta-level' representation required in order to infer that all combinations have been tried. I have no doubt that alongside the analogical representations there are very abstract descriptions.
Exactly how these should interact is an important research topic.
How can a machine be made to represent the process of sweeping
through a range of possibilities, subject to constraints? (For some
examples see (Funt 1977).)

Alan Bundy informs me me that his equation-solving system,
PRESS, cannot find a solution for 'x' in

$$x = \sin(x)$$

though people can. E.g. starting from a trigonometrical definition
of 'sin', we can derive the general shape of the graph of
'y=sin(x)', then superimpose the graph of 'y=x', notice that they
intersect only near the origin, then argue that it must be exactly
at the origin. Notice that visualising the approximate shape of the
graph is not the same as having an exact image. Neither does it
imply that the final result is approximate: a mixture of inference
methods can be used to achieve exactness.

How can we be sure we have exhausted all possibilities? In
general we can't. See Lakatos (1976) on the history of proofs of
Euler's theorem relating the numbers of vertices, edges and faces of
a polyhedron. But it is imporant not to confuse the demand for
heuristic power, which is what I have been talking about, with the
demand for rigour. Often rigour can come later, though total rigour
is unattainable except in the very simplest domains.

I have tried to indicate why it is not just because of
psychological limitations of human problem solvers that it is sensible to use a variety of representational systems in expert activities. This counters the view of some philosophers and mathematicians
that mathematics is essentially logic, and that any use of non-
logical methods of reasoning by human mathematicians is simply due
to their limited intelligence. In some cases the intelligent thing

to do is find a special-purpose representation, tailored to the
problem domain. Of course, it would be even more intelligent to have
a deep understanding of the nature of the representation and the
reasons why it is appropriate. It may prove best for this second-
order reasoning to use a quite different type of representation,
e.g. logic.

17. Using spatial structures in logical structures.

The fact that any visible notation has to be embedded in a
medium with its own geometry can blur some of our distinctions. For
example, spatial reasoning/perception can be used in analysing a set
of axioms, prior to constructing a proof. E.g. seeing a set of
implications as forming a sort of 'chain'. The axioms:

        P -> Q
        Q -> R
        R -> S

could be embedded in a larger set of axioms. By taking the ends of
the chain we get
        P -> S

and similarly for other transitive relations. So what looks like
logical reasoning using applicative representations, may in part be
geometrical reasoning using analogical representations.
        This is ultimately due to the fact that even an applicative
logical notation must be embedded in a usable, manipulable, medium.
In a structure like 'f(a,b)' geometrical relations between the components are used to indicate the relation of applying between the
function and the arguments. If an explicit symbol were required for
'apply', as in 'apply(f,a,b)', then for consistency we should
require this to be expanded as 'apply(apply,f,a,b)'. Aristotle
discovered this infinite regress in connection with the relation
between a predicate and its subject and decided this was not really
a relation. Without taking sides on that issue we can see that at
least the argument shows that if our notation is to be finite and
usable there must be a level of representation which is analogical
not applicative. The geometric/syntactic structure of a formula can
represent analogically the application of a function to its arguments: the application is pictured, not described. If it were always
described explicitly instead of being depicted then the unification
algorithm used in logic programming languages would have to be quite
different, and much less efficient.

18. Conjecture

Human spatial abilities underly many other more abstract
abilities, like medical expertise, mechanical or electronic fault-
finding, logical reasoning. For instance, the notion of a 'search
space' uses physical space as an analogical representation of part
of a process of solving a problem.
        All known animals which are good at logic, plannning, etc.
have visual apparatus (even blind people still have the relevant
part of the brain). But the converse isn't true. Will either be true

of intelligent machines?

19. Representing processes: simulation vs description

Simulations which run e.g. (Brown and Burton) form a special class of analogical and sometimes mixed representations. They should be contrasted with descriptions from which inferences are made. A collection of equations with algorithms for transforming some of the parameters can be an applicative implementation of a non-applicative, analogical virtual representation, i.e. the running simulation program, in which changes in datastructures or the values of variables represent changes in the thing represented.

Often a simulation of some kind gives the easiest and quickest means of providing an answer to a question about how a system would behave in certain conditions. But a simulation may not produce enough information to answer other questions, for instance about why it behaves like that, or what the preconditions are for its behaving like that, or what the range of variation of behaviours would be in a range of situations. For these purposes a more abstract, perhaps more logical, description may be helpful.

A flow chart can be regarded as a sort of 'frozen' simulation of a certain class of processes: projected from a space/time domain into a two dimensional spatial domain. The relationships are really more complex than this, since the process simulated may have several sub-processes, corresponding to one loop in the flow chart. A computer program will generally use a still more complex mode of representation, with a mixture of applicative and analogical representations together with a host of special-purposes notational conventions which may affect any of: (a) the process of reading in program text, (b) the process of compiling to a lower level language, (c) initialisation processes and (d) the process of running the program.

Natural languages use an even more complex mixture of representations, especially in spoken forms, where stress, intonation, volume and tempo may all interact with each other and with the words selected. Often mixed modes are used, e.g. sentences where time order or spatial order is represented analogically, along with explicitly named properties and relations.

20. Virtual machines and virtual representations

Often we seem to use objects in our minds which are like objects which exist in the physical world. A visualised map or diagram may be used for some of the same purposes as a real physical one. Sometimes an external physical map will be easier to use, because it is more detailed than an image, more stable, more easily traversed in all directions, and can have a different range of operations applied to it, for instance laying a ruler or other cut-out shape on it. Nevertheless, the status of mental maps, diagrams, models, is of considerable interest.

Introspective reports are not to be taken too seriously -- though they are often suggestive evidence. People often say they use a picture or image in performing some task. But they can't just use a picture or image. E.g. as they investigate relationships they must be making use of some specification of constraints (e.g. it must remain a triangle even though its shape changes.) The constraints may exist only in a compiled form -- another type of representation.

Moreover, even the claim to be using a mental picture or diagram cannot be taken literally. A literal mental picture would require a mental eye to look at it, and it would presumably produce its own 'internal' mental picture which would require another mental eye to look at it.....

One answer to this is to acknowledge that one sort of representation may be <u>implemented</u> in terms of another quite different sort, just as a computer may be a 'virtual machine' implemented by software or microcode in terms of some lower level machine. For instance a lot of picture-like representations in computer programs use two-dimensional arrays, which are actually represented at a lower level as a one-dimensional array or vector, and at still lower levels as complex patterns of switch states. What makes us justified in talking about a 2-D array is the availability of <u>procedures</u> which produce operations best interpreted in 2-D terms, such as scanning a row, or a column, of the array, or scanning all eight neighbours of an array element. In principle the array could even be implemented in terms of a logical database, and array operations implemented in terms of logical deductions. This would be quite acceptable as a lower level representation, if the logical virtual machine ran fast enough. (Very very fast!). Hayes (1974) made this point by referring to the need for an underlying medium in which a representation is embedded.

My point is that one can discuss the heuristic and other properties of a representation independently of how it is actually implemented -- and it may have totally different properties from those in an underlying virtual machine.

Of course, a poor implementation may have features (e.g. excessive space or time requirements) which undermine the advantages of the virtual representation -- a common trap for programmers unaware of the lower levels of the systems they use.

So when introspection suggests that we are using a certain sort of representation, the properties of that representation may be achieved by implementing it in terms of a quite different representation to which we may have no introspective access at all. Some of the differences can be brought out by simple experiments. For instance, a person who claims to be able to visualise written words will often find that he can read the letters off his image much faster from left to right than from right to left. This is not the case when the letters are in front of him on paper. Perhaps the discrepancy is due to the visual image being implemented in terms of list structures, or similar chains of binary associations between objects and the rest of the list. We have already noted that a list may function as an analogical representation of an ordered set of objects.

AI systems also seem to need a variety of layers of representations. Von Neumann computers seem to be well suited to this; will the same be true of other novel architectures, e.g. declarative machines?

21. Criteria for assessing a notation

Chomsky (e.g. 1965) distinguished several kinds of adequacy of grammars and grammatical theories. An observationally adequate grammar for a natural language generates all and only well formed strings of the language. A descriptively adequate grammar also assigns parse-trees which accord with the way users understand the language. Explanatory adequacy of a grammatical theory (for Chomsky) is concerned with the ability to account for how a language is learnt.

Chomsky's distinctions do not address the question whether one notation or grammar is more useful than another for the purposes of an intelligent language user, for he claimed not to be concerned with processing. But the attempt to formulate criteria for evaluating grammars was a precursor of the important task of formulating criteria for assessing formalisms for use in Artificial Intelligence. It is very important, however, that we distinguish two major rols, namely the use of a formalism in a working system and the use of a formalism for theorising about a working system and its task domain. Building explanatory theories requires a more abstract, more logical, language than building a working model or simulation. The requirements are quite different. For instance a working system has time constraints. Theoretical discussion may have quite different constraints, or none at all. A working system merely has to represent or replicate a class of behaviours. A theory has to say something about the relationship between those behaviours and others not produced, requiring a much higher level of abstraction.

Criteria for adequacy of representations used for a visual system were discussed by Marr and Nishihara (1978) and Marr (1982). They consider such things as whether the representation is easily accessible, i.e. readily computed from available input, general, i.e. able to cope with a range of cases, uniquely determined by the input, stable, i.e. resistant to changes of view or lighting, sensitive, i.e. able to detect and indicate small differences between scenes. These criteria (especially the last two), may conflict, and any selection will generally involve a trade-off. They did not discuss many other relevant criteria. For instance, their hierarchically organised representation makes it hard to represent spatial relationships between arbitrary parts of a structured object. So one finger can be related to another on the same hand quite easily, but not so easily to a finger on the other hand, or to the nose it is scratching. Criteria relevant to choice of a representation used for recognising objects may not be relevant to the goal of avoiding collisions with them, or the goal of picking them up without damaging parts. Of two tasks, one may require the representation of far less detail, and quite different spatial relationships.

For instance, it is an error to suppose that all the uses of vision require a representation of 3-D structure. Much motion control, for example, can efficiently be based on the monitoring of 2-D image structure.

Woods valuable essay on semantic nets (1975) discusses criteria for assessing them. However, he seems to assume throughout that what needs to be represented is what logic represents exactly. I have shown that this may not always be the case.

McCarthy and Hayes (1969) introduced three sorts of criteria more relevant to evaluation of general knowledge representations. Their criteria partly echo Chomsky's distinctions, perhaps

unintentionally. Consider an agent A using a anguage L in a world W.
a. Metaphysical/Ontological adequacy.
   Can L express everything that can be the case in W?

b. Epistemological adequacy (relative to agent A)
   Can L express everything which A needs to know about W?

c. Heuristic adequacy.
   Does L facilitate the <u>Processing</u> that A requires, better than
   alternative languages L1, L2,..., for representing the same
   world, W.

These criteria were presented as if they might be absolute.
That is, how the world actually is, and what A needs to know about
it, and the purposes for which A needs the knowledge are assumed
fixed, and then different languages are discussed. But we have seen
that how A needs to construe the world may depend on how much A has
already learnt, and what tasks or problems he has. So quite different representations may be needed at different times. This does
not, however, rule out a general theory of what the relationships
are between purposes, types of environment, and useful representations.
     Readers interested in exploring these issues should try for-
mulating criteria for selecting a notation for numbers. If the criteria include easy learnability, and other cognitive criteria, then
the first few Roman numerals may do quite well. However, once there
is a need to represent infinitely many integers or to multiply and
divide lare numbers; a different sort of notation becomes desirable.
     A more detailed analysis of criteria for assessing represen-
tation schemas would have to be far more careful than anything I
have seen so far in the AI literature. It would have to include a
survey of the different purposes for which formalisms may be used.
For instance we have already seen that the following two uses may be
incompatible:

A.   theorising about properties of a domain

B.   programming something to act intelligently in the domain

These generate very different requirements. I suspect that further
investigation will reveal a host of different sorts of criteria, and
that there will often be conflicts to be resolved by a systematic
analysis of trade-offs.

22. Some problems with FOPL

FOPL is rich, powerful, and the most general language we
have. But it is far from unproblematic. There are many difficulties
which I am not going to have time to go into in detail. Here are a
few old problems.

(1) Is <u>first</u> order logic enough? E.g. "Napoleon had all the quali-
    ties of a good general"

(2) Can actions/real relationships be adequately represented? This
    raises the problem of indefinite qualification. In English we
    seem to be able to say things which are indefinitely expandable
    in ways in which an assertion using logic would not be.

> Bill hit Joe
>   with a fish
>   last Thursday
>   on the head
>   hard
>   to hurt him
>   at the market

One common answer is implicit in the use of case grammars, but was originally suggested by Donald Davidson, I
believe. This is to extend the ontology, to include entities
called actions with a variety of properties and relations to
other entities.

> act(a) & type(a, hit) & agent(a, Bill) & object(a, joe)
> & instrument(a, x) & fish(x) & time(a, Thursday 5th Sept),
> & application_point(a, head(Bill)), & force(a, hard)....

Would a logical formalism allowing variadic predicates
be better? How would its semantics be defined?

(3) Problems arising out of the restriction to denotational (exten-
    sional) semantics have been discussed above.

23. Conclusion

I have tried to indicate, though in a sketchy and incomplete
fashion, some of the reasons why we need to explore the uses of different sorts of formalisms for different purposes. We need to understand how an intelligent system can choose between different formalisms, and how it can, on occasions, create new formalisms when doing
so would give new insight or heuristic power of some kind. The discussion suggests that the design of really intelligent systems is
going to be a very difficult and very complex task. If only Kowalski
were right!

Acknowledgement

Part of the work reported here was supported by a fellowship
from the GEC Research Laboratories. Despite our disagreements, I,
like many others, have learnt a great deal from Bob Kowalski.

REFERENCES

Bobrow, D. (1975). 'Dimensions of Representation', in D.Bobrow and
    A.Collins (eds) Representation and Understanding, Academic
    Press.

Brown, J.S. and Burton, R.R. (1975). 'Multiple Representations of
    Knowledge for Tutorial Reasoning', in D.Bobrow and A.Collins
    (eds) Representation and Understanding, Academic Press.

Bundy, A, Silver B, and Plummer D. (1983). 'An analytical com-
    parison of some rule learning programs' Proceedings British
    Computer Society Expert Systems Group Conference, Churchill
    College Cambridge.

Chomsky, N. (1965). Aspects of the theory of Syntax. MIT Press.

Eastman, C.M. (1971). 'Heuristic algorithms for automated psace
    planning' in Proc. 2nd IJCAI British Computer Society.

Funt, B.V. (1977). 'WHISPER: a problem solving system utilizing
    diagrams and a parallel processing retina', in Proceedings
    5th IJCAI, MIT.

Goodman, N. (1969). Languages of Art Oxford University Press.

Goodman, N. (1978). Ways of worldmaking, Harvester Press.

Hayes, P.J. (1974). 'Some problems and non-problems in representa-
    tion theory', in Proc. AISB Summer Conference University of
    Sussex, 1974 (out of print).

Johnson-Laird, P.N. (1983). Mental Models, Cambridge University
    Press.

Kowalski, R.A. (1980). contribution to SIGART newsletter No 70,
    Special Issue on Knowledge Representation, Feb. 1980

Lakatos, I (1976).. Proofs and Refutations, Cambridge University
    Press.

Marr, D. (1982). Vision Freeman.

Marr, D and Nishihara H.K. (1978). 'Representation and recognition
    of the spatial organization of three-dimensional shapes.
    Proc Royal Society B200,

McCarthy, J. (1979). 'First-order theories of individual concepts
    and propositions', in D. Michie (ed) Expert Systems in the
    Microelectronic Age Edinburgh University Press.

McCarthy, J. and Hayes, P.J. (1979). 'Some philosophical problems
    from the standpoint of Artificial Intelligence', in Machine
    Intelligence 4, ed. B. Meltzer and D. Michie, Edinburgh
    University Press.

Nagel E. (1961).   The Structure of Science, Routledge and Keegan
      Paul.

Scott, G.L. (1984).   'Obtaining the structure(s) of a non-rigid body
      from multiple views by maximising perceived rigidity' in
      Proc European Conference on AI, Pisa.

Sloman, A. (1965) 'Functions and rogators', in J.N. Crossley and
      M.A.E. Dummett (eds) Formal Systems and Recursive Func-
      tions, North Holland.

Sloman, A. (1971).   'Interactions between philosophy and artificial
      intelligence', in Artificial Intelligence 2,

Sloman, A. (1978).   The Computer Revolution in Philosophy: Philoso-
      phy Science and Models of Mind, Harvester Press and Humani-
      ties Press.

Sloman, A. (1979).   'The primacy of non-communicative language' in
      The Analysis of Meaning, Procedings 5 ASLIB Informatics
      Conference, ASLIB, London.

Wittgenstein, L. (1922).   Tractatus Logico Philosophicus, Routledge
      and Kegan Paul.

Woods W.A. (1975).   'What's in a link: Foundations for semantic net-
      works', in D.Bobrow and A.Collins (eds) Representation and
      Understanding, Academic Press.

IS A DECISION TREE AN EXPERT SYSTEM?

Simon A. Hayward
STC IDEC
Six Hills House,
London Road,
Stevenage,
Herts.

Abstract

One classic view of intelligent knowledge based
problem solving is that knowledge, particularly heuristic
knowledge, is applied to facilitate search of very large
problem spaces. This gives the paradigm of an intelligent
system as one capable of solving problems which cannot be
handled by "brute force computation". However Expert System
products are now becoming available commercially which generate
or use simple deterministic decision trees to produce
"decisions". These may be treated with scepticism or
indifference as "expert" systems. However neither MYCIN nor
PROSPECTOR, two prototypical Expert Systems, solves a
significant search problem.
It is important for the establishment of both research
objectives and commercial expectations that we further clarify
the function of knowledge in Expert Systems. The paper
attempts to assist this process by distinguishing between the
advantages of formalising knowledge in a computationally
tractable way, and using knowledge to reduce the computational
demands of problem solving.

1. Introduction

As the interest in Expert Systems continues to
increase the question of what defining characteristics are
possessed by such systems continues to haunt us. This concern
manifests itself in a number of ways, ranging from a limited
number of analytical or theoretical papers from specalists in
the field (eg Stefik et al 1982, McDermott 1983) through the
debates about AI methodology (eg Bundy/Olson 1983, 1984, Richie
& Hannah 1984/Lenat & Brown 1984) to press commentary ranging
from enthusiastic to sceptical. Alex D'Agapeyeff (1984) found
in surveying the commercial applications in the UK that it was
necessary to introduce a new term "simpler expert system" to
adequately categorise much activity. This term appears
necessary to describe systems which would be disclaimed by
purists as having no more than a coincidental link with AI,
while they do not appear to have grown from conventional data
processing or software engineering roots.

This situation is indicative of a problem in handling
the boundary (if one exists) between conventional data
processing systems and expert systems. The classifications of
researchers such as Stefik et al (1982) which concentrate on
the complex cases, do not elucidate this point since the
systems which are relevant in defining this boundary lie in
their first category of those with a small solution space,
reliable data and fixed reliable knowledge. This category is
passed over virtually without comment. However, it is at this
end of the spectrum that we must focus in order to answer the
questions of those approaching expert systems from the
perspective of data processing or software engineering, rather
than as AI researchers. It is in this arena that this paper
attempts to make a contribution.

2. Performance   Criteria for "Expert" Systems

It is curious that after about 10 years research in
the field (dated from MYCIN) it is still so difficult to
provide adequate definitions to delimit the categories of
interest. Part of this difficulty is caused by the emphasis on
system performance characteristics. This emphasis is
inevitable and proper since clearly the point of "Expert
Systems" is that they should exhibit "expert" behaviour. The
"definition" given recently by the Stanford school of
researchers (Brachman et al 1983) uses seven "dimensions" all
of which, with one exception, are essentially related to
performance characteristics. The exception is the use of
symbolic manipulation (in contradistinction to numeric
processing). There is also a reference, which the authors
confess to being vague, to problems being sufficiently
difficult or complex, but no explanation of how such complexity
is to be measured.
Important as it is, this emphasis on performance
characteristics is damaging to any taxonomic exercise since any
taxonomy which will help the computer scientist requires some
reference to system structure/internal behaviour i.e. how the
performance is produced (cf Simon 1981). Nevertheless it must
be recognised that the performance criteria cannot be ignored.
A recent trend, more apparent in the UK than the US (News item
1984) has been to abstract certain architectural features from
expert systems, for example rules and backward chaining, and on
this base to build systems which are clearly non-expert in
their performance.

3. Other Expert Systems Characteristics

A further complication in defining Expert Systems is added by another characteristic of these systems. This is the exploratory nature of the development techniques. Sometimes this is presented as a capability for rapid prototyping (Buchanan & Duda 1983) and sometimes as a more radical opportunity for incremental development of systems in little understood problem domains (Shiel 1983). It has been suggested that the power of the "expert systems approach" lies in this characteristic of the development process and not in the final system, which once completed (and thus understood) could be implemented with a conventional language and system architecture (Kowalski 1983).

The final possibility in defining expert systems is that they reflect a paradigm shift as characterised by Kuhn (1970) which opens the possibility of using the computer in "new" ways to carry out tasks not previously considered as candidates for computerisation. In this case a number of events would contribute to the paradigm shift; declarative programming, rule base/control structure division, incremental development, reducing hardware price/performance ratio and so on. However no one of these events is key but together they would contribute to a more general perceptual shift. If this were the case one could not expect to find specific criteria for defining expert systems in terms of performance or internal structure.

In practice all these perceptions are present in varying proportions in different views of the expert systems field. However it is important both for research and commercial exploitation of such systems to attempt to untangle the strands and in particular to answer the question as to whether there are any defining characteristics of expert systems in terms of computational structure or mechanism.

4. Use of Knowledge

One of the original conceptions behind the use of heuristic knowledge in expert systems was that such knowledge enabled a potentially very large problem space to be searched effectively. It was one answer to the problem of combinatorial explosion which affected classic AI tasks. From this grew the knowledge engineering "maxim": 'in the knowledge lies the power' (coined by Feigenbaum). This view grew very naturally from the early DENDRAL experience (Lindsay et al 1980) in which the molecular structure generation algorithm could be constrained using the knowledge of mass spectroscopy experts. However subsequent (now classic) expert systems such as MYCIN, R1 and PROSPECTOR do not follow this pattern.

These systems use specialised knowledge in their respective domains and exhibit powerful problem solving performance but none handles a significant search problem. In these cases the knowledge has ceased to be merely a tool for the control of complexity, but has become the entire basis of the systems performance.

The view of "intelligent systems" developed within the AI tradition suggests that they differ from conventional software by virtue of their ability to handle problems of unconstrained complexity, which are intractable using algorithmic computing. However the achievement of such capability must surely require more than systems which are simply knowledge based. Any useful system must be based on knowledge of some sort. In what sense therefore are MYCIN etc significantly different from conventional systems? The answer to this question is usually sought in the manner in which the knowledge is represented and used. For example the knowledge is explicit rather than implicit; it is held as "small" atoms which can be modified independently of one another; explanations can be generated and so on (cf Fox 1983). While these may well be useful characteristics it is far from obvious that they constitute a qualitative distinction between such systems and conventional systems. It is certainly possible to build substantial rule based systems, for example in the equipment fault diagnosis field (see Hayward 1984) which are deterministic decision trees. These could be programmed in a conventional manner, albeit with the possible loss of the advantages of expert systems for ease of development.

This author would suggest that the significant characteristic of expert systems in this case is not the particular representational or computational mechanism used, but the fact that some representation of the knowledge has been achieved. This is perhaps best illustrated by PROSPECTOR. The power of the system lies in the fact that a geologist's understanding of his field has been represented in a form which can be used as a basis for computation. In the case of PROSPECTOR the sophisticated probabilistic inference net provides a vehicle for the geological knowledge which probably could not have been achieved with conventional programming. However the key to PROSPECTOR'S expert behaviour lies in the skill of this translation into a computable form, not in any intrinsic qualities of the representational mechanism. A similar point can be seen for MYCIN. The various departures from a pure backward chaining rule based model (eg self-referential rules) are not failures to operate within a formalism which has a theoretical justification, rather they are an illustration of the power of a basic computational structure to cope with demands placed on it in performance of a particular task.

If it is accepted that the significance of these classic expert systems lies in the translation of knowledge into a computable form then it is easy to see how a spectrum arises from cases where the translation could not be achieved with conventional approaches, to those where it could be achieved but the expert systems "approach" is easier or more efficient in development terms, to cases where the domains had not previously been considered as a candidate for computerisation. In this last case the availability of the expert systems approach has resulted in a new perspective on the problem, but an Expert System may not in fact be required for its solution. This perspective clarifies a number of related issues. There has been a considerable debate about the nature and demands of the "knowledge engineering" task (eg Nii 1980). Given a spectrum of systems varying in the difficulty of the translation task, knowledge engineering will vary from a simple extension to the software engineer's toolkit, whereby he programs in a different way, to a highly demanding intellectual exercise in which the understanding of AI programming techniques is itself a minor element.

The second issue which can be clarified is the use of expert systems "shells". If the knowledge to be represented is of any real complexity then it is unlikely that it can be constrained within a predefined formalism. If it can then conventional techiques are adequate. The formalism may provide a useful starting point, but it will be essential to have the capability to extend or modify it to meet the demands of the particular knowledge to be represented.

5. Expert Systems and Search

The emphasis above on formalisation of knowledge clearly relates to performance criteria for defining expert systems. However if we return to a focus on how the knowledge is used then this may be more informative with regard to the question of system structure and mechanism.

Given the importance of search in the development of AI and the value originally placed on knowledge as a means of enabling effective search of large, complex state-spaces it is curious that virtually no attention has been paid to the type of search undertaken by individual expert systems and the role which the knowledge of the system plays in facilitating it. The sole exception as far as this author is aware is a paper given by McDermott (1983). This paper analyses some of the systems developed at Carnegie-Mellon University and produces a variety of metrics related to the use of the knowledge in the systems. However there is no theoretical underpinning for these metrics and it is not entirely obvious what they tell one about the systems concerned.

Conventional data processing systems could be
described in terms of search, although this would be unusual,
the reason being that the search performed by a conventional
system is trivial. At each decision node in the system it is
possible to choose a correct state transition (ie. the
programme branch) with certainty.   In the case of expert
systems, and indeed a wider class of AI systems, this is not
the case and the choice of next step is achieved using
heuristic (ie. uncertain) knowledge or by experimentation (ie.
backtracking) or a combination of the two. There is thus a
distinction between knowledge which is embodied in a system for
the purpose of defining the search paths and that which may be
needed to effectively search the space thus defined. In the
classic case of chess problems the knowledge required in the
first case is simply that which defines the legal moves,
whereas in the latter it is that which enables "good" moves to
be chosen. All systems embody knowledge in the first sense,
whether it be PAYE tables or office procedures. Conventional
systems do not use knowledge in the second way. Indeed
conversion of a problem to a form in which an algorithmic
solution can be given may be viewed as converting the problem
solving knowledge from a form which aids search, in the
conventional AI heuristic sense, to that which defines a
deterministic decision tree for solving the problem.

In the case of MYCIN and PROSPECTOR the search is
exhaustive but not trivial. This is because the search paths
are not deterministic. The problem spaces are not
combinatorially explosive, but the search is exhaustive
precisely because the consequences of decisions at each node
are not fully predictable. This is related to the probablistic
character of the assertions built into the systems. If there
were no uncertainty in the application of the knowledge (cf the
discussion of applicability factors by McDermott 1983) then the
search would be trivial and the consequent decision tree could
be coded in any conventional programming language.

This however is not quite the same as saying that an
Expert System is not needed for that particular task. At this
point we must consider the development of the problem solving
system (however undertaken), and this links together the two
dimensions of knowledge as described above. If the items of
knowledge being used in the domain are highly inter-linked,
that is the same piece of knowledge can be relevant in many
situations (ie. at many different decision nodes) or conversely
in a given situation it is difficult (to the point of
impracticability) to define in advance all the items of
knowledge which may need to be considered, then a development
problem occurs. The difficulty here is not in searching the
problem space once defined, but in defining the problem space
to be searched. The interaction of the knowledge may be
sufficiently obscure to require the type of incremental
development facilitated by expert systems development
techniques. This situation would appear to explain the rise of
R1 and the previous failure of conventional methods to solve
the PDP & VAX configuration problem (McDermott 1980).

In looking at the type of knowledge in relation to the search space created it is worth noting that a conventional system may exhibit a large space, because there may be many branch points and very many paths through the programme (witness the difficulty of conventional programme testing). However the state space will normally have a simple structure with nested sub-trees. The extent to which structured design methods are followed will show in the simplicity of form of the decision tree defined by programme. This is the opposite of the sort of tree one would expect to find in a powerful expert system.

Once again what we have here is a spectrum rather than a hard distinction and the need for expert systems techniques when considering marginal applications is likely to be in the eye of the developer (or funder). It may be that even simple problems can be solved more quickly by, for example, programming in OPS5 rather than COBOL. However we are now clearly in the area of debate about declarative v. procedural languages and that in itself is not germane to understanding expert systems.

Regardless of the quantitative rather than qualitative distinction proposed, it is important to appreciate that the distinction can be drawn. There is a danger that expert system techniques will be applied to ever smaller problem spaces. If this happens the original rationale is entirely lost, and the quantum jump involved in building systems requiring non-trivial search is overlooked. This jump arises not because of differences in the methods used to implement the system but because the task of converting the knowledge to a computationally tractable form is very much more difficult, ie. the difference lies in the knowledge not the representational method itself.

References

Bundy A./Ohlsson S (1983, 1984) AISB Newsletter 1983/1984.

Buchanan B.G, Duda R.O. (1983) "Principles of Rule-Based Expert Systems" In "Advances in Computers" Vol 22, ed Yovits M.

Brachman R.J, Amarel S, Engleman C, Engelmore R.S, Feigenbaum E.A, Wilkins D.E. (1983) "What are Expert Systems?" In "Building Expert Systems" ed Waterman, Lenat, Hayes-Roth, Addison Wesley.

D'Agapeyeff A. (1984) "Report to the Alvey Directorate on a Short Survey of Expert Systems in UK Business".

Fox J (1983) "Formal and Knowledge based
Methods in Decision Technology" Proc of 9th
Intnl Conf on Subjective Probability, Utility
and Decision Making, August 1983.

Hayward S.A. (1984) "Diagnostic Expertise and
its use in Commercially Viable Expert Systems"
Paper presented at ECAI 1984.

Kowalski E (1983) Private communication
December 1983.

Kuhn T (1970) "The Structure of Scientific
Revolutions" University of Chicago Press.

Lenat D.B, Brown J.S (1984) "Why AM and
EURISKI Appear to Work" Artifical
Intelligence 23 (1984).

Lindsay R.K, Buchanan B.G, Feigenbaum E.A and
Lederberg J (1980) "Applications of Artifical
Intelligence for Chemical Inference: The DENDRAL
Project" McGraw-Hill.

McDermott J (1980) "R1: The Formative Years",
AI Magazine 2,3.

McDermott J (1983) "Extracting Knowledge from
Expert Systems" Proc. IJCAI 1983.

News item (1984) Expert Systems Vol 1 No 1.

Nii H.P. (1980) "An introduction of Knowledge
Engineering, Blackboard Model, and AGE" HPP
Report HPP-80-29 Stanford University.

Richie G.D, Hanna F.K (1984) "AM: A Case Study in
AI Methodology" Artifical Intelligence 23 (1984).

Shiel B. (1983) "Power tools for Programmers"
Datamation Feb 1983.

Simon H (1981) "Sciences of the Artificial"
2nd ed MIT Press.

Stefic M, Atkins J, Balzer R, Benoit J, Birnbaum L,
Hayes-Roth F, Sacerdoti E. (1982) "The organisation
of expert systems: a prescriptive tutorial"
Artifical Intelligence 18, No. 2.

INTELLIGENT FRONT ENDS

Alan Bundy
Department of Artificial Intelligence
University of Edinburgh
Edinburgh
Scotland

Acknowledgements

This paper was first published in the Pergamon Infotech
State of the Art Report "Expert Systems" Pergamon Infotech Ltd (1984).
I would like to thank Bob Muetzelfeldt, David Probert and
Mike Uschold for their valuable comments on early drafts of this paper.
The research was supported by SERC grant, number GR/C/06226.

Abstract

An intelligent front end is a user-friendly interface to a
software package, which uses Artificial Intelligence techniques to
enable the user to interact with the computer using his/her own
terminology rather than that demanded by the package. Several such
systems exist and provide interfaces for finite element, statistical and
simulation packages, and the area is an important area of growth for
expert systems. In this paper we discuss the techniques required in an
intelligent front end and whether general tools can be provided for
their construction.

1. Introduction

An intelligent front end, IFE, is a kind of expert system.
It is a user-friendly interface to a software package which would
otherwise be technically incomprehensible and/or too complex to be
accessible to many potential users. It will be convenient to use the
term 'package', throughout this paper, to refer to the target of the
IFE, but this term is meant to be interpreted in a very general sense.
It might be a traditional software package, such as a finite element,
statistics or mathematical modelling system, but it might be a database,
a compiler or a computer network.
An intelligent front end builds a model of the user's
problem through a user-oriented dialogue, which is then used to generate
suitable coded instructions for the package. It allows users to explain
their problems in language familiar to them and then translates this
into a language suitable for the software package.
Intelligent front ends are likely to become of major
importance in the immediate future. The falling price of computers has
made it possible for a much wider audience to have access to them. A
large amount of existing software is potentially useful to this
audience, but the audience may not be able to use it. The software
that was built before the advent of cheap computers was designed to be
used by a small elite of computer experts and can be incomprehensible to
the layperson. IFEs promise to act as a translator between this

software and the lay user and, hence, enable the widespread use of
powerful software. If IFEs succeed they will be of major commercial and
social significance.
        The architecture of a typical IFE is given in figure 1-1.
The specification of the user's task or problem is extracted during a
dialogue between the user and the program. Instructions to run the
package are then synthesised from the task specification and the package
is run. The results of the package are then interpreted into the
language of the task specification and explained to the user as part of
the dialogue.

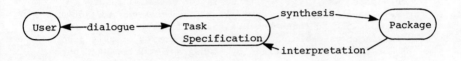

Figure 1-1:   A Typical Intelligent Front End

        The distinguishing characteristic of an intelligent front
end, as opposed to a merely rational or well-engineered front end, is
the explicit representation of the user's problem in the task
specification. It is this which enables the user to state the task in a
different terminology from that used by the package. In addition, an
IFE might also have a model of the user, representing, for instance,
the user's understanding of the package. It might also have a model of
the package, describing what kind of task the package can and cannot
cope with.
        Examples of IFE systems are:

- SACON, (Bennett & Englemore 79), which advises on the use of
  a finite element package;
- ELAS, (Weiss et al 82), which assists in the analysis and
  interpretation of well log data for determining the likely
  presense of hydrocarbons;
-    , (Barstow et al 82), which helps a petroleum scientist
  develop a mathematical model;
- ECO, (Uschold et al 84), which helps an ecologist build
  FORTRAN simulation models;
- ASA, (O'Keefe 82), which helps a psychologist find a
  suitable statistical analysis of his/her experiment;
- REX, (Gale & Pregibon 83), which assists in the use of a
  statistics package; and
- ADVISOR, (Genesereth 79), which is an automated consultant
  for MACSYMA.

        These example IFEs fit the idealised architecture of figure
1-1 with varying degrees of precision. For instance, many of them do
not have an explicit task specification, but instead integrate the
synthesis and dialogue subsystems into one. In fact, figure 1-1 has a
normative as well as a generalising aspect - we will argue that this is
how IFEs must be constructed if they are to free the user from the
language of the package.

In this ideal IFE the following kinds of Artificial
Intelligence and Expert Systems techniques are called for:

- Knowledge Representation, to represent models of the task,
  the user and the package;
- Problem Solving, to synthesise the package instructions from
  the task specification and to interpret the results of the
  package;
- Natural Language Understanding, which may or may not be used
  in the dialogue with the user.

Thus the IFE area involves the integration of several
different areas of AI. It also impinges on non-AI areas of Computer
Science.

- Man/Machine Interaction is concerned with the provision of
  well-engineered front ends and the experience of this area
  must be integrated with the AI techniques to produce the
  best possible system.
- Computer Aided Instruction has considerable experience of
  interfacing software to naive users. Intelligent CAI has
  experimented with techniques for user modelling. This
  experience must be harnessed in IFE building.
- Relational Database work has been moving into the IFE area
  as the user interfaces to large databases have become more
  'user friendly'.

That so many different areas of Computer Science have been moving in the
same direction tends to reinforce the argument for the significance of
this development.

The area of intelligent front ends has been made a research
theme of the UK government sponsored Alvey Programme for Information
Technology. Apart from the general promotion of IFEs, one of the main
aims of this theme is to develop general-purpose software to assist the
building of IFEs. The inspiration of this aim is the provision of
EMYCIN-type, expert system shells, which assist in the building of
diagnosis systems. IFEs are another kind of expert system. Can a
similar shell be provided? Failing this, can a meccano kit of
techniques be provided which can be rapidly assembled into an IFE?
Since the area of IFEs is wide and somewhat vague around the edges, can
we separate out a sharp sub-area for which such shells and/or meccano
kits can be more readily provided? In subsequent sections of this paper
we explore these possibilities, discuss what kind of software would be
required, and whether any of it is already available.

2. Types of Intelligent Front End

IFEs can be of many types depending on the package to be
interfaced to, the kind of user, etc. In this section we discuss some
of the dimensions of variation. This discussion draws on the report of
the first workshop of the Alvey IFE Theme (Bundy & Uschold 83).

In our definition we have assumed some conceptual distance
between the language in which the user prefers to describe his/her
problem and the language in which the operations of the package are

naturally expressed. For instance, in ECO the user specifies his/her problem in ecological terms, e.g. "deer graze grass", "deer biomass depends on respiration", etc, and this problem is represented in the task specification. The target 'package' is a FORTRAN compiler which requires input in the form of loops, conditionals, arithmetic expressions, etc. The task specification represents the user's view of the task and this must be translated into the language of the package by the synthesis subsystem.

In some early IFEs, e.g. SACON, REX and ELAS, the conceptual distance between the user input language and the package was minimal. In SACON and ELAS the small amount of translation required was done implicitly by the EMYCIN and EXPERT production rules, and there was no explicit task specification. Since EMYCIN-type shells* have no explicit mechanism for translation between representations and no explicit representation of the task, they are unlikely to be sufficient as shells for IFEs in which there is a large conceptual distance between user and package.

In future IFEs the conceptual distance between user and package may be so large that a sequence of task representations and translation procedures are required, analogous to the sequence of scene representations and translation procedures used in current vision systems.

The information provided by the user may not be exactly the information required to decide what instructions to give in the package, even after it has been translated into the language of the package. In this case some 'gap bridging' processing will be required. This might be done by inference in the task specification language using, for instance, an EMYCIN-type production rule subsystem. Some 'jumping to conclusions' may be required, which call for non-monotonic or default inference.

In some applications it may be possible to avoid communicating with the user in the language of the package. For instance,

- the user may have to choose between alternative inputs to the package, although even in this it may be possible to present the choice in the user's preferred terminology;
- the user may want to see the output provided by the package, although again the significance of this output might be explained in the user's preferred language; or
- the user may want to be instructed in the direct use of the package.

Another dimension of variation is given by the nature of the input to the package. This can vary from simple, one-line commands to arbitrarily complex computer programs. The more structured the input to the package the more processing is required of the synthesis subsystem.

* By 'EMYCIN-type shells' I mean a package whose inference engine is a production rule system. My assertion about what cannot be done in such systems should be interpreted as assertions about what cannot be straightforwardly done within the spirit of such systems. Most of these things can be done by exploiting tricks or ad hoc patches, but such tricks and patches will not lead directly to an understanding of how to build custom-made IFE tools.

AI planning and automatic programming techniques can sometimes be used
to synthesise such structured package-input. Since EMYCIN-type shells
do not embody such techniques they are unlikely to be sufficient for
IFEs in which the package input is highly structured.

If the IFE is aimed at a range of users of different levels
of skill, or if the user's skill can be expected to improve over the
course of a session, then it will be necessary to make the IFE
adaptable. This can be done in several ways.

(a) Users may have commands at thier disposal which can change
the dialogue subsystem. For instance, the IFE can give more
or less explanation and instruction to the user.
(b) These same commands may be called by the system after it has
interrogated the user about his/her skill level. (REX does
this, for instance.)
(c) The commands may be called by the system after it builds its
own hypothesis about the user's skill on the basis of
his/her performance in using the system.

(b) and (c) make progressively less demands on the user, and thus are
more suitable for the novice. If the default is set for the novice then
(a) also makes no demands on the user. (c) requires a user model to be
formed and maintained. A danger with (c) is that the users may improve
their skill levels faster than the IFE can adapt, resulting in hunting
behaviour.

3. Dialogue Handling

We can divide the problem of dialogue handling into two
parts:

(a) controlling the overall structure of the dialogue; and
(b) determining the mode of the interchanges.

In (a) we are concerned with what questions should be asked
and what answers given, when and by whom. In (b) we are concerned with
whether natural language, graphics, etc should be used to ask and answer
these questions. This factoring of the dialogue handling problem will
simplify the explanation of the range of techniques available.

One popular solution to (a) is to use a menu. This
determines a tree structure for the dialogue. Each non-terminal node
represents a multi-choice question from the program to the user and each
arc represents one of the possible answers to this question, which may
then lead to a further question. The terminal nodes represent actions
to be taken, e.g. instructions to be sent to the package, or information
to be stored in the task specification. The standard menu solution to
(b) is for the computer to ask the questions in the form of canned text
specifying a character for each of the possible replies, and for the
user to respond with one of these characters. Many IFE systems, e.g.
ELAS, REX,   , make use of menu-driven dialogue, but with much more
complex interactions with the user at each node.

3.1 The Control of the Dialogue

        Menu trees can be generalised to a directed graph structure,
which we will call the transition net (see figure 3-1). Joins in the
transition net will mean that there are alternative routes to the same
question. Loops will give the possibility of repeated asking of the
same question (we hope in different contexts). The current node of the
transition net summarises the findings of the program so far and allows
subsequent dialogue to be interpreted in the light of this context,
which keeps that dialogue brief. Workers in MMI, (Alty 83, Edmonds 82),
have produced aids to help the IFE builder design transition nets. For
instance, path algebras provide a formalism for representing nets and
these algebras are employed in tools for interactive net design.

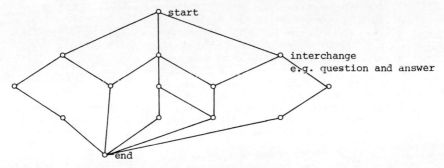

Figure 3-1:   A Transition Net

        A further generalisation of menus is to generate the
transition net dynamically as a byproduct of a problem solving process.
For instance, the search tree generated during a run of EMYCIN can be
regarded as a transition net. The terminal nodes represent questions
to be asked of the user or answered by laboratory data. The non-
terminal nodes represent questions to be answered by appeal to
production rules. SACON uses this technique. Dynamic generation of the
transition net means that it can be responsive to context and can be
radically different on different occasions (although each net generated
can be thought of as a subnet of some, possibly infinite, master net).
The cost of this flexibility is that the transition net cannot be
designed per se, but that design is restricted to the production rules,
etc, which generate the net.
        In all the above techniques the initiative remains with the
program. Users are constrained to answer the questions asked by the
program in an order determined by the program. The input from the user
is kept within narrow limits. This eases the job of the program
designer and may be welcomed by the novice user. However, it may not be
suitable for some kinds of IFE. In some domains the transition net may
not be a suitable representation of the contextual information required
to process the user's dialogue, for instance, this context may not vary
much during the session. Thus, it may be better for the user to have
the initiative and volunteer information for the program to store as the
task specification. We will call such a dialogue user-driven, because
the program does not know what is coming next. In user-driven dialogues

the mode of the user input must be constrained, or the program designer
will have an impossible job. ECO has a user-driven dialogue system.
Hybrid systems are sometimes desirable, especially where the
IFE is intended for users at different skill levels. The novice user
may prefer to be guided through the transition net, whereas the expert
user may prefer to use a user-driven dialogue to jump straight to the
desired node of the transition net.

In many IFEs the dialogue is controlled as a side effect of
some more dominant process, e.g. an inference process or the synthesis
of the input to the package. The ENYCIN dialogue can be thought of in
this way. We will see another example in section 4. Intelligent
Browsers provide another example. In RABBIT (Tou et al 82), for
instance, the dominant process is the attempt by the program to select
a few examples from a large database on the basis of the user's,
possibly changing, description of his/her needs. The dialogue is a
process of changing the user's description in response to the examples
provided by the system at each stage.

3.2 The Mode of the Interchange

We now turn to (b) - the mode of the interchange. This is
one of the main areas where the IFE designers must look to other
disciplines for help. The techniques chosen will depend on the domain
of the IFE and not much can be said in general, except to survey some of
the possibilities.

In addition to the keyboard input and VDU output available
on most computers, special hardware might be used to allow input/output
of graphics, touch screen, speech, etc. Each of these is a major area
of research in its own right and will not be dealt with here. In the
discussion below we restrict ourselves to text input/output. This may
range from simple canned text to natural language.

The traditional menu system outputs multi-choice questions
as canned text and the user responds with single character input. The
context is completely set by the current node in the transition net and
the user has no initiative at all.

To make use of a context, external to the transition net,
the program output must be dynamically generated in some language.
Similarly, to allow the user more initiative there must be a non-
trivial, user input language. These languages can be natural or
artificial. There is a continuum of possible languages - from a formal,
logical language, like predicate calculus, to a natural language, like
English. An artificial language which reads like a subset of English,
e.g. REX's pseudo-English query language, can combine the ease of
parsing of a formal language with the readability of natural language.

If the range of allowed user inputs is narrow then a formal
language may be more appropriate than a natural one for the following
reasons:

- Allowing some natural language input may mislead the novice
  user into thinking that any natural language input is
  allowed.
- Formal language statements are often shorter than the
  corresponding natural language ones and put a lighter burden
  on the non-expert typist.

- A simple _formal_ grammar is easily learned by users.

The tradeoffs between the two will depend on:

- the training time available for users to learn any formal
  language;
- the frequency with which users use the system;
- their typing skill;
- the range of user input required; and
- the availability of a suitable natural language parser.

This formal grammar can be as simple as a few phrases or
words. For instance, when answering SACON's question: "What is the
material composing the total wing?" the user is restricted to a range of
phrases like "high-strength-aluminium". SACON can be requested to list
the acceptable replies. ECO uses a simple template grammar. An example
template is: "<state-variable> depends on <process>", where <state-
variable> might be "deer-biomass" and <process> might be "respiration".
        Some IFEs, e.g. ELAS,   , use form filling or editing as
the mode of interchange. Several windows may be displayed on a bit map
display. One of these may describe the current overall state of the
dialogue. One may offer a menu for moving to another node of the
transition net. One may be a form with blank entries to be filled in
with information from the user, or with partially filled entries to be
edited by the user. This mode can be very natural and easy to use if the
forms correspond to the way in which the user usually thinks of his/her
problem, cf spreadsheets.
        The ADVISOR consultation system for MACSYMA avoids a lot of
explicit dialogue with the user by analysing the his/her initial attempt
to use MACSYMA. From this analysis, ADVISOR builds a plan of the user's
intentions which is then fleshed out by an explicit dialogue to form the
task specification. REX avoids explicit dialogue by analysing the
user's statistical data to determine whether its properties fit the
preconditions of the various statistical techniques available.

4. Translation, Synthesis and Inference

The synthesis subsystem has several related jobs:

1. to translate the task specification into the language
   required by the package;
2. to synthesise the structure required by the package as
   input; and
3. to fill in any gaps in the information provided by the user.

The first two of these jobs can often be tackled together by
using problem-reduction/planning/automatic-programming techniques to
instantiate and link together methods which represent package
operations. The last of these jobs calls for inference techniques, e.g.
deduction, production rules, non-monotonic reasoning, etc.
        For instance, suppose the package is a statistics package.
The methods might represent different statistical operations each with
its own preconditions and effects, and the instructions that will be
sent to the package. The language of the preconditions and effects will

be the same as that used in the task specification, whereas the language
of the instructions will be that used by the package. Thus the methods
provide a bridge between the two languages.
        To initiate the synthesis process the user's goals, stored
in the task specification, are compared with the effects of each method
until a match is found. Where there is a choice of method an
intelligent browser may be used to assist the user select a method. The
instructions associated with the method are then placed into the
emerging plan and the preconditions are either seen to be satisfied in
the task specification or are set up as new subgoals. The process
recurses until all the subgoals are true in the task specification. At
any stage, inference may be needed to bridge the gap between the
information in the task specification and that required by the methods.
Where the task specification does not already contain the required
information the dialogue handler may be triggered to request it from the
user. Thus the synthesis process provides an architecture for the whole
IFE - calling the dialogue, inference and translation processes as
subroutines, as required. The whole process is represented
diagrammatically in figure 4-1.

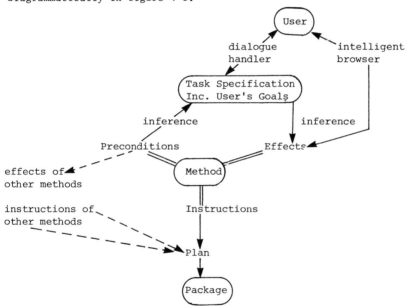

Figure 4-1:   The Process of Synthesising the Package Input

        , ECO, ASA and ADVISOR use this kind of means/ends
analysis driven synthesis of the input to the package. SACON and ELAS
use production rules to bridge the gap between the user's problem
description and the package input. The MECHO system used both
means/ends analysis and inference rules to synthesise sets of equations
from an English specification of a mechanics problem, (Bundy et al 79).

The same basic process can be used if the package requires: equations to solve; or procedures to interpret; or a plan to execute. The matching of the methods to the task specification via inference bridges the gap between the information provided by the user and that needed by the package and enables the translation into the package language and the building of the structured input that the package requires.

Production rules can also be used to translate, but are limited in their ability to synthesise. Translation can be done by having the condition of a rule match the task specification or input from the user and having the action of a rule call the package. ELAS works like this. However, the production rule system would have to be enhanced to enable the rules to build up a structured input to the package, rather than a series of simple commands.

5. Conclusion

Intelligent front ends are a commercially and socially important type of expert system requiring the integration of several areas of AI and Computer Science. This importance has been recognised by the UK Alvey programme.

The ease with which IFEs can be built will depend on the tools available to build them. Ideally, we would like to provide an expert system shell like the EMYCIN family of shells for diagnosis. EMYCIN itself has been used as an IFE shell, e.g. in SACON, but it has limitations as a general IFE shell. In particular, it does not have a problem reduction component which would enable it to handle two of the jobs of the sythesis subsystem: the translation of the task specification into the language of the package; and the synthesis of a structured input to the package. Nor does it provide for an explicit task specification.

But just as EMYCIN has proved an over-restrictive framework for the development of many diagnosis sytems, so an IFE shell is unlikely to be universally useful. For instance, if the IFE requires a broad-bandwidth communication with the package, e.g. with access to the package's error handler, then any IFE shell would require extensive tailoring and modification. More promising would be the provision of a meccano kit of procedures and subsystems which can be drawn from during the building of the system.

Among the candidates for IFE meccano kit are:

- Knowledge representation languages, e.g. relational/assertional database, frames, inheritance hierarchies.
- Procedures for dialogue handling, e.g. natural language front end, transition net building tools.
- Procedures for synthesis and inference, e.g. problem reduction, planner, automatic programmer, deduction engine, production rules, non-monotonic logic system.

Many of these are generally useful AI tools. Further research is required to see if they can be specially tailored to the needs of IFE. I suspect that the IFE area is coherent enough that it will be both possible and beneficial to develop special software for it.

References

Alty, J.L. (1983). Path Algebras - a useful CAI/CAL analysis technique. Research Report 125, University of Strathclyde.

Barstow, D., Duffy, R., Smoliar, S., Vestal, S. (1982). An Overview of PHINIX. In National Conference on Artificial Intelligence. Pittsburg, Pennsylvania.

Bennett, James S. & Englemore, Robert (1979). SCACON: A Knowledge-Based Consultant for Structural Analysis. In Proceedings of the Sixth IJCAI, International Joint Conference on Artificial Intelligence, pp. 47-9. Tokyo, Japan.

Bundy, A. & Uschold, M. (ed.) (1983). Intelligent Front End Workshop. SERC. Available from Mr W.P. Sharpe, Rutherford Appleton Laboratory, Didcot, Oxon, OX11 0QX.

Bundy, A., Byrd, L., Luger, G., Mellish, C., Milne, R. & Palmer, M. (1979). Solving Mechanical Problems Using Meta-Level Inference. In Proceedings of IJCAI-79, ed. B.G. Buchanan, pp. 1017-27. International Joint Conference on Artificial Intelligence. Reprinted in Expert Systems in the microelectronic age, ed. D. Michie. Edinburgh: Edinburgh University Press. Also available from Edinburgh as DAI Research Papre No. 112.

Edmonds, E.A. (1982). The man-computer interface: a note on concepts and design. Int. J. Man-Machine Studies, 16, 231-6.

Gale, William & Pregibon, Daryl (1983). Building an Expert Interface. Bell Telephone Laboratories, Murray Hill N.J., Unpublished.

Genereseth, M. (1979). The Role of Plans in Automated Consultation. In Proceedings of IJCAI-79, ed. G Buchanan, pp. 311-19. International Joint Conference on Artificial Intelligence.

O'Keefe, R.A. (1982). Automated Statistical Analysis. Working Paper 104, Dept of Artificial Intelligence, Edinburgh.

Tou, F.N., Williams, M.D., Fikes, R., Henderson, A. & Malone, T. (1982). RABBIT: An intelligent database assistant. In Procs. of AAAI-82, ed. D.L. Waltz, American Association for Artificial Intelligence.

Uschold, M., Harding, N., Muetzelfeldt, R. & Bundy, A. (1984). An Intelligent Front End for Ecological Modelling. Research Paper 223, Dept of Artificial Intelligence, Edinburgh. Also in Procs of ECAI-84.

Weiss, S., Kullkowski, C., Apte, C., Uschold, M., Patchett, J., Brigham, R., & Spitzer, B. (1982). Building Expert Systems for Controlling Complex Programs. In Proceedings of AAAI-82, pp. 322-6. American Assocaition for Artificial Intelligence.

TUTOR - A PROTOTYPE ICAI SYSTEM

Davies N.G., Dickens S.L., Ford L.
Logica UK Ltd, Betjeman House,
104 Hills Road, Cambridge CB2 1LQ

Abstract

Results from ICAI research have a greater bearing on expert systems development than is generally appreciated. The provision of an intelligent interface for an ICAI system that operates in tutorial mode is crucial since it must be able to support a dialogue in natural language and maintain a user model of students' states of knowledge if it is to teach sensibly. As the use of expert systems becomes more widespread with the increase in naive users that implies, an intelligent front-end is essential for a system which operates in consultation mode.

This paper describes TUTOR, a prototype ICAI system. Emphasis is on those parts which form the front-end : natural language interface, student model and teaching strategy. On the basis of an extensive sample dialogue TUTOR's current capabilities are evaluated.

1. Introduction and Background

With the current interest in ES the question arises whether the expertise in such systems can be used for educational purposes. There are only two systems of any note that attempt to 'transfer' expertise in the form of a knowledge base to users - namely, GUIDON (Clancey, 1979), and SOPHIE (Brown, Burton, and de Kleer, 1982). The TUTOR project is thus to be seen as a continuation of this line of research.

The overall project aim is to develop a prototype framework which can be adapted to provide instruction for a wide variety of subjects. Initially, for experimental purposes, it is being applied to a part of the Highway Code and is being developed on a VAX 11/750 in ESIL Prolog (ESIL, 1983).

2. System Overview

2.1 Domain

TUTOR aims to teach a student the
appropriate driving actions when in the vicinity of
traffic lights.
The variables that the student must take
into account are: traffic light colour setting;
distance; road condition; traffic condition and speed.
These allow the subject to be expressed by 33 rules in
all. A typical rule is:
  IF   you are near the lights
       and they are amber
       and the road is dry
       and you are in traffic
  THEN slow down.
TUTOR's task is made difficult because it
must sensibly choose from about 100 possible scenes to
present in order to best foster learning.

2.2 Natural Language Interface (NLI)

The NLI is based on a semantic grammar
(Burton and Brown, 1977) and is implemented in the
definite clause grammar (DCG) formalism (Pereira and
Warren, 1980). It handles 19 sentence types and
records its understanding of them in a discourse
history. Sentences may originate from either the
student or TUTOR. This latter point is important
since in other systems, such as SOPHIE, it is
customary for the NLI to only be concerned with the
user's input. Our decision to design the interface in
this way was motivated by two considerations:
a. establishment of communication protocols;
b. desirability of uniform maintenance of the
discourse history.
A characteristic of interactive systems is
the predominant verbosity of the system and the
difference in permitted expressive power of system and
user. We thus find systems displaying a lengthy text
of natural language and requiring a one-word answer
from the user, or even an expression in LISP or Prolog
notation. By constraining all communications through
the NLI we ensure:
- that the system does not become too verbose (since
to provide for lengthy sentences places a strain on
the NLI);
- that the student can perceive grammatically
acceptable communications by reference to TUTOR's
output (and thus learns the 'Lingua Franca').

Maintenance of a discourse history of both TUTOR's and the student's communications is desirable in the resolution of anaphora and ellipsis. However, our long-term aim is that TUTOR will be able to update the discourse history without recourse to the NLI.

2.3 Student Model

The importance of a student model in computer-aided instruction has long been recognised (Self, 1974) and its use in ICAI systems which incorporate a body of expertise is discussed elsewhere (Ford, 1984).
In our model there are two types of record:
- concept belief;
- cluster belief.
In the first of these we record success or failure on the part of the student to answer correctly a question which requires knowledge of a concept, e.g. light setting.
Prior protocol analysis revealed that the tutor taught 'clusters' of rules. For example, the tutor taught one 'basic' rule for when the student was far from the lights and a number of 'exception' rules to it. We have labelled these 'basic' and 'exception' rules as rule clusters.
The idea of rule clusters is more than of passing interest since a criticism of rule representation schemes is that they do not reflect how rules fit together (Clancey, 1983). By explicitly representing rule linkages TUTOR is afforded the possibility of reasoning about the clusters and taking appropriate tutorial action if the student shows a weakness in a particular cluster, for example.
Since each rule of the subject is associated with a particular rule cluster we are able to record cluster success or failure in a similar way to concept success or failure in the student model. For each of the two types of student model record a history of the last three assignments is maintained although it is only the most recent that presently influences tutorial action.

2.4 Teaching Strategy

The teaching strategy of the prototype deals with dialogue management; placing requests on the teaching generator for new scenes to be generated; and updating the student model.
In its dialogue management rôle the teaching strategy caters for the 19 sentence types handled by

the NLI.   These sentence types can be categorised as:
scenarios, queries, questions, answers and dialogue
pragmatics.

2.5 Teaching Generator

        The function of the teaching generator is to
generate a new scene consistent with:
- a genetic graph;
- the student model.
The genetic graph, first described by Goldstein
(1982), is a directed graph that is pre-determined
prior to system implementation. It is therefore a
static data structure. In our case, each node in the
graph represents a unique rule cluster, thus the graph
contains one node for each rule cluster. Linking the
nodes are arcs that are: directed; ranked; and
labelled. Each node will normally have many incoming
and outgoing arcs. The outgoing arcs form two
partitions. Arcs are labelled 'correct answer' in one
partition, and 'incorrect answer' in the other. The
ranking of arcs within a partition establishes a
priority in pursuing paths through the graph.
The teaching generator uses the graph to pursue those
rule clusters which the student has not mastered, and
is thus sensitive to:
- genetic knowledge (how new knowledge is acquired
from old);
- belief about a student's knowledge.

3.   Results

        We present below a fairly extensive dialogue
that has been achieved. 'Tn' and 'Sn' have been added
to what would appear on the screen to indicate the
originator of a message (tutor/student). We use 'n'
to enable specific messages to be referenced in
section 4. Graphic displays consist of a road
junction with windows showing the state of the lights,
road condition, etc.

Dialogue

T1: Welcome to TL2 TUTOR.
     I shall try to teach you about aspects of the
     Highway Code.
     Imagine that you are driving a car and ...
     you are far from the lights.
     the lights are green.
     the road is dry.
     there is no other traffic.

```
      what should you do?
S2:   how fast am i travelling?
T3:   i do not understand.
S4:   help.
T5:   the actions you can give as an answer are:
      continue; slow down; stop; go; get ready; and
      wait.
S6:   i would slow down.
T7:   no.
      you are still some way from the lights and road
      and traffic conditions are safe.
      have another try.
S8:   continue.
T9:   that is correct.
      you are now near the lights.
      the lights have changed to amber.
      there is now traffic ahead.
      what would you do?
S10:  slow down.
T11:  that is correct.
      you are now at the lights.
      the lights have changed to red.
      there is now traffic behind you.
      what would you do?
S12:  am i stationary?
T13:  you are moving.
S14:  is there traffic in front of me?
T15:  i do not understand.
S16:  is there traffic ahead of me?
T17:  there is traffic behind you.
S18:  i would slow down.
T19:  no.
      remember you are right at the lights.
      have another try.
S20:  stop.
T21:  that is correct.
      the lights have changed to red and amber.
      there is now traffic ahead of and behind you.
      you are now stationary.
      what would you do?
S22:  wait.
T23:  no.
      the lights will soon change to green.
      have another try.
S24:  help.
T25:  the actions you can give as an answer are:
      continue; slow down; stop; go; get ready and
      wait.
S26:  get ready.
T27:  that is correct.
      the lights have changed to green.
      what would you do?
```

```
S28: am i still at the lights and am i still
     stationary?
T29: i do not understand.
S30: am i at the lights and am i still stationary?
T31: you are at the lights.
     you are stationary.
S32: what are the lights?
T33: i do not understand
S34: are the traffic lights red and amber?
T35: the lights are green.
S36: where were we?
T37: you are at the lights.
     the lights are green.
     the road is dry.
     there is traffic ahead of and behind you.
     you are stationary.
S38: i would go.
T39: that is correct.
     you are now far from the lights.
     the lights are red and amber.
     what would you do?
S40: is the road dry?
T41: the road is dry.
S42: i would continue.
T43: that is correct.
     you are now near the lights.
     the lights have changed to green.
     there is now traffic ahead.
     what would you do?
S44: i thought there was traffic beind.
T45: i do not understand.
S46: i thought there was traffic behind.
T47: the traffic has turned off.
S48: i would slow down.
T49: that is correct.
     you are now at the lights.
     the lights have changed to amber.
     there is now no other traffic on the road.
     what would you do?
S50: i dont know
T51: you should stop
     because traffic conditions are safe for you to
     stop.
     the road has become wet.
     what would you do?
S52: i thought it was dry.
T53: there has been a thunderstorm.
S54: is there no other traffic and are the lights red?
T55: the lights are amber.
     there is no other traffic.
S56: if the lights were red i would stop.
```

```
T57: that is correct.
     but
     the lights are amber.
     so what should you do?
S58: what if the lights were green?
T59: you should continue.
     going back to the scenario i presented.
     what would you do?
S60: where were we?
T61: you are at the lights.
     the lights are amber.
     the road is wet.
     there is no other traffic.
     you are moving.
S62: okay
T63: what should you do?
S64: i would stop.
T65: no.
     you are right at the lights and the road is wet.
     have another try.
S66: i dont know.
T67: you should continue
     because with a wet road you would not be able to
     stop safely.
     there is now traffic behind you.
     what should you do?
S68: if it was dry i would stop.
T69: that is correct.
     but
     the road is wet.
     so what should you do?
S70: if it was dry i would stop.
T71: that is correct
     but
     the road is wet.
     so what should you do?
S72: what should i do?
T73: you should continue.
S74: why?
T75: because with a wet road you would not
     be able to stop safely.
```

4. Conclusions

Perhaps a useful way to evaluate the
prototype is to relate the dialogue in section 3 to
some of the issues that an ideal system should
address.

4.1 Model of the Expert

TUTOR evidently contains <u>some</u> expert knowledge of the domain. It is able to evaluate students' answers [T7, T9 etc.] and provide its own answers to a scene [T51, T67]. It can also answer queries about a scene [T13, T17, T31, T55] and relate scene changes to real world concepts [T47, T53]. Furthermore, TUTOR can justify an answer to a scene [T75] and explain why a student's answer is wrong [T23, T65].

But TUTOR's knowledge in all these respects is somewhat limited. It lacks a large body of domain knowledge that a student would undoubtedly wish to refer to. For example, TUTOR can only distinguish between 'moving' and 'stationary' [T13] – it has no real knowledge of speed [S2]. TUTOR also does not understand concepts such as braking distance, reversing, relative distance of the student's car and other traffic, and the driving actions of other traffic.

4.2 Human-Like Reasoning

TUTOR has the simplest of inference engines which relies heavily on pattern-matching. In determining the driving action for a particular scene TUTOR merely maps scene features on a rule set to determine the appropriate rule, and hence the driving action. We intend to explicitly represent the underlying causal model of the subject domain, thus affording TUTOR the possibility of providing more human-like reasoning when presenting explanations to the student for his wrong answers or justifications for its own recommended driving action.

4.3 Give and Take Problems

TUTOR exhibits some capability in this respect. It primarily 'gives' problems [T1, T9, T11 etc] but it can 'take' them, particularly when they are related to the current scene [S58, S72]. In practice a student can provide a completely new scene although this is not demonstrated in the dialogue. Presently, TUTOR returns to <u>its</u> problem as soon as it has given the answer to the student's problem, thus denying the student an opportunity to quiz TUTOR on its solution [T59].

4.4 "What if" Facility

The student is able to test his own ideas in two ways. Firstly, he can ask TUTOR what it would do in a scene he has (partially) constructed [S58]; and secondly he can offer his own solution to a scene of his choosing and ask TUTOR to evaluate his answer [S56, S68]. TUTOR's weakness in both situations is that it is too anxious to return to its own scene, thus denying further exploration by the student who may wish to specify another scene based on his earlier one.

4.5 Student Model

There are problems in representing the student's knowledge in terms of concepts (scene features) and rule clusters. Neither category of which can realistically be said to model the student's knowledge.
A further criticism of TUTOR's student model stems from the fact that it only records students' knowledge of the subject domain. There are other types of knowledge that it could usefully contain. An obvious candidate is the knowledge of the various facilities that TUTOR offers (in terms of conditional answers, scene modifications, the help facility and so on) and how they can be used. Thus we can envisage TUTOR presenting T5 immediately after T3 simply because the student has input an unparsable sentence and the student has yet to use the 'help' facility. In this way TUTOR could reveal all the facilities available to the student at appropriate points in a session.

4.6 Reasonable English Interface

TUTOR has a natural language interface, albeit for a small subset of language. Features of the interface are:
- ability to deal with multiple expressions of the same thing [cf S6, S10];
- ability to recognise compound semantic terms (e.g. traffic lights [S34];
- resolution of anaphora [S52];
- ability to handle co-ordination [S30].
Even with these facilities, however, its scope could be improved [cf S14, S16]. Also the NLI cannot deal intelligently with unexpected input, even when it is of limited semantic significance [cf S28, S30]. All input from the student is of course typed and thus prone to mistyping (also all students are human and

thus prone to mis-spelling) but the NLI does not
presently handle these phenomena [S44].

5. Summary

A prototype ICAI system has been described
which addresses the problems associated with providing
a user interface which is sensitive to the needs and
the current state of knowledge of the user. On a
dedicated VAX 11/750 response times vary between 2 to
16 secs with most responses taking 9 secs.
Since this paper was prepared an enhanced
prototype has been implemented which substantially
overcomes the problems identified in section 4.

Acknowledgements

This work has been carried out with the
support of Procurement Executive, Ministry of
Defence.
We have benefited substantially from
consultations with Steve Bevan, Bran Boguraev, Rod
Johnson, Squadron Leader Dave Lowry, Tim O'Shea, and
John Self, although neither the views in this paper
nor the limitations of TUTOR are attributable to
them.

References

Brown, J.S., Burton, R.R., and de Kleer, J. (1982)
'Pedagogical natural language and knowledge
engineering techniques in SOPHIE I, II and III', in D.
Sleeman and J.S. Brown (eds), Intelligent Tutoring
Systems, Academic Press.

Burton, R.R. and Brown, J.S. (1977) 'Semantic
Grammar: A technique for constructing natural language
interfaces to instructional systems', BBN Rep. No.
3587, Bolt Beranek and Newman, Cambridge, Mass.

Clancey, W.J. (1979) 'Tutoring rules for guiding a
case method dialogue', Int J Man-Mach Stud,11,190-202.

Clancey, W.J. (1983) 'The epistemology of a
rule-based expert system - a framework for
explanation', Artificial Intelligence,20,215-251.

Duda, R.O., Hart, P.E., Barrett, P., Gaschnig, J.,
Konologe, K., Reboh, R. and Slocum, J. (1978)
'Development of the Prospector system for mineral
exploration', Final Report, SRI International, Menlo
Park, CA.

Expert Systems International Ltd. (1983) ' VMS
PROLOG-1 Reference Manual', ESIL, Oxford.

Ford, L. (1984) 'Intelligent Computer-Aided
Instruction', in M. Yazdani and A. Narayanan (eds),
'Artificial Intelligence: human effects', Ellis
Horwood.

Goldstein, I.P. (1982) 'The genetic graph: a
representation for the evolution of procedural
knowledge', in D. Sleemnan and J.S. Brown (eds),
Intelligent Tutoring Systems, Academic Press.

Pereira, F. and Warren, D. (1980) 'Definite clause
grammars for language analysis - a survey of the
formalism and a comparison with augmented transition
networks', Artificial Intelligence,13,231-278.

Self, J. (1974) 'Student models in computer-aided
instruction', Int J Man-Mach Stud,6,261-276.

Shortliffe, E.H. (1976) 'Computer-based medical
consultations : MYCIN', North Holland.

LOGIC PROGRAMMING FOR THE LAW

W P Sharpe
Rutherford Appleton Laboratory

Abstract

         A report is given of a practical investigation into the
use of Prolog to represent legislation. The superficial correspondence
between legislative rules and logic is examined in the context of
building a pilot consultation system for the Statutory Sick Pay
legislation. It is shown that exploiting the surface correspondence
does not lead to a system of any significant power. Some of the
objectives that must be set for the design of an effective system are
discussed and the extent to which system building requires traditional
'programming' as well as 'knowledge engineering' is demonstrated.

1.   Introduction

         This paper reports on a practical investigation that was
undertaken into the representation of legislation using PROLOG as a
logic programming language. The piece of legislation chosen was the
Statutory Sick Pay (SSP) provisions contained in the Social Security
and Housing Benefits Act (1982) and associated SSP Regulations (1982).
This was chosen because of the widespread attention it received in the
computer press at the time of its introduction. Since it concerned
pay-roll programs of DP departments its provisions had to be
incorporated into those programs, which are written in traditional DP
languages (usually COBOL). The legislation was strongly criticised by
the DP community because of its complexity; it was said to be both
difficult to understand and difficult to implement. This legislation
therefore suggested itself as a suitable test-bed for the techniques of
knowledge based programming for which much is claimed for their ability
to tackle complex problems. The choice of logic programming language
was also quite natural. Regulations are expressed as rules, and indeed
Allen (1979) has proposed that a more explicit and carefully structured
representation of rules be used for the law. Logic is a natural and
powerful expressive tool for representing rules and would therefore
seem to be an obvious choice. PROLOG was the only practical system
available, and there is some interest in finding its limitations as a
logic programming language; but that was a secondary objective to
exploring how readily the logic rule approach could generate a system
of useful capability within the time constraints of the project.

The project was concerned not only with using the rule based approach to legislation but also with testing how readily the logic rules could be derived directly from the written legislation and how close they could remain to it while acquiring some useful problem solving ability. From one point of view one could argue that since the written law is not tailored to any one of its many domains and methods of application nor should its machine representation be. One would like to believe that the ability of logic to provide executable specifications would mean that even if this level of generality is not achieved it would at least be possible to represent the legislation once and include problem solving expertise by purely additive knowledge engineering. The project therefore started with this naive position and went through the following stages:

(1)   Direct representation of rules as close to their written form as possible with no particular problem task in mind. Identification of limitations.

(2)   Representation of rules in a form tailored to a specific top level problem goal in the style of the Supplementary Benefit program by Hammond (1983), but still keeping as close to the written form of the legislation as possible.

(3)   Representation of the legislation in a form powerful enough to tackle a number of real world case histories. The example problems were taken from the Employers' guide to SSP produced as an explanatory document by the DHSS.

In the course of this evolution the general target was a system that could be consulted in a fairly general and 'intelligent' way about the provisions of the legislation. As the project progressed it became apparent that to build such a system three categories of information would need to be explicitly handled. The inclusion of each type of information entailed going beyond the straightforward translation of the written legislative rules into logic rules, demonstrating that the natural match between the domain and the formalism was superficial only.

Firstly, the law is in general definitional rather than algorithmic in character. The definition of a concept is given rather than a method of discovering or establishing an instance of that concept. We may compare it with a **specification** of sortedness as distinct from an expert sorting algorithm, as discussed by Kowalski (1983). In the case of the law we are interested in preserving the original definition, alongside any problem solving strategic knowledge we have to bring to bear. In the British Nationality Act program developed at Imperial College (personal communication) it appears that the additional knowledge can be added as additional rules rather than as a modification of the definitional rules. Such a neat distinction proved impossible to maintain for SSP. The relationship between the problem solving knowledge and the definitional law is similar to that between the 'heuristic' and 'causal' rules in Clancey's (1983) analysis of MYCIN. The law is supposed to be a set of rules to which the behaviour of society will conform, it is a model against which a particular case should be made to fit. The description of the model however is not the best heuristic for diagnosing the peculiar characteristics of a specific case.

Secondly, to support our problem solving rules we need to establish some underlying conceptual framework for them to handle. The need for this in the representation of case law has been convincingly

shown by McCarty (1980) in his TAXMAN programs. The ill-structured
nature of case law comes from the great many ground facts relevant in
any new case and the 'open textured' nature of the high level concepts
involved in legal reasoning. Uncovering an appropriate conceptual
structure is the major component of McCarty's work and we find we must
undertake the same task for statute law. We cannot assume that because
the law is written down that there is no knowledge acquisition problem
in representing it. This conceptual framework will have to encompass
both common world concepts, of time periods, events, etc, and as our
system becomes more ambitious the social context which gives the law
its validity as a set of 'norms'. Studying this requirement will help
us understand the way we might design a system that can answer
questions both about the law, and about its application to cases.
Questions of the first type are:

>"What is the law on X?"
>"How does pregnancy affect entitlement to sick pay?"
>"What can I do if ...?"

Questions of the second type are:

>"What does the law prescribe about X in this case?"
>"What SSP is due for 12 May given ..."

The third type of knowledge to emerge as requiring
separate and explicit treatment was the knowledge required to produce
sensible dialogues during a consultation. Hammond (1983) has discussed
how, using the Query-the-User facilities (Sergot 1983), predicates can
be declared 'askable' to indicate that information could be asked of
the user when required. This 'call by need' approach was found to be
inadequate in its simple form for this project. At the minimum it
appears to be sensible to be able to generalise a specific question, eg
instead of asking "Was <person> sick on 12 May?" we would ask "How long
was <person> sick for after 12 May?" Specific problems that arose are
discussed later with a sketch of a solution in this case.
A consultation system that was to be used by a benefit assessment
officer in claimant interviews would certainly have to have a solution
to this problem.

This project has concentrated on the practical investigation of the
first two of the above three types of knowledge, with some observations
on the third. The remainder of the chapter describes the project
according to the three stages described above. Less than a third of
the SSP legislation was tackled in this study - that part directly
concerned with determining entitlement. The remaining two thirds range
over wide areas, such as records to be maintained by employers,
determination of disputes etc. In general these other sections possess
much less logical structure than the main part concerned with defining
the essential conditions of entitlement. To tackle them would raise
the problems of the three types of knowledge by an order of complexity
and would certainly also entail tackling representation of the deontic
concepts.

2.   The "Direct" Aproach

In order to qualify as a day for which SSP is due a day
must meet three basic conditions and must not be excluded by reason of
any of a number of supplementary conditions; the structure of the
legislation expressed in the first three sections of the Act is as
follows:

    employee_is_entitled_to_SSP_for(Day) if
            part_of_a_period_of_incapacity_for_work(Day) and
            within_a_period_of entitlement(Day) and
            is_a_qualifying_day(Day) and
            not is_excluded_from_SSP(Day).

We will consider in more detail the first of these three conditions.
Two rules contain the essential definition of a period of incapacity
for work (piw):

2 (2) In this Part "period of incapacity for work" means any period of
       four or more consecutive days, each of which is a day of
       incapacity for work.
2 (3) Any two periods of incapacity for work which are separated by a
       period of not more than two weeks shall be treated as a single
       period of incapacity for work.

Between them these two rules will demonstrate many of the problems we
encounter in the translation into a representation for an intelligent
consultation system. The statement of the first rule in the standard
form of logic is:

        $\forall(x)[F(x) \& \forall y[W(x,y) \rightarrow S(y)]] \rightarrow P(x)$
where
        $F(x)$ means x is a period of four or more days
        $W(x,y)$ means y is a day in the period x
        $S(y)$ means y is a day of sickness
        $P(x)$ means x is a period of incapacity for work

We can transform this by routine procedures into clausal form:

        $P(x) \leftarrow F(x), S(d(x))$.
        $P(x), W(x,d(x)) \leftarrow F(x)$.

In the transformation we have had to introduce the function $d(x)$ in
order to eliminate an existential quantifier. We have also ended up
with two rules, instead of one, which are not Horn clauses. It is
plain that we cannot render these clauses back into an intelligible
English form that still is an obvious expression of the original rule.
Nor are we able to use PROLOG as a problem solver since it is
restricted to the Horn clause subset of clausal form. It is possible
to derive a corresponding Horn clause specification but only by taking
a particular representation, eg lists, of the concept we are trying to
define and defining it as a recursive procedure. This takes us into
the issues tackled in the later stages of selecting representations and
procedures to search them. Before leaving this rule we also note that
taken together our top level goal and this one could not tell us
whether a day was in a period of incapacity for work.

A link is missing that must be expressed by the rule:

    part_of_a_period_of_incapacity_for_work(Day) if
          period_of_incapacity_for_work(P),
          part_of_period_(P,Day).

This is a trivial example of how we must insert 'problem solving' rules
in intimate relations with our legislative rules if they are to have
any pragmatic value. Further, we realise on reflection that in a
pragmatic sense the rule does not say what it means. It is quite clear
from the use made of the definition that a period of incapacity for
work is not just a consecutive period of sickness but the longest such
period. It begins when someone falls sick and ends when they are
better; a subset of a period is not properly speaking a period in the
sense meant there. To express this we must start to add still more
rules whose form is far from simple.
        The second of the above rules causes us even more trouble.
First of all, this is an excellent example of a rule conceptually
modifying one that has gone before to such an extent that the first
rule is almost useless. We must therefore throw away our direct
representation of the first rule and take the two together; the author
can think of no other way of dealing with "shall be treated as" other
than defining what a piw **is**. An appropriate definition might be:

        Periods of four or more consecutive days of sickness, separated
        by not more than two weeks, together comprise a piw.

Trying to express this in logic the following suggests itself:

        $\forall x \forall y \forall z [[W(x,y)\&W(x,z)] \rightarrow [FS(y)\&FS(z)\&\neg G(y,z)]] \rightarrow P(x)$

where

        W(x,y) means y is a day in the period x
        FS(y)   means y is one of four or more days of sickness
        G(y,z) means y and z are separated by more than 14 days of
                non sickness

Clearly, FS and G need further expansion, and this formulation suggests
that we would have been better off starting with a definition of a
part-piw and then defining how parts comprise a whole. This approach
is taken in our final representation. All remarks made above for the
first rule concerning the difficulty of expression in Horn clauses and
making contact with problem solving rules apply with even greater
strength to our now considerably more complex definition.
        The conclusion of this analysis is not that logic cannot
be used to represent the law. It is that a "direct" approach,
unmotivated by a conceptual representation of our task or problem
domain does not yield a representation of any pragmatic value, either
as a definitional structure or a problem solving tool. Further, that
the direct representation may fall beyond the scope of our Horn clause
problem solving mechanisms. The translation to logic was comparatively
simple and so the claim for logic of a certain 'naturalness' as a
specification language in this doman may be considered to be
substantiated. We now see how far beyond the specification of the **law**
we must go to specify a **system** that can apply it.

3. The "Single Goal" Approach

We have seen how to give some pragmatic value to our
representation we must constrain it to the Horn clause form and must
supply missing information to link the basic rules together. The
second approach to the problem was therefore to take the same initial
clause as before and treat it as the top level goal of a problem
solving representation. The process of representation is then driven
by the top down refinement of subgoals, and legislation is only
included if it is encompassed by this process. We find that the two
rules we considered above enter into our representations in quite a
different way. First of all we have:

        part_of_a_period_of_incapacity_for_work(Day) if
                day_of_sickness(Day), and
                one_of_four_or_more-days_of_sickness(Day).

The first subgoal can then be further refined according to the detailed
provisions in the Regulations for determining days deemed to be days of
sickness. The second subgoal contains the essence of the first of the
piw rules. No further refinement can be made without making some
further assumptions about the problem solving task. The simplest
assumption is that this subgoal will be resolved by the user and we can
therefore declare this relation to be 'askable'. To determine it with
respect to some database representing a case history would require more
rules to examine adjacent days and count them.
        Although the above encoding may appear quite trivial it is
the result of a design decision that had to be reached independently of
the legislation. A more straightforward rule, closer to the
legislation, would have been:

        part_of_a_piw(Day) if
                one_of_four_or_more_days_of_sickness(Day).

By including the additional subgoal it is possible to bring in the full
definition of a day of sickness (which comes down to five bottom level
goals to be declared 'askable'), before asking the generalising
question. In this way the user is lead through the detailed definition
for one day and then asked whether it belongs to a longer period of
such days. We must still include problem solving rules intermingled
with the definitional ones and we find that the bottom level goals that
result have a rather contrived air about them and may depend on a
context created by earlier 'askable' goals, eg:

        start_of_period_of_sickness_greater_than_four_days_ending_
                within_previous_fourteen_days(Day,Start)

Alternatives of more or less elegance could be produced but the points
are well made that problem solving rules are very different from those
derived directly from the legislation, and the retrieval of definitions
is a different task from applying the definition to a case history. We
conclude that this representation will be highly inflexible. A large
number of bottom level goals was generated and the highly specific
nature of many of them meant that they were unsuitable for a general
problem solver able to reason bottom up from data. It was quite

evident that this program could only possibly **show** that a day satisfied
some conditions, not **find** those that did.

The Query-the-User method has proved very successful in
other instances so we must explain why we had problems with it here.
The answer is clearly that the system's internal reasoning powers are
far too weak. It is driven back to the user for help with evey step
along the way. In fact the program is very little more than a decision
tree. It lacks any model for achieving coherence between the many
subgoals to be determined. Asking the user is all right if there is a
good match between his real world concepts and the goals that the
system must satisfy; in order to achieve that we must turn to the third
stage of the project.

4.   The "Conceptual" Approach

At this point it was clear that representing the
legislation for explanatory purposes and problem solving purposes are
two distinct tasks. Sometimes they can sit uneasily together,
sometimes they are in conflict. For this stage the original aim of
producing a problem solving system for the examples in the employers'
handbook was adhered to. A note on extending the system to the first
task is included at the end of the section. An attempt was still made
however to preserve wherever possible a distinction between rules that
defined the law and those that applied it.

The previous stages of the study had revealed that the
main problem lay in providing a powerful representation of events and
time periods. The SSP legislation, as the first rule shows, is all
about time periods and the relationships between them. What was needed
was a set of algorithms to complement the definitions. Just as a
specification of sortedness is essentially useless for sorting, so
general definitions of periods and events had no power to solve
problems. Analysis of the type of relationships between periods also
showed that it would be necessary to have different procedures for
'finding' and for 'showing' problems. Procedures that could show that
a number of days satisfied some rules would be combinationally
explosive, or non terminating if used to find a day. In most cases the
procedures could only be used one way because the operations entailed
arithmetic operations or tests that could only instantiate in one
direction.

A uniform set of procedures for representing and
manipulating time periods was therefore designed. Study of the
legislation derived that a period could be defined by a set of
cumulative definitions:

(1)   specific days, eg week begins on Sunday;
(2)   specific dates, eg tax year begins on 4 April;
(3)   some condition true on every day, and not on adjacent days,
          eg sickness;
(4)   restrictions on length (max or min) of a period defined by
          any of 1 to 3;
(5)   derivation or intersection of periods defined by 1 to 4;
(6)   linking of periods defined by 1 to 5, eg piw derived from
          sickness with gaps less than 15 days
etc

A small number of predicates are used to define the characteristics of each type of period found in the legislation. For example the definitions for a piw are as follows:

```
period_type(piw,linked).
period_sub_period_name(piw,sub_piw).
period_linkage(piw,14).
period_type(sub_piw,derived).
period_derivations(sub_piw,[sickness]).
period_min_length(sub_piw,4).
```

To handle these standardised forms of definition a small number of procedures are defined. There are two basic searching operations that are needed both for constructing a period from its definition and for answering the example queries. The first takes a day and the name of a period, and finds the period of the named variety that includes the day:

```
period_including_day(Period,Period_name,Day).
```

The data representation used for a period is a list of all the days in it. This allows linked periods to be handled as easily as non-linked ones. This procedure uses lower level ones that can generate dates forwards and backwards from the day of interest and uses the period definitions to test for inclusion. The second basic procedure for building up time periods takes a start and end date (a time frame) and searches for periods of a defined type within that time frame. Two versions are required, one to search from the start forwards, the other from the end backwards. This is written in such a way that when backtracking occurs it will find the next solution, returning the empty list when there are no more. This procedure is able to use the first one together with a few rules to adjust its time frame whenever a solution is found. For the rules that handle periods as part of other definitions it is useful to add one further procedure that collects up all the solutions within a time frame.

With the aid of these problem solving procedures a distinction can be maintained between those rules that define the law and those that apply the definitions. The latter must know about the data structures for periods and the procedures to handle them, whereas the former do not. For both of these types of rules the logic programming formalism appears to be natural and concise. It is only for the basic period searching procedures that the logic is less appropriate. The basic operations entail searching up and down lists in an efficient way that is more conveniently handled by an algorithmic language. Designing these procedures in logic was considerably more difficult than writing the other rules, and getting them to work was definitely a process of debugging rather than 'knowledge engineering'. The efficiency implications cannot be ignored either: the system as written could not handle an apparently simple example case in the form in which it was stated because it ran out of stack space in very deep recursions involving very large data structures. No doubt some ingenuity and a compiler that optimises tail recusion would help, but the conclusion that logic is not ideal for this type of operation appears inescapable.

The bottom level goals of this system are simpler and
relate directly to the data and legislation rules. They are all direct
equivalents of conditions found in the legislation, rather than
invented to fill problem solving gaps in it. It would be entirely
reasonable to declare all of them to be 'askable' of the user. By
establishing a conceptual framework for the problem solving, albeit a
simple one, we have put the problem solving back into the system.
        We can also now see how we could set about achieving a
more sensible dialogue structure for our problem solver. Take as an
example the definition of a period of entitlement. This is the most
complicated period definition but its interesting feature at this point
is that the period is ended by the first to occur of a number of
events: end of contract, start of pregnancy disqualifying period, start
of a period of legal custody, or end of piw (the usual case). The
problem solving rules first of all construct the intersection of the
current contract and the piw. This establishes a period within which
to search for the first instance of any of the other terminating
events. At this point it would not be sensible for the system to ask
of each day in turn whether it satisfies those conditions - it should
discover whether the event occurred in the period of interest, ie it
should generalise the question in the way that a human questioner
would. In order for this to be possible it would only be necessary to
introduce a new relation:

known(Period_name,Start,Finish)

that would record the period of time for which the data currently
available to the system represented a complete history. Then an
askable goal would only be asked if its history were not known for the
period in question. If it were asked then the 'known' relation would
require updating. Without a mechanism such as this we are not able to
cope with the statement in a typical example, where it says there is no
reason to suspect the (27 year old female) employee is pregnant.
PROLOG cannot represent negation directly, ie we cannot include 'not
pregnant' as an assertion to be used by the theorem prover. Negation
is implied from failure to prove a goal. By including the assertion:

known(pregnancy,_,_).

we would prevent further attempts to establish facts relating to
pregnancy. Even if we had explicit negation, the 'known' predicate
would serve to guide the process of generalising questions.
        Although we have gone a small way towards giving our
system problem solving capabilities and some possibility of improving
its dialogue at a rudimentary level, we have not yet tackled
representing the definitional aspect of the law for consultation,
distinct from problem solving. For example, the system can correctly
apply the rules that allow an employer to withold payment in lieu of a
waiting day for which notification of sickness was not given, but it
has no means to answer the question: "What can you do about the late
notification?". As another example, consider the rules defining a 'day
of sickness' that were discussed in the previous section. We saw there
how a dialogue could be contrived to take a user through the detailed
definition and then ask a generalising question. This was really a
trick, combining the two types of consultation and clearly does not

carry over into our new system. Once we have a conceptual framework
for some part of the legislation however we can incorporate procedures
to explain that framework. As a trivial example, if we redefined our
period predicates to look like:

        period(Period_name,type,x)
        period(Period_name,derivation,y)
          etc

then a query of the form

        ? - period(sickness,X,Y).

would recover the definitional predicates. Clearly we would want to
have some more sophisticated retrieval that could recursively unravel
all the dependencies and explain the relationship between them, but the
point is that by having a conceptual structure related to a user's
concept we have the germ of a consultation system on the concept of the
legislation. Part of the design of an extended system would be the
choice of basic concepts to which the explanation must be reduced, and
this level of justification would depend on the class of users.
            As a final point on our conceptual framework we note that
even when we are dealing with such comparatively simple things as time
periods and events the representation is quite complex. The nature of
the law is to always introduce exceptions to general rules; the system
allows for this in its representation of periods by including 'special
conditions' that can be applied after everything else. Even this
however does not deal with the rule that says that the end of a
contract does not terminate a period of entitlement if the contract was
terminated solely or mainly to avoid liability for SSP. To have
accommodated this would require the ability to attach whole clauses
where we only had predicate names. To introduce it as an afterthought
would require substantial reworking. We note that this would be a
traditional 'programming' rather than 'knowledge engineering' task.
The modifiability of rules pertains only to the direct expression of
the legislation, and we have now established just how much and how
little that can do for us.

5.   Summary and Conclusions

In summary therefore we observe:
(1)   A useful legal consultation system on any large scale will have
        to make explicit knowledge of four types: definitional, problem
        solving and dialogue. This knowledge is not made explicit by
        the direct representation of the legislation in logic.
(2)   A conceptual structure is essential for consultation on
        definitions and anything beyond trivial problem solving.
(3)   Problem solving may be separated into the application of low
        level procedures to general definitions. The general
        definitions and interfacing procedures are naturally written in
        logic, but the low level ones less so.

This project started with the perception of a match
between a technique, logic for rule based systems, and the domain of
legislation, and sought to investigate how far the technique would go
in helping to build a knowledge based system of power and flexibility.
The method was practical, the representation of a new piece of
legislation as a means of gaining insight into the problems involved.
The conclusions arise from making a number of distinctions which help
to assign the correct role for logic in the building of knowledge based
systems.

The most important distinction is the one expounded by
Newell (1982): that an intelligent system must be described at two
levels, the knowledge level and the symbol level. We must not confuse
the power of logic at the representational level with competence at the
knowledge level. Only by analysing each competence we require of a
system can we make the necessary knowledge explicit; until we have made
it explicit we cannot represent it; and until we have represented it we
have not given that competence to our system, whatever the
representational formalism.

We found that in order to build a system with any
competence in the legal domain we had to be specific about the
competence required - was it to explain definitions, reason about
cases, hold sensible dialogues with a user, etc? With a clear purpose
in mind the logic programming method proved to be powerful and easy to
use in all respects except the low level manipulation of data
structures. We found that even a simple problem solving system
involved a knowledge acquisition task, ie deriving some underlying real
world concepts pertaining to the tasks. We also noted that the easy
modifiability of the rules that represent the legislation would not
carry over quite so easily into our more powerful conceptual model. In
other words there is a good deal of programming as well as knowledge
engineering in building a knowledge based system in a complex domain.
It was apparent that extending a system to deal with all the law,
instead of just the parts displaying a high degree of structure over a
few basic concepts, would require conceptual models of far more detail
than we have at present. The TAXMAN (McCarty 1980) program shows just
how far one would expect to go away from the original expression of the
law in order to model the concepts adequately.

Our general conclusion from this study is therefore that
the match between the technique and the domain exists only at a surface
level and is perhaps inclined to deceive us into believing that in this
domain the epistemology of the knowledge level comes free with the
knowledge.

Acknowledgements

I am grateful to Bob Kowalski, Peter Hammond and Marek Sergot for
introducing me to the field of logic programming and the law, and for
their help in providing source material and discussing problems. This
project was undertaken as part of a Masters course and I would like to
thank Tom Addis for his very helpful comments on the original
dissertation. I am also happy to acknowledge the support of the
Science and Engineering Research Council.

References

1. Allen, L. (1979). Language, Law and Logic. Plain Legal Drafting for the Electronic Age. In Niblett, ibid.
2. Clancy, W.J. (1983). The Epistemology of a Rule-Based Expert System. Artifical Intelligence, Vol.20, No.3. pp. 215-251.
3. Employer's Guide to Statutory Sick Pay. (1982). DHSS. NI.227.
4. Hammond, P. (1983). Representation of DHSS Regulations as a Logic Program. In proceedings of Expert Systems 83, pp. 225-235.
5. Kowalski, R. (1983). Logic for Expert Systems. In Proceedings of Expert Systems 83, pp. 79-93. BCS.
6. McCarty, T. (1980). The TAXMAN Project: Towards a Cognitive Theory of Legal Argument. In Niblett, ibid.
7. Newell, A. (1982). The Knowledge Level. Artificial Intelligence, Vol.18, No.1, pp. 87-127.
8. Niblett, B. (Ed), (1980). Computer Science and Law. Cambridge University Press.
9. Sergot, M. (1983). A Query-the-User facility for logic programming. In Degano, P. & Sandwell, E (Eds), Integrated Interactive Computer Systems. North Holland.
10. Social Security and Housing Benefits Act 1982. HMSO.
11. Statutory Sick Pay (General) Regulations 1982. HMSO.